BOUNDLESS

BOUNDLESS

THE RISE, FALL, AND ESCAPE OF
CARLOS GHOSN

THE *WALL STREET JOURNAL'S*
NICK KOSTOV & SEAN McLAIN

HARPER
BUSINESS
An Imprint of HarperCollins*Publishers*

HarperCollins books may be purchased for educational, business, or sales promotional use. For information, please email the Special Markets Department at SPsales@harpercollins.com.

FIRST EDITION

Library of Congress Cataloging-in-Publication Data has been applied for.

ISBN 978-0-06-304103-5

22 23 24 25 26   LSC   10 9 8 7 6 5 4 3 2 1

For Grandad
—Nick

For Surya and Amartya
—Sean

Boundless intemperance
In nature is a tyranny; it hath been
The untimely emptying of the happy throne
And fall of many kings.

—William Shakespeare, *Macbeth*

CONTENTS

Contents

Part III

AUTHORS' NOTE

In the fall of 2018, Carlos Ghosn went from being one of the world's most prominent businessmen—an automobile executive crisscrossing the globe in his private jet—to being an alleged criminal in a Japanese jail cell.

A little over a year later, he became a celebrity fugitive. What had been a big business story moved to the front pages of all the newspapers.

Despite the slew of coverage, Ghosn remained an enigma. In particular, it wasn't clear whether he was the innocent victim of a corporate coup or guilty of a bevy of financial crimes (as Japanese, and more recently French, prosecutors alleged). In escaping from Japan, had he run away from justice or injustice? He had die-hard supporters and fierce enemies whose loud voices obfuscated the truth.

We wanted to get to the bottom of it all.

As reporters for the *Wall Street Journal,* we had front-row seats to the whole saga. We started covering the story on the day of Ghosn's dramatic arrest. It was a game of inches. Ghosn was in a jail cell and cut off from the outside world. There was so little to go on that Ghosn's declaration of innocence amounted to a scoop. Every document we could get our hands on or source we could reach was a small victory in trying to understand what had happened and why.

The trail took us from Tokyo to Paris via Lebanon, Rio, Oman, a Caribbean island, and the suburbs of Boston. What emerged most profoundly was the complexity of Ghosn's character: we found a man teeming with a blend of charisma and introversion, bombast and restraint, derring-do and conservatism, grand designs and petty obsessions, analytical excellence and irrational moves.

Ghosn's life was also the story of globalization, its opportunities, and its excesses. Born in the Brazilian jungle, he had risen to the top of the business world on the back of his talents and hard work. Once he arrived there, he found a rarefied space with almost no oversight.

This book draws on interviews with more than a hundred individuals who afforded us their time and patiently shared their knowledge and experiences. They include interviews with current and former executives at Nissan, Renault, and Michelin, board members, rivals, friends, and Ghosn family members. Many of them spoke on the condition that we would not use their name, a request we have respected.

The book also draws heavily on thousands of pages of documents, including previously untapped legal documents from Japan, France, Lebanon, and the British Virgin Islands, board minutes, audits, internal company reports, emails, presentations, surveys, and audio and video recordings. One stack of documents we consulted stemmed from a hard drive containing a trove of communications between a Lebanese lawyer, Fady Gebran, and some of his contacts, including Ghosn. Ghosn's lawyers have said that those documents were obtained by Nissan representatives without following proper judicial procedures, and that it was therefore impossible to guarantee their authenticity. In the course of our reporting, we were able to authenticate dozens of the messages and ascertain that the events or financial transactions described in them took place in real life. Furthermore, we never found a single discrepancy or any indication that other messages might not be genuine. Hence, we decided to use them in the book.

We used a process that has served *Wall Street Journal* reporters well for decades: the key people mentioned in this book have all been provided with an opportunity to comment on the revelations contained within these pages. We also followed a cardinal rule: "No surprises."

Ghosn himself sat down to answer our questions for several hours. He was forthcoming on everything, with the exception of matters related to Oman. He said he would reserve his answers for the French justice system, where he is facing a criminal investigation. That, of course, is his right. He also agreed to make some family members and friends available for interviews. His elder sister, Claudine, in particular was an invaluable source in piecing together Ghosn's early life.

As we got closer to publication, we sent an email to Ghosn's public relations advisers asking for Ghosn to review a number of facts and anecdotes that we planned to include in the book, and giving him another opportunity to comment on the specifics of the so-called Oman Route.

They came back to us with the following response: "Mr. Ghosn's counsels are of the view that the intended assertions for which comments are requested are inaccurate and/or incorrect and/or incoherent and/or put out of context." The statement said that Ghosn's legal counsel had advised their client not to bother reviewing our message.

Finally, while working on this story, we both developed some of the most intense source relationships we've ever had. It was a particularly difficult time for many of the people mentioned in these pages: families were torn apart, careers were ruined. Often, we conducted interviews while covid-19 had locked down the world, which added even more strain to those people's lives. Despite all that, they still spoke to us. Our conversations were sometimes emotional, leading to relationships that yielded both revelations and challenges. On occasion, those connections were impossible to maintain. Regardless of the trajectory of our correspondence, we will always be grateful and indebted to our sources. Without them, this book would not have been possible. Thank you.

Nick Kostov, Paris
Sean McLain, Tokyo

CAST OF CHARACTERS

Carlos Ghosn: Forged the Renault-Nissan Alliance and was one of the greatest auto executives of all time before his arrest in Japan

Family

Rita Ghosn: Ghosn's first wife and the mother of his four children, Caroline, Nadine, Maya, and Anthony

Carole Ghosn: Ghosn's second wife

Rose Ghosn: Ghosn's mother

Georges Ghosn: Ghosn's father

Claudine, Sylvia, and Nayla Ghosn: Ghosn's sisters

France

Behrouz Chahid-Nouraï: Finance chief at Michelin

François Michelin: Michelin's owner and CEO

Louis Schweitzer: Ghosn's first boss at Renault

Patrick Pelata: Ghosn's classmate at École Polytechnique and later his number two at Renault

Alain Dassas: Nissan's finance chief during the financial crisis

Frédérique Le Grèves: Ghosn's chief of staff at Renault and Nissan

Mouna Sepehri: Longtime Renault executive

Emmanuel Macron: Minister of the economy, industry, and digital affairs and later president of France

Martin Vial: Head of Agence des Participations de l'État (APE), which manages France's interests in corporate assets

Jean-Dominique Senard: Replaced Ghosn as Renault chairman and head of the Alliance

Nissan and Japan

Hiroto Saikawa: Replaced Ghosn as Nissan CEO in 2017

Greg Kelly: American who acted as head of Ghosn's CEO office until 2015; arrested along with Ghosn in 2018

Hari Nada: British Nissan lawyer who replaced Kelly as head of the CEO office in 2015

Toshiaki Ohnuma: The head of Nissan's secretariat, which handled pay-related issues for the board of directors

Hidetoshi Imazu: Former head of manufacturing at Nissan who became the statutory auditor who launched the investigation into Ghosn

Toshiyuki Shiga: Ghosn's former second in command at Nissan, until he retired and joined Nissan's board of directors

Hitoshi Kawaguchi: Nissan's head of government affairs who aided Imazu in his investigation of Ghosn

Lebanon

Fady Gebran: Ghosn's childhood friend and personal lawyer

Amal Abou Jaoude: Gebran's assistant

Carlos Abou Jaoude: Lebanese lawyer

Ziad Gebran: Fady Gebran's youngest son

Middle East

Suhail Bahwan: Omani billionaire in business with Nissan

Divyendu Kumar: General manager of Suhail Bahwan Automobiles in Oman

Khaled Juffali: Saudi billionaire in business with Nissan

Escape

Michael Taylor: Former Green Beret and security expert

Peter Taylor: Michael Taylor's son

George-Antoine Zayek: Lebanese former militiaman

BOUNDLESS

Prologue

Carlos Ghosn contemplated the box in front of him. Freedom.

It was a large black wooden crate with steel reinforcements on the edges, the sort of case a band would use to transport large speakers or instruments.

Ghosn was listening to instructions from Michael Taylor, the former Green Beret he had hired to help maneuver the getaway.

Taylor was explaining, step by step, what the auto titan would need to do: Climb into the crate, and stay still. Let the lid be lowered. Once secured, the trunk—and he—would be in motion. Inside his box, he would be loaded onto a private jet with the rest of the luggage.

Ghosn was well versed in the private-jet lifestyle. He had flown everywhere on his Gulfstream as chief executive of two carmakers, Renault and Nissan. He was accustomed to flying high above the clouds, lounging on a plush leather seat. This would be a new experience.

If all went well, Carlos Ghosn could be having brunch in his sprawling vineyard in Lebanon by the following morning—spirited away by Taylor, freed from the clutches of Japanese justice, thousands of miles away from the financial crimes of which he had been accused.

Though the box offered the potential of freedom, it also represented abject desperation. If anything went wrong, he was guaranteed to end up on the front pages of every newspaper in the world, a laughingstock. Worse than his humiliation would be his inevitable destination: straight to jail, again, but this time with no chance at bail.

Still, staying and arguing his way through the morass of the Japanese courts seemed a far more devastating fate. He had been locked away in their system for more than a hundred days, enduring daily interrogations by prosecutors during which he was not allowed a lawyer.

He was facing serious criminal charges, having been accused of orchestrating a complex flow of money between Nissan, the Middle East, and his own pocket. Beyond the criminal charges, his carefully honed image had been ripped to shreds as Nissan and Tokyo prosecutors had steadily leaked damaging bits of information, ensuring that Ghosn-as-villain had been front-page fodder for months.

He was facing a lengthy legal battle, and he wasn't sure he'd live long enough to survive the ordeal. Even if he funneled all his resources and contacts into his day in court, he knew that in Japan prosecutors won over 99 percent of trials.

Escape, even if it meant living as a fugitive for the rest of his life, was preferable.

*   *   *

Carlos Ghosn had been the world's most prominent car man of the first two decades of the twenty-first century. To the astonishment of nay-sayers worldwide, he had forged two middling carmakers into a global powerhouse, the Renault-Nissan Alliance. But Ghosn never felt that he had been adequately compensated. Over the years, he had watched as people of lesser talent had made millions more than he did. It had grated on him to the point of obsession.

Since the financial crisis of 2008, he had started to take matters into his own hands, exploring numerous schemes to secretly pay himself what he thought he was worth. Ten years later, he had been ready to push through his last great act as an executive—a merger between the French and Japanese carmakers—before sailing off into the sunset aboard a 120-foot-long yacht. As part of the deal, he would be entitled to a massive payday, one that would enable him to retire as a very wealthy man.

By Ghosn's account, a plotting group of Nissan executives had prevented that by conspiring to orchestrate his downfall. His careful plans had been thwarted by a dramatic, unexpected arrest. His supporters had evaporated at an alarming rate. His friends in Davos would neither protect nor defend him.

The betrayal from his companies burned most acutely. He had given Nissan, in particular, so very much. The prior year, Hiroto Saikawa, Ghosn's handpicked successor, had unveiled a stainless-steel statue more than sixteen feet tall for Nissan dubbed *Wheels of Innovation*, which Saikawa called "a retrospective on Mr. Ghosn's 17 years of leadership." On the night of his mentor's arrest, that same man told the world that Ghosn had abused his position to line his own pockets (eventually, Ghosn's companies accused him of misappropriating more than $100 million).

Stripped of the trappings of corporate power, Ghosn had been reduced to a presumed criminal before the law, a status he deeply resented. He was not going to admit defeat so easily. And he had more than his own name and integrity to protect. The Ghosn family had made its fortune far from its native Beirut, spanning back two generations and originating in the Amazonian rain forest. Carlos Ghosn was the clan's greatest scion. To end his storied life in ignominy would be failing the legacy of his grandfather and tarnishing the reputation of his children. He would rather risk his life than accept such a fate.

Back in the hotel with Taylor, from the corner room on the forty-sixth floor, large windows offered a view of the vast Pacific, partially framed by the twinkling lights of Osaka. It seemed less as though he was on top of the world and more as though he was teetering on the edge of it. He climbed into the box.

"Breathe slowly," Taylor reminded him as he lowered the lid.

Then everything went dark.

PART I

PART 1

1

Self-Made

The steamship carrying Abdo Bichara Ghosn and his wife, Milia, glided to a halt at a small clearing along the muddy Madeira River in the heart of the Amazonian jungle.

He had heard stories about the fabulous wealth locked in the dense rain forest: the *Hevea brasiliensis*, or rubber tree, was the best source of latex in the world, its white secretions turning adventurous men into overnight millionaires.

Rubber had been noticed during early European expeditions to the Western Hemisphere, when explorers had seen natives using the milky substance to make waterproof coverings for their homes. But more than a century would pass before John Dunlop and the Michelin family discovered that the rubber could be used to make tires for bicycles and automobiles. Around the time Bichara and Milia arrived in the Amazon, Ford Model Ts were rolling off the assembly line in Detroit, heralding the boom in rubber demand that was making men in the Amazon fantastically rich.

Bichara had seen one of the many posters plastered across cities on nearly every continent, advertising the easy riches to be found in South America. A similar siren call of instant wealth had recently drawn daring or desperate types to the American West to pan for gold.

The legends were many. Rubber barons had started building mansions among the vines, lighting expensive cigars with hundred-dollar bills; their wives dripped with jewels. To build homes with their new-found wealth, the engineers, traders, and merchants of the rubber boom imported the finest materials in the world—Italian marble, ceramics from France, linens from Ireland—to construct and adorn their bustling community. Its epicenter was the growing city of Manaus, where they built the world-famous, still standing Teatro Amazonas opera house, some five hundred miles inland from the south Atlantic Ocean.

By the time Bichara Ghosn, a heavyset man with a black mustache and a severe countenance, arrived in 1910, Brazil's rubber trade had reached such heights that men and equipment were being sent even deeper into the jungle. He and his wife, Milia, a slight but resilient Lebanese woman with thick hair and dark eyebrows, finally alighted from their boat another five hundred miles up the river from Manaus, at a humble hamlet called Porto Velho (Old Port in Portuguese). It was little more than a hot, dusty shantytown. Though it lacked such luxuries as paved roads and modern conveniences, there were signs that something big was under way.

Thousands of men had swarmed to the banks of the river, throwing up new buildings at a frenetic pace. They were engineers, doctors, surveyors—but mostly they were laborers, there to fell trees and lay tracks. The goal was to build a railroad that would circumvent portions of the river too treacherous for carrying rubber by boat.

Where others may have perceived bleak and inhospitable terrain, Bichara sensed possibility. And indeed, the railroad endeavor would be his pathway to realizing his grand ambitions.

Laying tracks in the remote, sweltering jungle was even worse than it sounds. The main threats were malarial mosquitoes, but laborers also had to contend with poisonous snakes and giant paraiba catfish that attacked their canoes, leaving them prey to deadly electric eels. Ants built structures up to five feet high and venomous spiders were the size of crabs. More than four thousand workers were toiling in

Porto Velho by the time Bichara arrived. One in ten would die that year.

That didn't prevent men and women from dozens of countries from traveling up the river. They hailed from the Caribbean, from Spain and Germany, from as far away as China. Some were veteran builders of the Panama Canal. Others, such as Bichara, had no intention of laying a single mile of rail but saw in Porto Velho an opportunity for a fresh start.

Bichara had actually come by way of the United States, where he had arrived a decade earlier. Boys such as Bichara, a Maronite Christian, had been sent out from his home country in droves at the start of the twentieth century. Lebanon was still part of the Ottoman Empire, and Maronite families were often targeted by the military during compulsory military enrollment drives. He traveled to America as a teenager, illiterate and penniless, and worked as a street hawker, peddling sundry goods in Rhode Island.

Bichara worked his way up to a modest living, but the Amazon presented a much faster route to success than the one he was on in America. Soon after they had settled in South America, he took advantage of the basic commercial skills he'd gleaned from his time in the States and set up a large general store on a prominent street corner in the heart of their new, upstart jungle hometown. The most lucrative products he sold were diesel for the boats that plied the river and salt, used to preserve food in the tropical climate.

The railway was finally finished in 1912. The cost had been great, most tragically in terms of human lives. Thousands of workers had died in the construction of what they called the Devil's Railroad. And, ultimately, any triumph derived from its execution was short lived. Soon after the last track was laid, the same steamships that had enabled the movement of men and goods to complete the railroad rendered it obsolete.

The British had been trying for years to smuggle rubber tree seeds out of Brazil and establish plantations elsewhere but had failed because the journey was too long and arduous. With steam-powered travel, they had now succeeded. Seedlings made it from Brazil to England and from England to Singapore, and within a matter of decades, huge plantations sprang up in Malaysia, Sri Lanka, and eventually tropical Africa. The price of rubber plummeted, and Brazil's share of the rubber trade shrank.

The impact on Brazil was devastating. Manaus was reduced to poverty; its illustrious opera house shuttered its doors in 1924; those who could fled with their riches. But just enough rubber still flowed out of the jungle to keep local traders such as Bichara in business. In a diminished pond, he was a bigger fish.

Construction began to take on a semblance of order in Porto Velho, a town that had so recently been little more than a haphazard collection of single-story huts. Telegraph poles permitted easier communication with the outside world, and Bichara's business continued to grow. He saved enough to build a warehouse and an impressive upgrade: with two stories and ornate decorations on the facade, his new shop was the first building in Porto Velho to be made entirely of brick. He called it Monte Libano, or Mount Lebanon.

Bichara was a savvy businessman. Though he lacked a formal education, he could recite by heart each customer's debts. With the larger warehouse, he had the space and foresight to make massive orders from Manaus near the end of the rainy season, when large ships could navigate the swollen river. When other stores ran out of stock during the dry season—when the river was low and traffic was difficult—Bichara sold his goods at a premium.

The region was still dangerous. One of Bichara's business partners, his brother-in-law, fell into the river and was never seen again. The family assumed that he had been eaten by one of the many black caimans that populated the waters. Giant reptiles notwithstanding, the region and its businesses maintained their appeal, so much so that a Brazilian airline started flights to the remote area. Bichara became the local representative of the airline company, adding to the clout of his business.

In the span of thirty years, Bichara Ghosn's uncommon mettle had blessed him and his family—now a flock of eight children—with all the success he had dreamed of in the wild frontier of the New World. On October 10, 1939, he passed away. At his deathbed were three of his sons. The other five children, along with their mother, were living in Lebanon due to the lack of decent education offered in Porto Velho.

Bichara was a practical man with practical concerns. As such, his parting words of advice for his sons were not dripping with sentimentality. He told them:

Always buy real estate on the corner, because it's worth more.
Go back to the homeland to find your wives.
Never argue with a taxi driver or a priest.

His sons listened carefully. Each would go on to run successful businesses of his own. And the Ghosn clan expanded, reared on legends of Abdo Bichara's trailblazing life in the Amazon. His descendants felt that a grand destiny had been conferred there, in the malarial jungle of the early twentieth century. Their family story took root in the extraordinary promise of transcending borders and boundaries, of refusing to be hemmed in by limited visions, of observing landscapes in search of opportunity, and of having the tenacity to chase their greatness.

Future Ghosns thought themselves self-made men and women. Several would venture out to build something out of nothing, just as Bichara had.

They were special. And they were compelled to dare.

*   *   *

Bichara's youngest son, Georges Ghosn Bichara, was not among the three successors at his father's deathbed. Though born in Brazil and initially raised in a large house on a corner plot, he, like all of the Ghosn children, was schooled in his familial homeland, in a seminary in the Lebanese city of Jounieh, a short distance north of Beirut.

Georges was a jovial child who loved life in the seminary, especially singing the Maronite Mass. His older brothers had gone back to Porto Velho, where they ran the family business. After Georges graduated, they decided that their kid brother had lived the easy life long enough; they wanted him back in the jungle.

When he returned to Porto Velho in his early twenties, Georges worked with his brothers. The shift from the vibrant coastal city of Beirut to the tangled isolation of the Amazon was stark, but he adapted quickly, seeking out excitement wherever he could find it. Of immediate concern to his family was the pace at which Georges was starting to chase after the women of Porto Velho.

To keep the gossips and protective fathers at bay—and to honor their departed father's second commandment—within a matter of years Georges was sent back to Lebanon to find a wife. His first stop was with a parish priest in central Beirut, at St. Elias Cathedral, located next to an all-girls school. He asked the priest to introduce him to some young women, assuring him that he had the best of intentions. In keeping with the traditions of an old-world courtship, the priest contacted the school and asked for a short list of appropriate candidates. The requirements were that the woman must be recently graduated and from a good family.

Georges visited the young women at their homes, with the priest and a relative of the priest as chaperones. Among the young women was Rose Jazzar. Georges always noticed the texture of a woman's skin. When he walked into the room, he was immediately struck by Rose's clear complexion, the sight of which was an uncommon luxury in the drenched jungle from which he'd recently returned. Rose noticed his stare and thought Georges was a handsome young man, with his strong build, thick, dark hair, and evident confidence. But he was moving back to Brazil, having merely returned to the homeland to find a wife, and she wasn't keen on the idea of moving halfway around the world to live in effective isolation.

Moreover, physical sparks went only so far. Georges was a bon vivant with a love of cigars, good food, samba, and poker. Rose was conservative and serious minded, with a taste for classical music, French culture, praying, and bridge. It didn't seem like a match. But Georges was smitten, and nothing if not persistent.

A few weeks after their initial meeting, Georges heard from the priest that Rose's brother was in the hospital. The priest, stepping into matchmaking capacity, told Georges to go pay Rose a visit. He did just that, but not before rushing out to buy a large box of chocolates. Rose was touched by the considerate gesture and agreed to see the somewhat roguish charmer again. They began dating, and Georges soon proposed marriage.

Three months after the proposal they were married, on January 8, 1950, by the Maronite patriarch in Jounieh. They spent their honeymoon in Rome, where Rose happily strolled through the Vatican. But her pious, leisurely bliss ended the moment their plane landed in Rio de Janeiro. It was Carnival time, and the city was a vibrant, exuberant open-air dance floor. Rose was shocked by the flagrant display.

The good news for Rose was that they would not be staying in Rio for long. The bad news was . . . everything else. On their flight into Porto Velho, the plane flew low over the Amazon. The pilots wanted to show the newcomer some of the authentic sights and sounds—including the alligator-like caiman sunning themselves on the banks of the river.

Like many before her, Rose had a hard time adjusting to life in Porto Velho. She yearned for culture, education. Trying to occupy herself, she meticulously planted a garden outside their home, and overnight it disappeared, devoured by an army of ants. But despite all appearances of delicacy, she was a steely person. Having been born in Nigeria, then raised in Lebanon as one of eight children, she knew how to adapt to changing circumstances. She was going to make the best of it, starting by creating a family. Within a few years, on March 9, 1954, their second of four children was born.

They named him Carlos Georges Ghosn Bichara.

To navigate such harsh terrain as an adult during that era was intensely challenging. To be an infant and young child, subject to an untamed environment, was unimaginable. In Porto Velho, young Carlos was often ill, suffering from—among other ailments and symptoms—frequent diarrhea, which his mother attributed to his drinking dirty water. The family doctor—then the only doctor in Porto Velho—proposed that the Ghosns move to a less brutal climate for the sake of their toddler's health. The incisive Rose saw it as her exit route. And she leaped at it.

"Georges, I'm going back to Lebanon. My son is going to die here!"

2

The Father

Georges, Rose, Carlos, and his older sister, Claudine, left Porto Velho for Beirut in 1955.

After settling the family in their homeland, Georges commuted back and forth to Porto Velho for several years. While home in Beirut, he established a business importing and exporting products as well as trading currencies. Georges and Rose had two more daughters, both born in Lebanon.

The Ghosns lived a privileged life. They had a driver, Reizkallah, whom the children loved and who not only taught Carlos swear words in Arabic but encouraged him to shout them at people on the road. They attended church as a family on Sunday morning before spending the afternoon at Rose's mother's home. The extended family was large, and the Ghosn children loved playing with their cousins, who became like siblings to them. Children in Lebanon had Thursday afternoons off from school, so Georges made a routine of taking that time off from work to spend it enjoying his children. He would take them to the coast, where he'd stroll along the shoreline as Carlos and his elder sister ran around him. On overcast days, he'd take the children to his sister's house in Jounieh or to one of Beirut's cinemas to catch a matinee.

Summers were spent in Broummana, a vacation town outside Beirut, where Marie, their maternal grandmother, had a house large enough for her eight children and all her grandchildren. The cousins would explore the lush pine forest that surrounds the town or ride their bikes along the mountainous dirt paths.

This glowing, comfortable, carefree existence—perched upon the Mediterranean, surrounded by their close-knit family—was shattered in the spring of 1960, when an unexpected tragedy struck the Ghosn family. Six-year-old Carlos and his older sister, Claudine, puzzled at the stream of anxious people coming into and out of their home in Beirut. Their mother refused to offer any explanation and instead instructed the children to pack their bags swiftly, as they were being sent to their grandmother's house.

Given Rose's silence and the fact that they couldn't yet read the headlines atop the front pages of every newspaper in Beirut, the children had no idea that their father had been arrested. For murder. The story of Georges Ghosn's crime would grip Lebanon throughout the summer.

On Easter Sunday, Georges had driven the family's white Peugeot 403 into the mountainous regions east of Beirut. Beside him in the car was a childhood friend whom he knew from his seminary days, a priest named Boulos Masaad.

In addition to his import-export business, Georges and Masaad were partners in a secret enterprise: they were smugglers, bringing in diamonds as well as gold from Africa. Georges also smuggled in currency to supply and bolster his foreign exchange business.

The plan had taken shape in Nigeria, where the two had run into each other by chance years before. They had rekindled their friendship and hatched the idea to smuggle contraband. Georges would provide the funds to acquire diamonds and other valuable goods. The priest would hide them beneath his cassock, taking advantage of loose border controls for trusted religious officials. The plan worked, and Masaad was soon making regular runs.

At the start of 1960, however, the relationship between the two men soured. For their latest round, Georges supplied the cash to Masaad, who in turn was supposed to procure a large amount of diamonds. That time, Masaad had concocted the scheme and was requesting enormous sums of money for the run, igniting Georges's suspicion and leading him to believe he was being conned.

On April 17, Georges picked up Masaad and told him they had important business in Damascus. About twenty miles outside Beirut, near the town of Sofar, they reached a crossroad. On Georges's signal—two short beeps—a man appeared, bearing both a rifle and a revolver. He forced the priest out of the car and led him sixty feet from the road.

The man with the guns was Selim Abdel-Khalek, a local tough guy hired by Georges to intimidate his old friend. Georges was tired of the fights with Masaad and, having chosen to ignore his father's third rule, uttered to his brothers on his deathbed, wanted to send a message to the priest. Masaad refused and started to walk away. Abdel-Khalek promptly fired a shot that penetrated the priest's kidney. Masaad doubled over and fell to the ground. Bleeding profusely, he called out for help.

What happened next would be hotly debated after Georges's arrest.

The prosecution initially claimed that Georges had then taken the revolver and fired a second bullet into Masaad's skull. But Georges always maintained that it was Abdel-Khalek who had fired both shots.

A man from a nearby village passed by and saw the Peugeot parked along the side of the road. Thinking it odd that a car would be parked along such a lonely stretch of road at night, he wrote down the license plate number: 1403.

Fearing they would be caught, Georges and Abdel-Khalek didn't take the time to bury Masaad's body or cover up the killing. They split and fled the crime scene, with Georges climbing into the car that would incriminate him, driving home for a bath, and later going to a casino along the coast.

The next day, Georges flew to Cairo for a business trip. By then, investigators were hot on his tail, having found Masaad's body and followed up with the eyewitness, who had given them the license plate number of the suspicious Peugeot.

The moment he stepped off the plane from Cairo on April 21, 1960, he was grabbed by police and taken directly to custody outside Beirut. He was detained in Baabda Prison. He denied killing Masaad but admitted he had been running a smuggling operation with him.

Three months later, in July, prosecutors filed their indictment, accusing Georges and Abdel-Khalek of the murder of the priest, and seeking the death penalty for both.

In early August, after sawing through the iron bars of Baabda Prison, eight inmates (including Abdel-Khalek) escaped. According to two of the inmates who were later caught, Georges had engineered the plan, complete with paying off the guards in exchange for their smuggling a saw to one of the captured inmates. The deal was that in return for delivering the tool that enabled his freedom, Abdel-Khalek would take full blame for the murder, once they were out, one of the inmates said.

Georges vehemently denied any involvement in the escape, but the saga became even more theatrical from there. One of the escapees who had been apprehended claimed that Georges's wife, Rose, had provided the funds used to pay for the escape, delivering cash to Georges during her visits to him in prison. Rose herself was apprehended in Broummana, where she had been staying with the young Carlos and his sister. She was put into solitary confinement in Baabda Women's Prison.

The children were again sheltered from the reality of that terrifying turn of events. They knew that something was different that day only because they were sent to the house of their tutor, Mademoiselle Alice, who usually came to their home for the lessons.

While being interrogated, the wide-eyed Rose told the authorities that their car had been stolen and she knew nothing of the escape plan. She was released the next day and never faced charges. Meanwhile, Georges was transferred out of Baabda Prison after organizing a hunger strike to protest a shortage of food in the prison, the supply of which had been cut off as a security measure following Abdel-Khalek's escape.

They sent him to another jail in Beirut, La Citadelle. That did little to tamp down public intrigue, however. By the start of the trial in October, the story was still front-page news in Lebanon. Three buses and fifteen taxis carried people from Ashkout, the murdered priest's small town, to Beirut to attend the trial.

Abdel-Khalek was still at large but never took the full blame for the murder. At trial, Georges argued that Abdel-Khalek had framed him for the murder over a grudge over a land dispute. The judge didn't buy it. Georges was found guilty and sentenced to death. He was thirty-seven.

A few years later, however, his death sentence was commuted to fifteen years of hard labor. In the revised sentence, a judge reviewed the evidence and determined that Georges had only asked Abdel-Khalek to force Masaad to sign a document acknowledging his debt, not to shoot him. The killing was ruled an accident.

After almost three years on the run, Abdel-Khalek was eventually taken into custody again. He was found guilty of murder and given a life sentence.

*   *   *

Around the time of his father's arrest, Carlos Ghosn was enveloped in the most protective cocoon available, one that would ideally shield him from the mania of his family's drama. He was enrolled at the Collège Notre-Dame de Jamhour, a private all-boys school run by Jesuit priests and one of the best schools in the Middle East.

The campus, perched atop a hill with views of nearby Beirut, had recently been renovated. The Jesuit brothers sought to provide a world-class education, conducted in French, on a par with that of the most elite schools in Europe. Its alumni went on to the highest levels of business and government in Lebanon.

Naturally intelligent, Ghosn was a good student but not at the top of his class. Still, he was gifted enough to be placed among the brightest students, who studied Latin in addition to Arabic and English. History was the one subject where he exerted himself and demonstrated a genuine fascination. He inhaled history books, particularly those of the ancient Greek and Roman variety. He had an insatiable passion for tales of great men—not the legends of King Arthur or Odysseus but Alexander the Great, the Caesars, Napoleon Bonaparte—men who had sought out boundaries in order to cross them.

As a teenager, Ghosn's ambitions matured. He settled into his growing personality and started considering where he would go to university, maybe even in Paris, where his mother had often dreamed of living. In high school, he began thinking more seriously about his career, coming to the realization that if he wanted to be successful, he would have to devote himself to math and literature, just as he had to history. In tandem with his growing ambition for his future was an increasingly dynamic competitive streak, one that the Jesuits nurtured and encouraged. At Jamhour, the Jesuits publicly ranked the students on their performance and gave out awards to top performers. Ghosn started to compete for all of them, and by the second year of high school, he became determined to achieve the top score in every exam.

There were two sides to Carlos, which is hardly uncommon for a high-achieving adolescent, especially one with an absent father and a close bond with his mother. Marathon study sessions were offset by sessions of hanging out with friends who were obsessed with the Who and the Rolling Stones, and underage joy rides to Al Hamra, the buzzing nightlife district of the city known as the Paris of the Middle East. It was a golden age of a place soon to be plunged into unrest and despair.

As he reached the end of his time in high school, Ghosn became increasingly focused on academic success. His ambition crystallized on getting to France. Believing that the next few years would determine the rest of his life, he wouldn't even let friendships stand in his way. In junior year, students had to take their Lebanese baccalaureate exams, and the school gave them a month off to prepare, which led many of the kids to form small groups for cramming at the monastery. One of Ghosn's closest friends, Farid Aractingi, expected that he and Ghosn would go off together. But when he asked about their plans, Ghosn said he was going with another student, who wasn't his friend.

"Come on, Carlos, you're going with *him*?" Aractingi asked, devastated.

"Yes," Ghosn said. "He's a hard worker. You, you're a dilettante."

During his final year, a cousin recalled how he and Ghosn went over to the home of a distant relative of theirs. While they were there, they received a call from their grandma Marie's home, where Ghosn was staying at the time. The message was clear: "You'd better hurry home." Ghosn complied, the cousin said, rushing back to the house. When he arrived, Ghosn's father was there waiting for him. Georges had been released from prison early for good behavior. Ghosn could hardly remember a time in his life when his father hadn't been in prison. It was an emotional moment for the Ghosn family.

The reunion wouldn't last. Four months later, as Ghosn was preparing for his final exams, arguably the biggest moment in his young life, his father was arrested again. Georges was caught with $34,000 in counterfeit US dollars. Following his release, he had promptly traveled to Italy and bought a printing press. With it, he and a group of accomplices had printed more than $1 million in fake US dollars, which they had tried to circulate through Lebanon and Brazil. Georges pleaded not guilty but was convicted and sentenced to another three years in jail.

In his dad's long absence, Ghosn had grown up as the man of the house but had done so in what was essentially a matriarchal home, with three sisters and a strong bond with his mother. He had good relationships with his sisters and with his grandmother. Rose was a caring mother, but she was firm in her insistence on academic excellence, and much of Ghosn's success at school came under her attentive eye. However strict she was about his education, she loved him deeply. She had a habit, which lasted into his teenage years, of checking nightly that her only son was sleeping soundly.

Ghosn inherited Rose's keen analytical mind and her knack for numbers. On holidays with his sisters and cousins, he loved to play board games, especially Risk. He had something of a formulaic strategy that he opened with every time. He would always start in Japan and slowly build up an army from there.

Whatever pain Ghosn felt about the absence of his father he buried away. He never spoke of it, and his friends knew not to ask. However suppressed that anguish was, after his father was incarcerated for the second time, Ghosn became notably more rebellious. He had always been a joker, doing things such as bringing a device to school that made the sound of a cow and setting it off in his desk to confuse the teachers and make his classmates laugh. With age, his jokes sometimes took on a cruel, arrogant edge. He rankled at the staid practices of the Jesuits and what he saw as their blind adherence to tradition. A classmate, Elie Gharios, said he and Ghosn painted DOWN WITH OLD PEOPLE on the wall of a school building, targeting the elderly priests who ran the school, one of whom Ghosn bullied mercilessly.

The string of insults from the young man proved to be too much for the Jesuits, and they kicked Ghosn out of school, even though he was due to finish within days. And while Ghosn's test scores were good enough to merit acceptance at the elite preparatory schools in France, the priests refused to recommend him to the most prestigious Jesuit school in the west of Paris.

Instead, Ghosn opted for Collège Stanislas de Paris, still a famous French prep school that counted Charles de Gaulle, Christian Dior, and Prince Albert of Monaco among its alumni. It was hardly a bad outcome for a kid from Lebanon whose family name had been tarnished by a father convicted of murder. In France, there is an intermediate station between high school and some elite universities. Stanlislas was that stop, and getting into the preparatory school offered Ghosn a pathway to the country's vaunted institutions of higher learning.

After interviewing his teachers at Jamhour to make sure that Ghosn was worth the investment, two of his uncles agreed to pay for his studies. In the fall of 1971, young Carlos Ghosn flew to Paris for the first time.

3

The Outsider

When Ghosn first arrived in Paris in 1971, he found the French capital to be unwelcoming, even demoralizing. He was homesick for the warmth of Lebanon, the emotional, social, hot-blooded Beirutis whom he knew and understood. To a lonely teenager, Parisians were more rational, more distant, colder.

It didn't help that he was suddenly in a different academic league. Failing certain classes was a shock for the star of Jamhour. But his wits had won him a place at the elite prep school for a reason. Soon, the principal at Collège Stanislas noticed Ghosn's talent for math: he had a knack for finding simple solutions to complex problems. He suggested that the École Polytechnique, with its strong science and engineering programs, would make a worthy target for the young man. Ghosn took up the challenge. His ambition merging with a definitive opportunity was all the motivation he needed.

He buried himself in work. His sister Claudine was studying in Paris at the same time. Though they were close, finding a couple of hours in her brother's timetable to attend a movie or grab coffee felt like a small miracle. For two years, Ghosn's life revolved around his desk in his student room and the local cafeterias, where he could grab a quick meal for a few francs.

In the spring of 1973, he took his first crack at the École Polytechnique entrance exam but didn't make the cut (this is very common, akin to people taking the bar exam). He decided to go back to Stanislas and try again the following year. He wouldn't miss twice, but only by the skin of his teeth. He had received an abysmal grade in industrial design, which in other years would have disqualified him from entry.

It wasn't until he got back to Beirut that Ghosn learned that the fierce competition for entry to École Polytechnique that year had worked in his favor. One physics test, which he had passed, was so ferociously difficult that the admissions officers had had to change the rules and accept applicants with disqualifying grades. When Ghosn told his mother that he was in, she was beside herself with joy. And when he returned to Paris, he was no longer a nervous applicant.

The reformed high school rebel, having completed a successful, if challenging, three years preparing for his entrance exam, walked through the tall, dark green gates of the famed École Polytechnique, under words etched in stone during the reign of Napoleon Bonaparte:

POUR LA PATRIE, LES SCIENCES ET LA GLOIRE.

For the homeland, sciences, and glory.

It was January 1975. Now twenty years old, Ghosn was finally where a young man of his intellect belonged. Founded in 1794 for military engineers and built up by the French emperor himself, École Polytechnique had evolved into much more than an engineering school in which to earn a uniform and learn military tactics. Nearly two hundred years into its existence, it had become a preferred school for would-be masters of the French-speaking universe.

Exceptionally exclusive, it seldom admitted more than three hundred applicants a year. Its assumption was that nearly every one of those students would turn into someone. Graduates from this incubator of scientists, statesmen, and entrepreneurs included three presidents of France; three Nobel laureates; Ferdinand Foch, the supreme Allied commander in World War I; and André Citroën, the founder of the eponymous automaker.

What all these notables had in common, however, was that they were Frenchmen. Carlos Ghosn was an outsider from the moment he stepped inside, one of only eight foreigners to enter the school that year.

Ghosn lived in student digs, where residents were assigned rooms by their sport, and he was grouped with three others who had chosen soccer. His new roommates had arrived at École Polytechnique four months prior. Like the other French students, they had begun their school year in September 1974, when they had been handed two military uniforms, given military haircuts, and thrust into a train to the south of France for their requisite military training. They had returned in January as officers, while Ghosn arrived as a foreigner and a civilian.

*   *   *

For all its fields of instruction, École Polytechnique was still a military school and operated as such. Students woke at 7:00 a.m. to the sound of a bugle and the sight of a daily flag-raising ceremony. They were expected to learn to march like soldiers, an exercise completed in full military regalia, including the Napoleonic-era bicorne. A *polytechnicien*'s most public duty is to open the military parade down the Champs-Elysées every year on Bastille Day.

Ghosn was a dutiful participant, though he was excluded from some exercises and activities because he wasn't French. Still, he enjoyed the academic and social life that blossomed around the martial center of gravity. He played soccer several times a week and earned his first nickname, "La Branche," as Ghosn means "branch" in Arabic. (The nickname was quickly supplanted when a Venezuelan terrorist known as "Carlos the Jackal" went on a killing spree in Paris, and classmates returned to calling him Carlos, with an added wink to the bad guy.) He had an active nightlife, sneaking out to go to bars after the school gates closed at 10:00 p.m.

Every year, the top graduates went straight into the French public service, almost as a matter of course. In the 1970s, that future was considered far more prestigious than going into business. If those alumni played their cards right, it could lead them to the Elysée Palace.

Ghosn had little interest in such a path. He wanted to go into business, as he believed it would offer him more freedom, enable him to take more initiatives—and ultimately make him more money. In any event, even if he had wanted to dedicate himself to the service of the French Republic, an important obstacle stood in his way: he wasn't a French citizen. He would always be excluded from its prime posts.

In part because he wasn't competing with his classmates for the brass ring of French government service, Ghosn saw little need to study long hours to get the best grades. He could just enjoy life in his own way. He took math courses with Laurent Schwartz, the first Frenchman to receive the prestigious Fields Medal. He studied economics under Thierry de Montbrial, who captivated his attention with his lectures.

Away from the classroom, Ghosn saw the appeal of broadening his horizons beyond the exclusively French ambitions that transfixed his classmates. He made evident a growing fascination with the culture of the United States through a social initiative he called Tables Américaines, packing local dinner tables with Americans so that École Polytechnique students could improve their English and the Americans could hone their French. Ghosn had studied English, but he wanted to speak it as well as he spoke Portuguese, Arabic, and French. The evenings inevitably went beyond the finer points of conjugation and often spilled into the bars of the Latin Quarter until the wee hours of the morning.

The eating and drinking club served Ghosn well. When forty École Polytechnique students went to the United States in 1976, they leaned on their Tables Americaines contacts. Ghosn used the opportunity to drop into the University of Colorado in Boulder for a seminar on American culture (though he was more impressed by the Martha Graham Dance Company practicing on the grass outside). While there, he went with a couple of friends and three of the dancers to a student bar, knocking back potent Harvey Wallbangers for his first experience being seriously drunk.

On that trip, Ghosn also paid a visit to a friend he had met in Paris who lived in Santa Cruz, California. She had told him that her family was middle class, but when Ghosn turned up at her place it was a huge villa with four cars in the garage, including a Porsche and a Mercedes. This is how the American middle class lives? Ghosn thought. He hadn't seen anything like it in Brazil, Lebanon, or France.

When he returned to Paris from the land of opportunity, the country had just emerged from what would be known as Les Trente Glorieuses—the three decades of growth and technological progress following World War II. Graduates of École Polytechnique could envision their future prospects with confidence.

Back home in Beirut, however, things were deteriorating. The carefree Lebanon in which Ghosn had grown up, the cosmopolitan playground of jet-setters, was being dragged into the conflicts that surrounded it. By the spring of 1975, Lebanon had spiraled into civil war. First, it was just worrying headlines that Ghosn read in Paris, scanning newspapers while studying at the Sainte-Geneviève Library, across the square from the Panthéon; or in conversation at one of the student cafés that lined the sidewalks surrounding École Polytechnique. But then it hit close—very close—to home.

Rose, who worked at the Portuguese Embassy, was driving home with Carlos's sister Nayla, then in her final year in high school. Gunmen at the checkpoint sprayed the car with bullets and shouted for the occupants to get out.

"Where do you live?" one of the men asked Nayla.

Terrified, unsure how he might react if she said her family lived in the Christian part of Beirut, she kept silent. One of Rose's colleagues, who was in the car, showed his diplomatic passport and warned that if anything happened, there would be a serious incident. After muttering among themselves, the gunmen let them through.

Rose, still shaking, decided then and there that the family needed to leave Lebanon. That night, she called Carlos and his sister Claudine, who was also in Paris.

"Your younger sister is coming," she told them. "Get somewhere with an extra room."

In the end, she came, too, along with Georges, who had recently been released from jail for a second time.

Ghosn was concerned for his friends who were still in Beirut, and he cared deeply about his family and their well-being. But unlike some of his fellow foreign École Polytechnique students, he took little interest in the politics of that particular conflict. Leave it to others to obsessively discuss the turmoil. Leave it to the various newspapers to align themselves with warring ideologies. While other foreign students harbored dreams of taking their new knowledge back home to improve the lives of their countrymen, Ghosn had little time for or interest in discussions of Marxist and anti-imperialist theory. He was interested in progress, in advancing his own position in life, just as his grandfather had: by finding and building his own prosperity.

Ghosn maintained a pragmatic stance about the war erupting in his homeland. He perceived it as being irrational and wasteful. And for a mind like Ghosn's, his inability to grasp the logic behind the conflict made it easy to distance himself from that devastating chapter of Lebanon's history. His country had gone from a cultural hub of prosperity in the 1960s to a smoldering pile of ash. And to what end? To whose credit?

It was a waste of energy, a waste of resources, a waste of value—for all the people involved and for the country. And so, for the time being, Lebanon could burn itself. It wasn't going to burn him.

As Ghosn turned away from Lebanon, even the pronunciation of his name changed. Instead of the Arabic *Hoh-sun*, he adopted the more French *Gohn*, not as a conscious statement but more because the French found the pronunciation easier.

His successes at École Polytechnique helped fuel his new confidence. He moved on to study economics at the École des Mines, another palace of Parisian higher education, founded by Louis XVI. The lonely prep school kid was gone. The cocky kid from Jamhour was back, with a new polish of refinement.

Those around him couldn't help but notice his disruptive, rambunctious nature. Gilbert Frade, his director of studies, respected his big personality but felt compelled to say something. "Look," he told him in his office, "one day you'll be a great captain of industry, but for now stop acting like the boss. I'm the boss."

*   *   *

His teachers were right. Ghosn wanted to go fast. He wanted to run things, he wanted to lead things, and he felt sufficiently unencumbered to seize his potential.

He was ready to start. The only question was where.

Ghosn looked at France. He looked at the United States. He especially looked at Brazil, which was on the way up, and he knew he would have a competitive advantage there because of his French training and language. He knew he was talented, and he felt imbued with the certainty that he could compete with the elites of the world.

Early one morning, in the fall of 1978, Ghosn's phone rang. The caller was persistent, forcing the late riser to peel himself off his mattress. On the other end of the line was a man with a thick accent, who introduced himself as "Hidalgo." Without pausing for long, he said, "We have a project in Brazil . . . if you allow us, we'd like to see you in Clermont. We'll pay for the ticket. Come whenever you want."

Ghosn, an avid phone prankster, thought that one of his friends was pulling his leg. "Okay, thank you very much," he responded and hung up the phone. Later in the day, Ghosn took a call from his sister Claudine. She had recently received a call from Hidalgo, and had given him Ghosn's number.

The Spaniard worked for the French tire maker Michelin. The once modest family-run company had grown into a global empire. Its directors had asked Hidalgo to find young engineers who would be interested in helping spearhead its expansion in Brazil.

Before the end of the day, Ghosn called Hidalgo back to apologize. "What can I do for you?" he asked.

4

Wartime General

Ghosn walked past rows of tires several times his height, the huge kind mounted on earthmovers and mining haul trucks. His shift had started at 4:30 a.m., and it was time for a break. It was bitterly cold and pitch-black outside. Workers gathered in the break area over plates of andouillettes—fragrant French sausages filled with pork intestines—that they washed down with red wine.

Ghosn found the food repulsive at that time of the morning, but he was eager not to stand out. He picked at his andouillette and took small sips of his glass of wine. As well as sharing their hearty meals, he played cards with the workers during breaks.

Following the telephone conversation with Hidalgo, Ghosn had signed up with Michelin, but his Brazilian dream would have to wait. The tire maker's headquarters were in Clermont-Ferrand, a medieval city in central France. Its main factories were in the surrounding region of Auvergne, known for its chain of volcanoes and its rustic cattle breed, Salers.

The family-run Michelin was still managed according to nineteenth-century paternalistic principles, under which employers provided their workforce with everything from housing to medical care to holiday camps. White-collar recruits were expected to go through a toilsome training course—one from which even the founder's grandson and chief executive officer, François Michelin, hadn't been exempted—that required them to spend time working on the factory floor. When it came time to be assigned to a department, Ghosn requested manufacturing.

As part of his training, Ghosn had to prepare rubber for making the tires, in essence bridging his Amazon roots with the future he was carving out. His job was to slice the rubber, put it into molds, and roll it up. Those were not skills he had been taught at École Polytechnique.

At the end of his first week at Michelin, Ghosn needed a ride back to Paris. A colleague he'd met said he could join him and his wife. By the time they dropped Ghosn off some five hours later, the colleague's wife was dazzled. "If he doesn't end up president of Michelin, he'll be president of Brazil," she said.

Her forecast was not far off. In the early 1980s, Michelin was expanding fast around the world. Skilled managers were in short supply, forcing the company to make battlefield promotions. After only three years at the company, Ghosn was put into command of a factory in the blue-collar town of Le Puy-en-Velay, overseeing six hundred employees. By age twenty-seven, he was one of Michelin's youngest-ever plant managers.

Ghosn treated those years like a management school, worth more than a whole stack of MBAs. He soaked up information from the practical men working around him and playing cards across from him, carefully observing how they thought, how they related to the hierarchy, their minimal tolerance for bullshit, what they hid from their supervisors, and how they made fun of them. Ghosn was a social chameleon who moved comfortably between the boulevards of Paris and the conveyor belts of Michelin's factories. It wasn't long until his star quality—manifested in his swift problem-solving prowess and the respect bestowed on him by workers and executives alike—came to the attention of François Michelin. In 1983, Monsieur Michelin, as employees referred to the boss, asked the tire maker's chief financial officer, Behrouz Chahid-Nouraï, to take Ghosn under his wing and coach him to become an executive.

The half-Iranian Chahid-Nouraï was a veteran of the management consultancy firm McKinsey and the investment bank Lazard. He set about teaching his new protégé what he called "the McKinsey way": analyze a problem, find a solution, and distill the insights into a slick presentation. Such incisive methodology appealed to Ghosn's sensibilities.

Taking note of Ghosn's talents, Chahid-Nouraï threw him into the deep end by presenting him with a crisis facing the company. The French government had pressured Michelin to save a competitor called Kléber-Colombes from collapse. So Michelin had become the unwilling owner of 90 percent of France's second largest tire firm. Kléber-Colombes was losing around a million French francs a day, putting Michelin's own financial health at risk. The obvious fix was to shut down Kléber-Colombes, but the Michelin CEO, unwilling to alienate the government, had already ruled out that option.

Digging into the problem, Ghosn found out that although Michelin was light-years ahead of everyone else on passenger car tires, Kléber-Colombes actually had an edge in the tractor tire segment. Ghosn proposed a simple solution: give priority to Kléber-Colombes for farm tires and let Michelin focus on making passenger tires.

The biggest obstacle would be convincing François Michelin. The boss was a tire snob who believed that only Michelin could produce proper tires. Giving Kléber-Colombes priority over a section of the market was provocation. Ultimately, however, Monsieur Michelin agreed to give Ghosn's idea a trial run.

*   *   *

The recipe at Kléber-Colombes did wonders, and Ghosn was soon onto his next job as head of research and development for heavy-duty tires. The title wasn't glamorous, nor did it roll off the tongue. He was a master of tires, not the universe. But to Ghosn, being recognized as a master of anything signaled that matters were falling into place. He was on the right trajectory. His career was moving—fast. Perhaps it was time to start sorting out the rest of his life.

Rose had always told her son that he should marry a Lebanese woman. His grandfather would have agreed. Rose didn't trust women from other countries to follow him around the world and build a strong family, as she had done for Georges. She had been through quite a lot and had still managed to keep the family together.

In September 1984, Ghosn met someone whose sudden appearance seemed serendipitous. After playing a bridge tournament in Clermont-Ferrand, he went to Lyon with a friend to visit an old Jamhour classmate. Their host's wife was also Lebanese, and her younger sister had just arrived. Her name was Rita Kordahi. She was nineteen, and it was her first day in France.

Far from attempting to court her, Ghosn, twelve years her senior, devoted the evening to arguing with his friends over bridge tactics, then fell asleep. Rita thought they were crazy to fight so vehemently over a card game, and none of what transpired between the two of them suggested romance.

But two weeks later, Ghosn invited Rita and her sister to his house for a party. Rita, a petite brunette, had never had a serious relationship. She had grown up in the war-ravaged version of Beirut, carrying two backpacks to school—one holding books, the other holding clothes in case she couldn't return home. Ghosn could relate to that, having heard the stories from his own family. But she had lived it. This was a woman bearing no grand delusions about life or romance. Barely nine months after meeting, Rita and Carlos had a civil wedding in France.

It needed to happen fast, because Carlos Ghosn was going back to the country of his birth—Brazil—and if Rita was going to join him, she would need a visa.

*   *   *

Michelin had first entered the Brazilian market seven years earlier, at the time when Ghosn joined the company. In a meeting with shareholders, his eyes shining, François Michelin had described Brazil as a promised land. The market for truck tires was twice as big as France's and trucks clocked thousands of miles per week.

But the Brazilian business had turned into a disaster for Michelin. Sales were okay, but the Brazilian economy was facing severe turmoil. The company's bookkeepers were straining to account for the hyper-inflation that was leading to massive losses. By 1985, matters were so dire that Chahid-Nouraï was openly discussing pulling out of the Brazilian market entirely.

"We're going to lose our shirt in there!" he told his boss.

François Michelin didn't want to just give up, so Chahid-Nouraï suggested a Hail Mary pass: Why not dispatch Michelin's management prodigy, the thirty-one-year-old Carlos Ghosn, to Brazil to straighten things out? Again, François Michelin was hesitant. He feared that Ghosn lacked experience. But Chahid-Nouraï had full confidence in the young manager and ultimately pushed the decision through.

And just like that, Ghosn returned to his true homeland.

In Brazil, Michelin's sales team was bleeding the company dry by selling tires on three months' credit. With the cruzeiro tanking by the day, any profits had turned into losses by the time the payments hit Michelin's account.

Now Michelin would impose payment up front. When a nervous salesman told a customer about the change, the latter smiled. "Ah, finally the penny has dropped for the French."

There were other issues. In order to fight inflation, the Brazilian government was imposing price controls, preventing Michelin from increasing its prices even as the costs of raw materials were soaring. Ghosn set up a dedicated team to badger technocrats until they cleared Michelin's demands.

Once a month, Ghosn flew back to Clermont-Ferrand to present to François Michelin and other top managers. He prepared with Chahid-Nouraï, who made suggestions, often telling Ghosn to strip out numbers to make it more accessible for the boss.

Through Ghosn's presentations, Chahid-Nouraï and other executives followed each step of the recovery. Quickly, the thirty-two-year-old managed to rein in and control the crises facing Michelin. By 1987, Ghosn could even boast a profit for the Brazil unit—a relatively small one but big enough that François Michelin himself wanted a closer look.

*   *   *

In May 1988, François Michelin visited Brazil and took a tour of the empire. "The old married couple would like to visit Brazil," Ghosn had been told. Bernadette Michelin wanted to do some sightseeing. She had been studying the Michelin green guide, part of a series of books launched decades earlier to get people to use their vehicles and wear out their tires so they would have to buy more.

Then sixty-one, François Michelin was a tall, fastidious man with swept-back gray hair. The grandson of Edouard Michelin, who had founded the company a century earlier, François Michelin took over as chief executive in 1955, and established himself as the patriarch upon whose say-so everything depended. Though respected for his innovation, he was a creature of habit. He drove the same ancient Citroën 2CV, short for *deux chevaux*, or two horses, to work every day for years. He wore his shirts and coats until they fell apart.

To Ghosn, François Michelin quickly became a kind of father figure, and the relationship provided him with his first opportunity to study a captain of industry. Ghosn paid as much attention to his boss's flaws as he did his virtues, while also taking note of their shared instincts. Like Ghosn, François Michelin was a staunch globalist. Despite having been born and raised in Auvergne and having left his hometown only reluctantly, he believed that his duty was to expand his company around the world, to ensure that it would survive, even if it came at the expense of French jobs. "A boss is designated and named to grow the company," he would say. "If you don't have that in your genes, you're not a boss."

They also shared a distrust of politicians. The chief executive had once stopped Charles de Gaulle, a man to whom very few said "non," from visiting the inside of one of his plants in Clermont-Ferrand.

For all their aligned instincts, the two men were very different. One of the affable boss's greatest quirks was his detachment from money and material things, a lack of interest Ghosn never understood. François Michelin also hated balance sheets and the accountants who made them.

One Sunday during his trip to Brazil, François Michelin and Ghosn went to mass together at the Catholic church. As they were leaving, the patriarch patted his pockets and realized that he didn't have any cash on him. He turned to his country manager. "Monsieur Ghosn, do you have a little bit of money?"

Not knowing what it was for, Ghosn opened his wallet and gave his boss $100, figuring he was a rich man and that that would be sufficient for whatever he needed to buy. Outside the church, François Michelin turned and handed the money to a nearby beggar, who was standing there with outstretched hand. Ghosn was amazed. Here was one of the biggest executives in the world who seemed to exhibit little sense of the value of money.

François Michelin had managed to turn his company into a global giant, but Ghosn evaluated the messes that he credited to his boss's disdain for numbers: Kléber-Colombes; Brazil; fires that the ever-expanding Michelin team had to put out annually. To Ghosn, profit mattered. Money mattered. He regarded it as the simplest measurement on his ultimate scorecard, for both companies and people. The more you had, the better you were.

*　　*　　*

François Michelin had an ulterior motive for visiting Brazil: he needed to see whether Ghosn was senior management material. He had an important job in mind. Michelin was going to acquire the US tire maker Uniroyal Goodrich for a vast sum, enough that the failure of the company could sink Michelin. He needed a manager in the United States he could trust.

A few months after he returned from Brazil, François Michelin called Ghosn. "I'm going to buy Uniroyal Goodrich, and I want to send you to the US to run the company," he said.

The offer caught Ghosn off guard. He had spent three frenetic years in Brazil, first focused on rescuing Michelin's business, then battling to expand it. He was only starting to reacquaint himself with his birth country. Ghosn's first child, Caroline, had just been born. At the family apartment in Ipanema, Ghosn's relatives poured through the door constantly—his parents, his sisters Claudine and Sylvia, and their husbands—with such regularity and comfort that Rita sometimes felt she had married ten people.

Moving to the United States would mean breaking up the family and removing what had become their de facto home base. Ghosn dreaded telling his mom. She delighted in her new grandchild and in the family being reunited after decades of strife, separation, and uncertainty. But Rita pushed him to go; he simply had to take the job. It was a massive promotion, and, truth be told, she didn't mind the idea of putting some distance between herself and the in-laws.

*   *   *

Carlos, Rita, and Caroline arrived in Greenville, South Carolina, in the spring of 1989. Michelin had picked the southern city for its US offices in large part because there were no unions. Unionized workers were considered disruptive and costly, holding too much sway over compensation patterns and business decisions. The quiet urban center suited Ghosn just fine: less distraction, less drama, just the job at hand.

In September 1989, Michelin agreed to buy Uniroyal Goodrich for $1.5 billion, creating the world's largest tire company. The deal would triple Michelin's market share in North America, giving it one-fifth of the global tire market.

Ghosn got to work analyzing Uniroyal Goodrich's books, searching for the company's inefficiencies to devise solutions that might capitalize on hidden potential. Among the litany of issues he discovered was the difference in pay between the two companies. Despite the fact that he was the overarching boss at that stage, dozens of employees at Uniroyal Goodrich earned more than he did. He was making around

$200,000, a decent salary for an employee of a French company but equal to a middle manager's pay at Uniroyal Goodrich. The disparity was also on display. Uniroyal Goodrich executives all had freshly cut flowers delivered to their offices every day. At Michelin, executives had wooden chairs and spartan desks.

"Wait a minute . . . why do we have those salaries?" Ghosn asked his HR team. His question was genuine; at first blush he didn't know whether the Michelin team should be making more or if Uniroyal's was wildly overpaid.

It was an echo of Ghosn's visit to California years earlier, to his friend's supposedly "middle-class" house with four cars. But it was Ghosn's first exposure to one of the underlying dynamics that had produced such a bounty—the drastically different pay scale of US corporations. This couldn't stand, Ghosn thought. There couldn't be two pay scales between Michelin and Uniroyal Goodrich executives. Michelin was going to have to raise its own executives' salaries—including his own—in North America.

His decision was met with resistance. If Michelin matched US salaries, none of the French executives would ever return to France, Ghosn was told. If they didn't raise the salaries, no executives would be returning to France anyway, he responded. They'd all jump ship long before.

Ghosn got his way. Although the gap between Michelin and Uniroyal Goodrich wasn't completely closed, the US salaries at Michelin increased.

The pay disparity, both in number and on display, was symptomatic of one of the big challenges of the merger. The two companies were rooted in vastly different cultures—Ghosn's task was to join them in corporate matrimony. Michelin was a family-run company whose patriarch preached modesty and insisted upon traditional values. Uniroyal Goodrich's executive team were cigar-chomping New York finance sharks who knew the numbers and kept a close eye on the stock market. In the words of one Michelin executive, it was like marrying a virgin and a hoodlum.

For Ghosn to make the unlikely marriage work, he would need to understand the US company better. There were a million and one reasons why Uniroyal Goodrich was struggling, but Ghosn zeroed on the biggest one: its factories. As he pored over the data, it became apparent that all but one of Uniroyal Goodrich's seven North American factories were worthless. The previous owners had starved the plants of the funds they needed to modernize and stay competitive.

Ghosn began wielding the ax, closing several plants and cutting jobs at others. But unlike Michelin, Uniroyal Goodrich had powerful unions at several of its US facilities. In Fort Wayne, Indiana, things turned ugly. Ghosn wanted to keep the plant running but with a sharply reduced workforce. The union refused to negotiate. The plant manager relaying Ghosn's orders was being harassed. He received death threats. Someone sent him a bullet in the mail. His daughter was bullied. His wife was hassled at the shopping mall.

Ghosn tried starving out the union by withdrawing funds and shifting production to other plants, but the union didn't crack. After three months of fruitless negotiations, Ghosn told the plant manager, "You're going to go back, and you're going to give the plant closure notice." The maneuver worked. Soon after the threat, the plant resumed production with roughly a third fewer workers.

Only a decade earlier, Ghosn himself had been working night shifts on the factory floor in France. He realized as well as anyone that job cuts were painful, but where he differed was in his ability to replace sympathy with cold logic. Market forces were brutal enough that he felt his choice was simple: either cut some jobs or lose them all.

At the Fort Wayne plant, the shell-shocked manager acknowledged the success created by Ghosn's firm hand. "I don't know what kind of peacetime general he is," he said, "but he's a great wartime general."

*   *   *

Ghosn cut a strange figure at Michelin in the United States. The French expats were wary of his forceful tactics, which seemed very un-French. They gave him the nickname "Le Requin," or "The Shark." "Don't mess with this guy," they'd say. "If he grabs hold of your arm, he'll keep chewing and chewing." But Ghosn's allies grew in number as the company's profits increased, and his critics became less vocal.

Ghosn didn't fit the mold of a typical tall, broad-shouldered American CEO, either. He was short—though he developed a stance in which his calves always seemed contracted, as though he was ready to spring into action at any moment. He appeared bookish, with thick-rimmed glasses and bad suits. But whatever he lacked in style he made up for with his magnetic personality: he was energetic and captivating and could be counted on to deliver his message with clarity. He never minced words, nor was he vague about his intentions: everyone had a clear target, for which they were held accountable. Even when a tornado flattened Uniroyal Goodrich's plant in Ardmore, Oklahoma, Ghosn flew in with an ambitious timetable for its return to production.

After two and a half years on the job, Ghosn agreed to his first media interview, which he gave to *Modern Tire Dealer.* Mistakenly writing that his name was pronounced "goon," the trade publication described Ghosn as "somewhat of a mystery man" but stressed that he had won the respect of US managers, many of whom were much older.

Indeed, Ghosn was still in his thirties. But with increasing ease and enjoyment, he was starting to rub shoulders with the movers and shakers in US auto society. Running the branch of a major car parts maker, Ghosn found himself mingling with other CEOs. Just as he had studied the habits of factory workers, he took mental notes on how those men ran their businesses. He especially loved the way Bob Lutz, the outspoken Chrysler Corporation CEO, talked. Once Lutz stood in front of a group of Michelin executives and questioned why anyone would have purchased one of his company's vehicles in the past, as they had been so inferior. Ghosn loved such confidence and candor. He related to the steely criticism that Lutz cast on his own business. Ghosn respected honest assessments, black-and-white facts. That was why he loved math: the clarity of its answers. There are no excuses, no delays. With math, either equations are correct or they aren't.

*　　*　　*

After a few years in South Carolina, the Ghosns bought their first house, moving into an upmarket development in Greenville. The house cost $645,000, for which they took out a large mortgage. It was a stately four-bedroom home, one of the largest in the development, set back from the main road. It sat on a sprawling 6.5-acre lot, which Rita loved. Caroline now had a sister, Nadine, and the two of them had plenty of room to run around outside. Two more children, Maya and Anthony, would be born in short order.

Ghosn was running one of the largest employers in town but he imagined that the community would be surprised to learn how little he was being paid, given his title and growing status. Rita drove a Mazda minivan as she shuttled the kids to school and to sports practice. Ghosn's friends, fellow executives, drove Porsches.

Despite all his successes, his steadfastness in confronting Uniroyal's deficiencies, and his burgeoning reputation, Ghosn was still making well under half a million dollars a year in the mid-1990s, whereas the CEOs of carmakers like Chrysler and GM were making several times that. Ghosn had been aware of their pay packages but also had enough self-awareness to appreciate that these executives were in a different league. Ghosn was working for a supplier, not a carmaker. And he wasn't a CEO.

Still, he was nothing if not ambitious and was constantly at work composing a vivid and detailed mental picture of how the power brokers in his world operated. While he was calculating and observing the trajectories of success of those around him, it dawned on the Lebanese transplant (living in the United States, working for a French company) that he had enjoyed a meteoric rise during his almost two decades at Michelin—but he was about to hit a glass ceiling. He was not a man who appreciated boundaries.

In 1996, François Michelin began planning to retire and prepared to hand over greater responsibilities to his son Édouard. The elder Michelin had sent his son to North America to be mentored by Ghosn, who put him in charge of the plants and truck tire sales. Ghosn understood that Édouard, not him, would soon lead the company.

Rita was a pragmatic, perceptive woman. She could see that Ghosn was at a dead end, so she pushed him to leave. "There is no more space for you," she told him plainly. While mulling over her assessment, he got a call from a headhunter who had made a similar calculation.

A fellow graduate of École Polytechnique, the headhunter told him that a certain car company was looking for a new number two, who would have the possibility of getting the top job if he performed well. Ghosn was intrigued. He soon learned that the carmaker was Renault, another French company. But everyone understood that moving from a supplier to an actual carmaker was a massive leap. Still he hesitated. One didn't leave François Michelin lightly. He would take it as a personal affront. Ghosn loved the elderly Michelin and didn't relish the idea of burning that bridge.

*   *   *

On a Saturday morning in 1996, Ghosn met the CEO of Renault, Louis Schweitzer, in his office in Paris. The two had met once before, when Ghosn and Chahid-Nouraï had presented their plan for the rescue of Kléber-Colombes to Schweitzer, who was a government official at the time.

Schweitzer was impressed with the forty-two-year-old Ghosn. In addition to his already stellar career, Ghosn had visible strength, drive, and most of all a strong magnetism. The two men spoke for two hours. By the end of the talk, Schweitzer told Ghosn that the job was his if he wanted it.

A few weeks later, Ghosn was again on a flight to France, steeling himself for what he was about to do in Clermont-Ferrand. Predictably, when Ghosn told his mentor he was resigning, François was hurt. He took it as a betrayal, later asking a young executive, "Why is he leaving me?"

It was a sad note to end his time as a Michelin man. Ghosn's departure was announced in a laconic company news release. But the factual, if passionless, recitation of his triumphs underscored a simple truth: Carlos Ghosn was a battle-hardened global executive. He had the gene; he was prepared to lead.

5

The Birth of the Alliance

Louis Schweitzer gazed out over the Seine, trying to divine the future. The former civil servant couldn't see it from his current post, but he knew that just up the river and around a bend, about eight miles from the Cathedral of Notre-Dame, sat Île Seguin, the island that housed the company's oldest factory.

Once a symbol of France's postwar recovery and industrial ambitions, the factory was now an abandoned husk. The last vehicle had rolled off the line half a decade earlier, in 1992, and the works now lay dormant. It was a painful chapter to close, but the factory had become a symbol of everything wrong at Renault: it was owned by the state, run by bureaucrats, with line workers who were members of one of France's most notorious rough-and-tumble unions.

Schweitzer was aiming to write a new page: Renault was no longer fully owned by the state, having been privatized under Schweitzer's watch.

Still, a headline in the business monthly *L'Expansion* from a few years earlier continued to stick in Schweitzer's mind: "Renault Too Small, Too Alone, Too French." It was especially memorable because Schweitzer didn't entirely disagree with the diagnosis.

Merger frenzy was sweeping the globe in the spring of 1998. Consultants and bankers were pushing companies to marry, pointing at all their competitors that were out shopping for a partner. Conventional wisdom was that you either got bigger or got trampled.

Schweitzer, a blue-blooded patrician who counted Jean-Paul Sartre among his relatives, wasn't immune from the market pressure. But he also had reason to be confident.

Thanks in part to Ghosn, now more than a year into his tenure, France's largest carmaker was having a rare moment of financial strength. As planned, Ghosn had whipped the company into a lean profit machine. So much so that Renault had built up a pile of cash and was hunting for an acquisition target that would put it in the automotive big leagues and ensure its long-term survival. Also, a deal with Volvo had fallen through at the last moment, and the cash Renault was going to use for that deal was still burning a hole in Schweitzer's pocket.

Nissan was high up on Schweitzer's short list of potential targets. Several years earlier, he had discussed deals with Fiat in Italy and Daimler in Germany, but talks had gone nowhere. Meanwhile, the US carmakers were too big and too strong to do a deal with a small French carmaker.

That left the Koreans and the Japanese. Schweitzer and most of his colleagues at Renault preferred the Japanese. They had better cars and had managed to break into the US market. Nissan was also in serious trouble. The company was bleeding cash and piling on debt. Its market share was shrinking.

On paper, a deal with Nissan was perfect. Renault wanted a strong presence in Asia and the United States, and Nissan had both. Nissan's engineers were world class, and the company had a reputation for building high-quality vehicles (well-known perennial sellers such as the Maxima), the likes of which astounded Renault engineers. The problem was that Nissan was more focused on building cars its engineers found interesting and impressive, such as sports cars and powerful sedans, rather than those that an average consumer wanted.

On May 6, 1998, the *Wall Street Journal* broke the news that Daimler-Benz AG and Chrysler Corporation were discussing a merger in what would be the largest car industry deal in history. Schweitzer, along with the heads of every other car company worldwide, had immediate concerns about the impact it would have on Renault's business.

The combined company would employ more than 420,000 people and produce around 4 million vehicles a year, everything from Chrysler minivans to Mercedes sedans and Jeep Wranglers.

Publicly, Schweitzer downplayed the importance of the Daimler-Chrysler merger, saying that Renault was strong enough in Europe to compete with the new automotive giant. But in the closed conference rooms in Renault's headquarters at Boulogne-Billancourt, making an acquisition and doing a deal were put forth as a pressing imperative.

In June, Schweitzer sent letters to the heads of Nissan and Mitsubishi asking if they wanted to have a discussion on strategy. Both companies agreed to open talks. Renault had to decide which it preferred.

In the early summer of 1998, Schweitzer gathered his top lieutenants, including Ghosn, in the lounge of the Hôtellerie du Bas-Bréau in Barbizon, a quaint village an hour's drive outside Paris. They debated the pros and cons of both. Most of the executives felt that if Renault was going to spend time and effort forging an alliance, it should go for the bigger, more ambitious deal, which was with Nissan. The project was code-named Pacifique.

Nissan had no choice but to talk. It was in dire straits. At its headquarters, the air conditioners and some of the elevators had been shut off in order to keep the lights on. For years, the company had been kept afloat by banks in Japan, but a recession in Japan had led to a rise in loan defaults, which had dried up the credit market. Japan's famed bubble era, marked by rapid growth and easy credit, had come crashing down at the worst possible time for Nissan. The company had amassed $22 billion in debt and a host of uncompetitive products. There would be no more bailouts.

Schweitzer boarded a flight to Tokyo to meet his counterpart at Nissan, Yoshikazu Hanawa. He laid out his broad vision for the partnership, then left the ball in Nissan's court. In September, Hanawa flew to Paris, where the two executives formally agreed to negotiate. The companies each assigned a hundred people the task of hammering out the details of a deal. Schweitzer asked that the negotiations be exclusive.

*   *   *

Everything seemed to be going smoothly—until a meeting in Singapore in November 1998. At the meeting, Hanawa told Schweitzer that Nissan was keen to do a deal but that Renault was not the only potential partner. Nissan had also opened talks with the newly merged behemoth DaimlerChrysler and with Ford, which had recently taken a controlling stake in another Japanese carmaker, Mazda.

Schweitzer was devastated. Standing in the tropical drizzle after the meeting, he forecasted that Renault had maybe a one-in-ten shot to close a deal. He keenly felt the company's relative weakness in the automotive world: Ford was cash rich and had a foothold in Japan; DaimlerChrysler was a behemoth with the prestige of Mercedes to boast. Schweitzer reckoned that his only shot was appealing to the pride of the Japanese.

He explained to Hanawa that he envisioned an automotive *partnership* between the French and the Japanese companies, rather than a merger. In the aftermath of Renault's doomed attempt to acquire Volvo, Schweitzer had learned that many of the Swedish workers hated Renault. They felt as though the French were bullying them, trying to erase what made their company unique. Schweitzer had resolved to do things differently this time. He still assumed that Renault would be the senior partner in the arrangement. It was, after all, bringing the money. But he wanted to ensure that it wouldn't feel that way. If DaimlerChrysler's pitch was going to be "Marry us, we're rich and prestigious," Renault's pitch would be "Marry us, we will respect you and your ways."

Schweitzer made his proposal in the form of a mock press release. The headline read: "Renault and Nissan Join Forces." The two-page document outlined how Renault would pay $5 billion for a stake in Nissan. Renault would appoint three Nissan board members, who would act as chief operating officer, chief financial officer, and head of product planning. Now he needed a final touch to ensure that Renault would stand out among richer and more powerful suitors.

So when the time came to get down onto one knee, Schweitzer brought out Carlos Ghosn.

*   *   *

Ghosn had arrived at Renault almost two years earlier, when the French company was struggling to keep its costs under control. The company had recently unveiled a plan to the public to save around 3,000 francs per vehicle. Ghosn had looked at the plan and tore it up.

Renault had never really been a profitable, healthy company. Historically, it had become known as much for its labor-friendly policies as for its cars. When Renault had been in the red, it had had to go hat in hand to the government for bailouts. The joke in France was that you paid for a Renault car twice: once at the dealership and again in your income taxes. When Schweitzer had entered the scene, he had sought to change things.

The government retained a significant stake in the company, and much as Schweitzer had tried to get the union to adopt more reasonable demands and focus on the bottom line, he could only do so much. That was why he had brought in Ghosn. He needed help with slashing costs, an art the young Ghosn had already mastered at Michelin in France, Brazil, and the United States.

Ghosn quickly got to work devising a plan to improve the company's profitability. He worked backward, calculating that the company would need to save about 20 billion francs by 2000 if it wanted to be competitive. That worked out to 8,000 francs per vehicle.

When he told Schweitzer about his revised plan, Schweitzer looked at his young manager, trying to decide whether he knew what he was doing. The company wasn't going to get out of its hole without some measure of sacrifice or risk. The plan was ambitious, he noted, but possible. Ghosn agreed. He spoke with the unflinching confidence that compelled people to believe in him.

Soon after, Ghosn presented an extremely straightforward suggestion to kick off his plan: close three plants. Just like that. Schweitzer respected Ghosn's bold plan but realized that he would have to rein in his charge. He compromised, and in the end they agreed to close a single factory, which was in Belgium. The CEO was right to be cautious. The decision led to a fierce battle that earned Ghosn his next nickname, "Le Cost Killer," which stuck with him for his entire career.

Simultaneously, Ghosn set about breaking the rigid bureaucracy within Renault. He handpicked junior staff from a variety of departments, forming new teams tasked with ferreting out wasteful spending. The young, hungry managers weren't shackled by corporate politics. They had fresh, modern visions of what needed to be done to make money. New cross-departmental teams were formed to break fiefdoms and circumvent tired power centers. Salespeople weighed in on manufacturing; engineers went after finance. His goal was to get everyone thinking about how the company operated as a whole.

Each department was tasked with reducing its costs, and there were regular check-ins with Ghosn to track their progress. After several months, Jean-Baptiste Duzan, who had a preeminent role in the company as the head of purchasing, was among the team members gathered in a meeting room with Ghosn. When the executives totaled up their collective work they realized they would save the company some 19.2 billion francs. "My God, we've managed it, it's incredible!" Duzan thought.

The team was tired but exhilarated by their success. Ghosn looked at the total. "Are you sure?" They all nodded. He praised them for their hard work. Then he looked around the room, and instructed them to go back to their teams. "We need to get to twenty," he stated. He had promised—and expected—100 percent.

*   *   *

It had taken Ghosn months to construct his 20 billion–franc plan at Renault, but the payoff would extend far beyond the slanted sides of the rhombus logo known to nearly everyone in France. Now, the work was on show for a Japanese audience.

On November 11, 1998, Ghosn outlined for Nissan's Japanese executives the cost-cutting miracle he'd pulled off at Renault. His two-hour presentation was met with stony-faced silence. Staring at the sea of stoic Nissan executives in the room, Ghosn had no idea whether they were impressed or completely bored.

Ghosn soon learned that he had indeed made a strong impression on Hanawa, who told Schweitzer after the presentation that if Renault and Nissan made a deal, he was keen for Ghosn to oversee Nissan's recovery efforts. Another Nissan executive, Toshiyuki Shiga, was also impressed. He, too, was rooting for Ghosn, having been struck by his inimitable energy and passion.

Ghosn's performance, though impressive, wasn't a golden ticket. Renault was still competing with the Germans. By January 1999, it was struggling to even secure a meeting. Increasingly, the French suspected that Nissan was keeping them around as insurance, in the event the DaimlerChrysler deal fell through.

Alain Dassas, a finance executive at Renault, was having a conversation with Nissan executives when Shiga received a quiet message. The Japanese manager abruptly halted the meeting and escorted Dassas and his colleagues out. The Renault team was told that the Daimler executives had shown up early, so, unfortunately, their meeting would have to continue later. Renault negotiators took it in stride, knowing that they were not the favored candidate and that if they wanted to stay in the race, they would have to swallow their pride and be patient.

Plenty of people at Nissan were rooting for DaimlerChrysler. Young Nissan executives were abuzz with excitement at the prospect of working alongside the engineers who had made the Mercedes-Benzes they all lusted after. No one lusted after Renaults. In fact, they valued Renault engineering somewhere near the bottom of the automotive industry.

On March 9, the Renault team flew to Japan to start another round of negotiations, though some of them presumed that it would be their last meeting. Nissan had set a deadline for talks to wrap up by the end of that month, when it would close its books for the financial year.

Nissan's affections had so clearly waned that Renault lawyer Mouna Sepehri took to carrying an agreement to terminate the negotiations in her briefcase. It was Daimler's deal to lose.

The next day, the Renault team in Japan got an urgent phone call from Schweitzer, who was at the Geneva International Motor Show. DaimlerChrysler had just announced that it was pulling out of talks with Nissan. The trip to Japan was supposed to last two days, but an excited Schweitzer told the team that they would be staying longer. "You should go to Nissan headquarters right away, they are waiting for you. Now we have to sign," he said.

At Nissan, the mood was dour. The company's share price had tanked after news broke of DaimlerChrysler's withdrawal. Nissan desperately needed the cash, but DaimlerChrysler had decided it wasn't worth the money. Nissan had been jilted at the altar and was now faced with the prospect of having to settle for its second choice.

Renault didn't want Nissan to feel that way. At the beginning of the meeting, the head of Renault's legal department stood up to deliver a speech, reassuring Nissan that Renault was sincere in its offer of a partnership rather than a takeover. "We'll continue to treat you as an equal," he said.

Shiga, who had recently shuffled Renault executives out of meetings to accommodate the Germans, stood up and bowed. All that was left to do was for Schweitzer to get confirmation that he had his best man on the job. He called Ghosn into his office and said he wouldn't do the deal, which many felt was doomed to fail, unless Ghosn agreed to go to Japan. "In my mind, there's only one person who can go to Japan to do this, and it's you. If you won't go, I won't sign."

The stakes were high for both men. If Nissan went on to fail under Renault control, Ghosn would take the fall and be out of a job. Then again, so would Schweitzer. Moreover, Ghosn had taken the job with the ambition of eventually ascending to be CEO of Renault (with such conviction that, by Schweitzer's recommendation, he had taken on French citizenship so that he would be able to do so). And if he agreed to the new position, success could result in a far grander throne.

Schweitzer laid out the perks of the job in Japan and told Ghosn to let him know what it would take to send him there. Rita wasn't thrilled. The family had returned to France from the United States less than two years before. She was finally feeling settled, having found a permanent home—a stately, centuries-old country château outside Paris in the idyllic village of L'Étang-la-Ville. She was looking forward to doing renovations. Now her husband was talking about moving them again—to Japan? Rita pushed him to demand the biggest paycheck he could justify.

The company was on the ropes. It needed Ghosn's expertise in turning around companies, she reasoned. If it worked, Nissan would rake in cash. Why shouldn't the Ghosn family rake it in as well? Money wasn't exactly tight, but turning an ancient château into a modern family home took significant resources. More to the point, she knew her husband was worth it. Even if she did get the money, however, she still wasn't sure about Japan for her and their children.

Over lunch in one of the small dining rooms at Renault's headquarters, Schweitzer and Ghosn discussed how many people Ghosn wanted to bring with him, who they would be, and his conditions. They agreed that he should be provided with housing, and, in addition to a basic salary of close to $1 million, Ghosn asked for 10 million Nissan shares over the next three years, worth about $30 million at the time. He aimed high, but he was also a realist: he figured he had a fifty-fifty chance of success at the job. If he failed, Nissan would go bankrupt, he would be out of a job, and his shares would be worthless. If he succeeded, the value of the stocks would skyrocket. His pay, he felt, should match the significant risks he was taking.

Schweitzer thought it was a huge amount, but he wasn't there to bargain with his number two. He agreed to pass it on to the Japanese and picked up the phone. Hanawa asked Schweitzer whether he had accidentally tacked on an extra zero to the number of shares Ghosn wanted. "No," said Schweitzer. That was how much it would cost to get Carlos Ghosn to Japan.

Hanawa agreed, at least to the amount. He wasn't there to bargain, either. But Nissan refused to pay his salary in dollars, as Ghosn had requested. He would have to make do with local currency.

Ghosn had one final condition: his wife would have to agree.

Schweitzer sought out the assistance of a Japanese woman to organize a trip to Japan for Rita and the kids. The woman was under pressure from everyone at Renault to make sure that Rita saw the very best Japan had to offer. She came through, as by the end of the trip, Rita agreed that she would go.

The deal between Renault and Nissan was signed on March 27, 1999, in one of the auditoriums of the Keidanren, Japan's premier business association. Schweitzer had been true to his word to Nissan. There wasn't a single Renault logo in sight.

*   *   *

Few people believed that the partnership had much of a shot.

Ford CEO Jacques Nasser said his company had little interest in companies such as Nissan: "We're not in the mood of swapping our hard-earned cash for someone else's hard-earned liabilities."

DaimlerChrysler had walked away, perhaps a result of some colorful advice from its former colleague Bob Lutz, the man Ghosn had long admired. Lutz had warned DaimlerChrysler not to do a deal with Nissan. If it wanted to spend money on Nissan, it should put $5 billion in gold bullion onto a barge, paint "Nissan" on the side, and then dump it all overboard into the Pacific. That way, he said, it would lose only $5 billion. Most suitors looked at Nissan and saw a pile of debt. They looked at Renault and saw a pile of something else. Let them have each other, they thought.

A few days after signing, following a news conference at the New York International Auto Show, all sides were at pains to emphasize that it wasn't a merger—at least not yet.

The French were afraid of the debt. (It was the reason why Renault had bought only a 37 percent stake in Nissan, giving it control but ensuring that Nissan's $20 billion in debt wouldn't end up on Renault's books.) Meanwhile, the Japanese were afraid of, well, the French. No matter what kind words Renault offered, it was embarrassing. Nissan made incredible cars; it had world-class engineers; yet its executives had run the company so poorly that even in the hottest merger market in the industry's history, no one wanted it. It grated on the company's employees to think that the company was now the property of a French company and, to a certain extent, of the French state.

Still, Schweitzer told a huddled group of reporters that the Alliance *might* turn into a merger someday, if the conditions were right. Across the room, Hanawa spoke to a separate group of journalists, assuring them that such a day would never come. "It's a different alliance. It's not a merger. It's not a takeover," he said through an interpreter. "It will be like this for a long time, for forever."

Asked how the new partnership could survive given the apparent disagreement over its future, Hanawa sought to lighten the tone. "Well you know, in a relationship, a man and a lady can have different opinions about what the relationship means," he quipped.

6

Turnaround

Carlos Ghosn began his seduction of Japan perched on a comfortable chair in front of an audience of twenty million potential customers. The setting was TV Asahi's *News Station*, where he would be grilled by one of Japanese television's most aggressive newsmen, Hiroshi Kume. The top-rated anchorman thrived on attacking Japan's power brokers and took visible glee in cutting into his subjects with his acerbic wit. There would be no softball questions tonight.

Ghosn's arrival in the spring of 1999 was perceived with as much apprehension and curiosity as might follow an alien invasion. Many in Japan thought it impossible for its companies to be run by foreigners. They were too conservative, too idiosyncratic. Everyone, from CEOs to street sweepers, wanted to hear from this foreign man who was foolish enough to doom himself so publicly. He was about to lead one of Japan's most vaunted companies, Nissan, in one of the nation's biggest industries. If he stumbled, the failure would match the stakes: spectacular.

The Japanese car industry had led the crushed nation out of its post–World War II malaise and had been the primary engine behind Japan's relatively swift recovery. When the country had become the world's second largest economy in 1967 and there had been talk of the country overtaking the United States, it was the strength of Japan's car manufacturers that had made the notion believable.

Cars designed and built by Japanese hands had upended the car

business in the 1970s, when sales of small, fuel-efficient Japanese vehicles exploded in the United States following a spike in gas prices.
Vehicles churned out by Detroit were celebrated for their design
and horsepower but rarely for their quality or fuel efficiency. Toyota,
Honda, and other rivals changed that, selling well-made cars at a price
that seemed impossible to their competitors. As Japanese carmakers
stole market share in the United States, Detroit started mimicking
the way Japanese companies made cars. That spread from the US Rust
Belt to Wolfsburg, with the companies that had created the modern
automobile turning into pupils of the upstarts from Japan.

Despite the positive psychological cargo hauled in the trunks of Japan's cars, its captains of industry received as much prime-time television coverage as their global contemporaries: about zero.

So Ghosn's invitation from one of Japan's most popular interviewers
added electricity to the outsider's recent arrival on the scene. Nissan's
PR team had warned Ghosn that Kume would try to eat him alive and
had urged him to conduct his first TV appearance on the much gentler
public broadcaster, NHK, the dull but safe option. Ghosn, never one to
prioritize caution, chose to plunge into the deep end.

Kume wasted no time. He opened his prime-time slot by comparing
Ghosn to another foreigner who also had dark, prominent eyebrows,
who happened to be huge in Japan and was starring in Nissan com-
mercials at the time.

"He looks like Mr. Bean, doesn't he?" Kume said.

"But," the interviewer added, "this is a man of huge ability."

Nissan was in dire shape, and everyone knew that Ghosn was the
man brought in to save it. The difference was that most people presumed he would almost certainly fail, whereas Ghosn felt that his
whole career had prepared him for the challenge and that he had a decent shot at succeeding. Ghosn had saved Renault, Kume told viewers
while pointing at a chart, by closing the Vilvoorde factory in Belgium
at the loss of three thousand jobs. "Will the formula used at Renault be
used at Nissan?" he asked through a translator.

Ghosn gathered himself under the studio lights.

"There is no formula," he answered. "Renault is Renault, and Nissan is Nissan. You cannot keep up unused capacity for a long time. That doesn't work in any industry. But I do not think you could energize Nissan just by focusing on reduction." That said, he insisted that the firm would need to return to making attractive, competitive products. If not, drastic measures would be necessary.

Kume was enjoying himself—the wunderkind from Renault was proving feisty. He might make for good television. Though he had been the risky interviewer choice, Kume actually reinforced Ghosn's all-star qualities, branding him as a ruthless worker to people who appreciated a tireless work ethic.

That ethic was quickly noted, as evidenced by the company and Japanese media soon referring to him as "Mr. 7-Eleven." Ghosn quickly proved that the nickname wasn't hyperbole. Indeed, he worked from 7:00 a.m. to 11:00 p.m.—and he loved that people knew it. He was known predominantly as "Le Cost Killer," but he much preferred the other moniker. He lived out of a suitcase, staying in a hotel down the street from Nissan's headquarters in the swanky Ginza district, a tightly packed section of Tokyo that could pass for midtown Manhattan. At work he sat alone in a converted conference room on the fifteenth floor at a desk installed for him. He arrived each morning long before most of the staff and turned off the lights when he left. He eschewed the normal corporate hierarchy, meeting directly with middle managers who had strong ideas and tapping younger employees for input on how to fix the company.

Over the first few months, Ghosn toured Nissan's factories in Japan. He was accompanied by a flock of TV cameramen and reporters who documented the new foreign manager at work. Donning the turquoise jacket and cap of the line workers, Ghosn moved up and down the production line with an interpreter, interrogating workers. He met with hundreds of people.

Ghosn had selected two dozen young executives at Renault to join his team, giving them thirty-six hours to decide whether to follow him to Japan. When they arrived, he charged them with unearthing everything that Nissan was doing wrong. As at Michelin and Renault, he put into place cross-departmental teams, bringing together executives from different parts of the company under young managers to break down fiefdoms. Nissan had some of the best engineers in the world but was straining under a bureaucracy that killed off any initiative. Ghosn asked each team to come up with ideas on how to run the company more efficiently.

After touring Japan, Ghosn began to pile up air miles as quickly and as plentifully as his office hours. He flew to Nissan facilities in Europe and the United States, interviewing employees to make his own diagnosis on what was ailing the company.

Ghosn homed in on the US market. It was huge and had an enormous profit potential. Why were the sales there so weak? Ghosn discovered that Nissan would bring out a new model in Japan, then wait eighteen months before launching it in the United States, long after the hype had faded and sales had started tapering off.

Patrick Pelata, Ghosn's trusted lieutenant from Renault, gave his Japanese counterparts a week to come up with a solution. When he heard their fix, he marched into Ghosn's office, dumbfounded. The Japanese team had proposed to delay Japanese product launches by a year and a half to ensure that the vehicles would go on sale in all markets at the same time. Everything felt backward.

On a visit to the Nissan plant in Smyrna, Tennessee, Ghosn, sitting around a table with Pelata, the plant manager, and a few others, was baffled to learn that the US subsidiary was holding hundreds of millions of dollars in cash in accumulated profits. Its executives didn't trust the Japanese executives running the company back in Tokyo. Ghosn and Pelata just looked at each other, stunned. That would need to end.

Nissan's asset list was even more baffling. Ghosn put two of his French executives, Thierry Moulonguet and Dominique Thormann from Renault's finance department, on it. Their mission was to work out what Nissan actually owned. They asked for a list, and though it was delivered, it seemed to change every day, sometimes fluctuating by as many as thirty or forty stakes in other companies. The French finally settled on a number, one that seemed unfathomable. The Japanese carmaker held stakes in 1,394 other companies.

Thormann worked for weeks trying to finalize the list. "How in the heck did we end up owning these things?" he asked his Japanese colleagues. The answer was in the very nature of Japanese corporations: they bound themselves together into interlinked groups known as keiretsu and had shareholdings in one another. The idea was that interdependence and diversification could provide extra security and hedge against any downturns. Nissan was linked to its suppliers, so if one company fell on hard times, the keiretsu could bail it out.

The arrangements made no sense to Ghosn. Nissan had no business owning stock in a bunch of its supplier companies, let alone a supermarket chain (which it did). Selling off those stakes would be an obvious way to raise cash and pay down the company's hulking debt.

Still, nothing jumped out at him quite like the prices Nissan was paying suppliers for parts. As a former parts maker at Michelin, he knew what they should cost. And the idea of trying to save money by switching off the air-conditioning at headquarters in the summer or leaving his secretary short of stationery while paying 20 percent more than Renault did for steel or a transmission left him dumbfounded. Ghosn determined that the whole company was penny wise and pound foolish, especially considering that its US counterparts were famous for squeezing their suppliers for annual reductions.

Although those findings were startling, the implications of Nissan's dysfunction were significant. Taken together they meant that the company, despite its atrocious debt level, was in a much stronger position than anyone appreciated.

By October 18, 1999, Ghosn's Japanese diagnosis and treatment plan was complete. Ghosn strode confidently onto an elevated stage, dressed in a charcoal gray suit and patterned tie. The sign behind him read "Nissan Revival Plan" in both English and Japanese. His brow furrowed above his rimless glasses, Ghosn told the more than six hundred Japanese and foreign journalists that Nissan was sick but not beyond saving. Swinging his hand down like an ax to emphasize each point, he laid out his plan.

Five underused plants would be shut. Twenty-one thousand jobs would be cut. He put purchasing at the center of his plan, saying that Nissan was targeting a 20 percent cut in costs over three years by centralizing purchasing decisions and buying some parts in bulk with Renault. Nissan's roster of 1,145 suppliers of parts and materials needed to be cut in half. Finally, he announced, Nissan's keiretsu would be dismantled. Out of nearly 1,400 companies, Ghosn said, only in four of them did Nissan's shareholding seem to him "indispensable."

Then, reading from a teleprompter, he switched to halting Japanese. "I know how much effort and pain is coming, but believe me, there is no other way," he said.

That level of cost cutting would have hit any company hard, but in Japan, where plant closures and layoffs rarely happened, Ghosn's Revival Plan was an absolute shock to the system.

The plan didn't contain any Western-style firings—payroll would be reduced by buyouts and early retirements—and there was almost no pushback from the powerful Nissan unions, which appreciated the gravity of the situation facing the company.

To prove he wasn't kidding about any of his plans, Ghosn said that he and his entire executive committee would resign if Nissan failed to meet three targets: returning Nissan to profitability by 2000, cutting debt in half by 2002, and increasing Nissan's operating profit margin to 4.5 percent by the end of the Nissan Revival Plan in 2002.

Not even the Renault executives had known that Ghosn was planning to make a pledge to quit, should he fail. Thormann was among those who had made the snap decision to follow Ghosn to Japan. His wife had put a promising career in medicine on hold to accompany her husband six thousand miles from home, and now Ghosn was saying that he and other executives were prepared to pull the plug after the first year if they weren't successful? Thormann knew that he'd taken a risk in coming to Japan, but this was a clear manifestation of just how precarious his gamble had been.

By early 2000, however, Ghosn and Thormann both knew that it was no longer a fifty-fifty bet. Nissan's financials were already looking far better than anybody—including Ghosn and his team, who were scratching their heads and trying to understand why the numbers were looking so good so quickly—had expected. Ghosn's plan for Nissan had the makings of one of the most spectacular industrial turnarounds in the history of the auto industry. It was just a matter of seeing it through.

It wasn't lost on Ghosn that despite their initial shock, the Japanese had braced themselves, quickly recovered, and even seemed to welcome the pain necessary to realize his promise and profit. It was as if someone were articulating something they all knew deep inside—and they were finally free to act on it.

Weeks after Ghosn had announced his plan, Nissan's executive in charge of purchasing, Itaru Koeda, who only uttered the bare necessity at executive committee meetings, took the floor. "We want to cut costs by twenty percent in one year; not in three years," he said. The other executives swiveled their heads around, looking at one another in surprise. Even Ghosn was caught off guard. That was three times as fast as he had asked for. In the engineering department, all fifteen thousand employees stopped their projects for a month to work on how they could contribute to achieving the targeted cost cuts. Pelata quickly realized that such a commitment was typical of Nissan. The company was bold and could do big things. Its employees just needed to be sure they were being led in the right direction.

Carlos Ghosn wasn't just leading a charge; he had people running alongside him.

"The Nissan guys are coming to me and proposing cost savings of twenty percent while at Renault it was a huge effort to get them to save three percent. Where do you think I'd rather be?" Ghosn asked a colleague.

Nissan had found what it needed: a man with a lucid, plausible plan.

And Carlos Ghosn had found a place where people jumped to attention when he told them what needed to be done. To Ghosn, Nissan's potential under his command was boundless.

*   *   *

Ghosn was promptly rewarded for both his diagnosis that Nissan's problems were self-inflicted and thereby easily curable and his incisive marching orders, which would enable him to make good on his targets.

It was a world apart from how he was treated in France, where he was dealt with almost like a bureaucrat. To say nothing of the talk shows and the press conferences with journalists hanging on his every word in Japan, there were everyday luxuries and gestures of respect there: when Ghosn first arrived, he didn't know that Nissan managers had their own elevator. When he stepped onto the ones for the rank and file, he noticed that nobody got off when it stopped and the doors opened. The same thing happened on the next floor, and again until the doors opened on the management floor. No one would dare get off before the boss. He no longer coveted the fresh-cut flowers of US higher-ups. He finally had all the trappings of a high-powered auto executive, including being driven around in Nissan's luxury limousine, the President.

With the wind at his back, Ghosn smashed his first target. In 2000, Nissan posted a $2.7 billion profit, its largest ever, which astounded the business world. Bob Lutz, who'd said that Chrysler would be better off dumping $5 billion of gold into the ocean than investing in Nissan, admitted that his analysis was wrong, but for only one reason: Carlos Ghosn.

The success was Ghosn's, but it was also Japan's. As far as many people in Japan were concerned, the country had passed its peak a decade earlier. The island country had grown into the world's second largest economy, briefly holding the status of the world's largest car producer, until the world had woken up and started fighting back. Even its seemingly untouchable market leader faced skepticism, with the media publishing headlines such as "Toyota's Midlife Crisis" just months before Ghosn arrived in Japan.

Many Japanese lamented that the good times were over. But the unlikely arrival of Carlos Ghosn revived their hope that there might be a brighter future for the country after all. Through the revered qualities of diligence and discipline, he had saved a storied Japanese company from certain doom.

The optimism he inspired made him an instant celebrity, a fame that took on strange forms. A remix of a popular 1960s song, "There's a Tomorrow After All," was revived with new lyrics: "My new boss is French . . . this is my chance. I should start studying again." Ghosn became the symbol of change. *Ghosn-ryu*, or Ghosn style, became shorthand for tough Western-style restructurings of Japanese companies; he was asked for photos and autographs whenever he went to his favorite coffee shop or dined out with his family at the local yakitori restaurant on Sunday evening. But though his status had been elevated overnight, he didn't find the attention overwhelming. Quite the opposite: after all the work he had done across three continents, much of it unseen, he felt he deserved such recognition and regard. He was, in many ways, an icon—and he even had a comic book to prove it.

One of Japan's major manga publishers, Shogakukan, contacted Ghosn and informed him that he was its next subject. These weren't just comic books for kids—manga strips about successful entrepreneurs were what young salarymen read for inspiration during their commute. If Ghosn cooperated, the publisher told him, he would have some say over the content. If not, "We'll do it anyway, and we'll have total freedom."

Ghosn phoned Masayoshi Son, a billionaire tech entrepreneur who had already been made into a manga. "Collaborate!" Son told him. "I didn't, and the mangas were a catastrophe for me." Ghosn spent more than eight hours talking to the manga writers and provided numerous family photos.

The admiration extended beyond his being a superexecutive extolled in coffee jingles and comics. *Time* magazine named Ghosn the "most influential global business executive," ahead of Bill Gates. He was named Asia's businessman of the year by *Fortune* magazine. After attending a World Cup semifinal in Saitama in 2002, Ghosn was so mobbed by fans wanting photos and autographs that it took him more than twenty minutes to walk down twenty steps. But the most personally humbling accolade came from Japanese prime minister Junichiro Koizumi, who said on the campaign trail that he wanted everyone to challenge orthodoxy, just as Carlos Ghosn did.

As Ghosn's celebrity rose alongside Nissan's share price, he huddled with executives at the company's advertising agency, the Madison Avenue powerhouse TBWA. Ghosn was becoming the poster boy of Nissan. He told them that if it would help, they should go ahead and work on his image. TBWA had more than a thousand people on the Nissan account, and its job soon involved integrating what they saw as Ghosn's personal values—dynamism and innovation—into those of the Nissan brand.

It helped that Ghosn was becoming more presentable all the time. He lost twenty pounds. His hair got thicker. He had eye surgery in Lebanon to cure his shortsightedness, allowing him to ditch his bookish eyeglasses. The drab outfits, which had been the subject of such ridicule at Renault that his leaving gift had included a selection of colorful ties, were gone. The guy who had arrived in Japan looking like a math professor now turned up at car shows in expensive tailored suits befitting a true global elite.

*　　*　　*

Back in France, Ghosn's level of celebrity attention came as a shock.

In July 2000, Renault executives almost fell off their chairs when they discovered a large spread about the Ghosn family in *Paris Match*, the glossy bible of the upper classes. Photos showed Ghosn holding court with his four children at the breakfast table in his Tokyo apartment, striding past two rows of bowing Japanese employees, and strolling around town with his kids, mobile phone stuck to his ear. Readers learned that Ghosn "lives in an enormous duplex with views over Tokyo," that Rita was a good tennis player, and that Ghosn's son, Anthony, collected Pokémon cards.

Aghast, Schweitzer reprimanded Ghosn for the first time.

Remembering François Michelin's warning to him that Ghosn needed watching—he had never explained to Schweitzer exactly what he meant—the Renault CEO had made a point of ringing Ghosn every Monday to check in.

The Monday after the *Paris Match* spread appeared, the line from Paris to Tokyo burned. "You should never have done it," Schweitzer fumed. "In France there is a great respect for industry leaders, but stars are not approved." Ghosn listened. He was new to this game. To him, *Paris Match* was just another magazine among the many he had given interviews to in Tokyo.

He promised to be more careful in the future.

The following year, Ghosn and Schweitzer had a second disagreement. In October 2001, Ghosn published a book about Nissan's revival in Japan titled *Renaissance*. Schweitzer was fine with that. He had no problem with Ghosn's celebrity in Japan as CEO. He presumed that it could help Nissan sell cars. But that was never the status he had wanted Ghosn to hold in France. The following year, Ghosn collaborated with a French journalist to coauthor his autobiography, opting for the title *Citizen of the World.*

That title amounted to a hill Schweitzer at least wanted to have a battle on. He felt that the future head of Renault should be anchored in French society, not a citizen of the world. The term also holds a negative connotation in France, serving as a neologism for the global elite who forgot their duty to the motherland.

That earned Ghosn another Monday scolding. "I strongly disapprove," Schweitzer told him. "'Citizen of the world' . . . it does not fit the boss of Renault."

Schweitzer asked Ghosn to change the title, but his number two refused. To Ghosn, the disagreement highlighted a fundamental difference between the two executives. He felt that Schweitzer viewed Renault as a French entity that was expanding globally, whereas Ghosn saw Renault as a global company born in France. Schweitzer thought that the argument also reflected their differing beliefs about the nature of the Alliance. It was not an "alliance of equals," according to Schweitzer, because Renault controlled Nissan. Ghosn made it clear that he thought otherwise.

*   *   *

In 2001, Schweitzer came up with an idea to put a legal structure atop Renault and Nissan, a move that would have taken them a step closer to being a single company. He hired two law professors to push help through the so-called Project Métis, the French word for "mixed race."

Ghosn was immediately suspicious. He felt that Schweitzer was trying to give Renault more sway over Nissan—and he was right.

Ghosn argued that forcing Nissan and Renault into a merger risked destroying the Alliance before it could live up to its promise. Each company had its own history, its own culture, which were especially important in a place such as Japan, where your job became your identity. The company, to which so-called salarymen in Japan devoted every waking hour, became their tribe. Changing jobs or hopping between companies was almost unheard of, and a merger would be tantamount to an admission of failure. Schweitzer was wandering into a potential minefield. Forcing the two companies to eventually become one wouldn't cut it, not unless Renault became a more attractive partner. Ghosn knew how much the engineers at Nissan looked down upon their counterparts in France. In more ways than one, Nissan was the better carmaker and arguably, under Ghosn's control, the better company.

Ghosn fought fiercely to kill the project, finally agreeing to the formation of Renault-Nissan BV, a subsidiary in the Netherlands jointly owned by Renault and Nissan that would help manage the Alliance, rather than oversee either company. It was something of a mini-Hague or United Nations for a collective company of very different cultures, both corporate and national. It would serve as a forum, an outlet, a gathering place for discussions—nothing less, nothing more.

The two companies also renegotiated the terms of their partnership in a document they called the Restated Alliance Master Agreement, or RAMA, which froze their shareholdings in an attempt to ensure neither could seize control of the other.

When word reached Japan about Ghosn's ability to fend off deepening control by Renault, his acolytes at Nissan began to look at him not just as the savior of their company but as the protector of their independence.

*　　*　　*

Back in France, it was clear to Schweitzer that despite Ghosn's penchant for celebrity, and their differences over Project Métis, his protégé had done remarkable work at Nissan. Renault's CEO moved ahead with his plan to hand over the reins at the French carmaker to Ghosn ahead of his retirement.

In 2004, however, with his appointed return-to-Renault date approaching, Ghosn approached Schweitzer. He had decided that Nissan wasn't ready for him to go. "I don't think we're mature enough, and I think a lot of the work could be lost if we do it now," he told Schweitzer.

Instead, Ghosn requested that Schweitzer stay on at Renault for four more years. Schweitzer said no. The only alternative, then, Ghosn said, was that he himself run two of the world's largest carmakers simultaneously. After all, Schweitzer couldn't refuse to postpone his retirement *and* force Ghosn to give up Nissan. The idea struck Schweitzer as absurd. Because it *was* absurd. How could any man, even a man like Ghosn, possibly run two companies separated by eight hours and six thousand miles?

But there was little time or room to maneuver. Schweitzer wanted out, which meant he was stuck. He ultimately agreed, on the condition that it would be a short-term arrangement, to be continued until

Ghosn could prepare his successor at Nissan. Ghosn promised to do so as fast as possible.

*   *   *

On April 29, 2005, Schweitzer and Ghosn stood side by side at a specially called meeting of shareholders to vote on Ghosn's joining the Renault board of directors ahead of his appointment as CEO. When the time came to take photographs for the gathered press, Schweitzer pursed his lips, smiled stiffly, and symbolically handed over the Renault keys to Ghosn, who accepted them with no trepidation.

7

Two Briefcases

With two companies under his stewardship, Ghosn saw the contents of his calendar double overnight. In May 2006, he presided over Renault's annual shareholder meeting in Paris, and now, in June, he was ten thousand miles away, overseeing the AGM of another Fortune 500 company. As he stood behind a bank of microphones in a giant convention center in Yokohama, a fast-growing metropolis south of Tokyo, Ghosn shifted into Nissan mode. After thirty years of redevelopment, the once smog-ridden rail hub and shipyard had morphed into a jungle of gleaming office towers. Ghosn viewed it as a perfect new home for Nissan—even if it belonged to a cluster of nautically themed buildings and he was trying to sell cars. Inside the Pacifico building, designed to look like a clam, Ghosn faced more than fifteen hundred shareholders, all of whom had as much reason to celebrate as to be nervous.

Having recovered from a near-death experience, Nissan was now expanding around the globe. In 2003, a few years after his arrival, the company had signed a deal with Dongfeng in China, where sales had tripled since the deal had been signed. Nissan was also making headway in the Middle East, with billionaire sheikhs signing up to sell the company's vehicles.

One, named Suhail Bahwan, had flown all the way from Oman for a visit and refused to leave Japan without shaking Ghosn's hand. Bahwan turned around and promptly built the world's largest Nissan showroom, just outside Muscat.

Despite those triumphs, Nissan's most recent annual earnings report was somewhat disappointing, tarnished by a slipping market share at home and an underperforming stock price. Ghosn took the floor, intending to reassure the shareholders, but the attention of those in the room was focused on a more pressing question: Was Ghosn going to stick around at Nissan?

Surely he couldn't continue to run two global behemoths, in two very different countries, at the same time. Ghosn was evasive about his succession plan. "We have enough talent," he told the shareholders. "When the time comes [for me to leave] you will not be disappointed by whoever is leading the company."

Not only was Ghosn increasingly convinced that he could continue to run both companies; in a sense, he simply had to. He had cut costs at Renault. He had rescued Nissan from bankruptcy. Nobody else in the world could maintain the bizarre construction of the Alliance or bridge the significant divide between the two wildly different companies. He wasn't going to hand over the reins now that things were going well—barring the earnings blip and share price slump, both of which, he trusted, would be fleeting.

After years of belt-tightening, Ghosn was also having some fun. He had loosened the purse strings, in part by relaunching one of Nissan's legendary models, the GT-R sports car. Ghosn had big ambitions for the vehicle and was personally involved in every aspect of its production. It was being redesigned from the ground up to compete with legendary German sports cars. His obsession with building the best sports car that Nissan's money could buy had already gotten him a dose of unintended publicity and trouble with Rita when he had hit a motorcyclist in a Porsche 911 he was test driving. One of Ghosn's children had been in the car. The rider had suffered only minor injuries, but the image of the Nissan CEO driving a Porsche had attracted plenty of media attention.

Still, the famously frugal chief had told Nissan engineers that he wanted a world-class vehicle, no matter the cost. That included the marketing and PR budgets. *National Geographic* was invited to film a documentary touting the game-changing vehicle. Nissan also hired Jim Marshall, a motorsports turned rock photographer who had shot musical legends such as the Beatles, Bob Dylan, and Janis Joplin, to tail and photograph Ghosn.

"Please be confident. We are confident," Ghosn told shareholders. "We have a very strong and very attractive product pipeline coming."

Ghosn wrapped up the shareholder meeting in Yokohama, then prepared himself to go tend to issues seven time zones away. After having dinner at home that night, he packed his bag and headed to the airport shortly before midnight to board Nissan's private jet. Sixteen and a half hours later, at 8:30 a.m. in Paris, he was sitting in his airy executive suite at Renault's headquarters in Boulogne-Billancourt, a building nestled between a highway and the Seine west of Paris. In front of him were several stacks of paper that had accumulated since his last visit.

Upon arrival in Paris, Ghosn had gone through a now-familiar routine: he had stashed his black briefcase containing his Nissan documents and opened an identical briefcase containing his Renault files. The two, which he swapped back on return trips, symbolized his new life: a foot in both worlds, each accompanied by a briefcase to keep him abreast of the respective issues that required his attention.

His striding through the door at Renault's headquarters always sparked a buzz of activity. All of Ghosn's top managers were summoned to a brief one-on-one session with the boss. Heads of product planning needed to talk about budgets; human resources officers wanted to hire from a competitor. Ghosn's number two at Renault, Patrick Pelata, regularly had a list of more than a dozen topics he wanted to talk to Ghosn about but would pick the three or four most important for their monthly one-on-one meeting, then deal with the rest himself.

Though Ghosn felt he was managing the needs of both companies, his lieutenants thought otherwise. Some quietly complained about his schedule, but none was willing to openly bet against the man who had pulled off seemingly impossible feats for both companies.

To prove any doubters wrong and take advantage of an opportunity for self-promotion, Ghosn invited the press to shadow him on a lap of his transcontinental circuit. *Forbes*, the *Wall Street Journal*, and *Businessweek* dispatched correspondents, who followed the executive through his taxing hopscotching. The consensus among them was that Ghosn's life, however crazy, was well controlled. He worked thirteen-hour days and spent forty-eight hours a month on a plane with the special tail number N155AN. He was stretched to his physical limit, sure, but the results appeared to be worth it.

*   *   *

As well as wooing the press, Ghosn had an innate ability to schmooze with politicians and bureaucrats. Most usually left him alone anyway, since Ghosn provided them with what he knew they wanted: jobs and growth. And so most of them, whether they hailed from the United States, China, or Japan, were effusive in their praise.

The only people seemingly immune to Ghosn's charms were the French, particularly French politicians and civil servants. The distaste was mutual. Like Ghosn, they had been educated in the *grandes écoles*. Unlike Ghosn, many had gone straight into government, where they'd landed at ministries or state agencies.

Ghosn knew that it wasn't smart to antagonize the French government. The state remained Renault's largest shareholder and had representatives on the company's board—which was why, on that particular visit to France, despite dreading the inevitable lecture, he paid a visit to the French finance minister. He also needed to sound out the French state on a sensitive issue: Ghosn was in secret talks with the largest shareholder of General Motors to bring *the* behemoth of the automotive world into the Renault-Nissan Alliance. The GM initiative was unprecendented. If the deal went through, no other automaker would have as firmly established roots in the three main markets: the United States, Europe, and Asia.

Ghosn knew that French authorities would be loath to back him. The government had few objections to Renault's relationship with Nissan, given the French carmaker's dominant position in the deal. But GM was a different animal, one that already had operations sprawling across Europe. This time, Renault wouldn't be in the driver's seat. Though he knew it would be a tough sell, Ghosn felt it was necessary, a crucial ingredient to help him assemble the global empire he now saw within his reach.

On June 30, having conquered jet lag, Ghosn arrived at the "Fortress of Bercy," as the seat of France's Ministry for the Economy and Finance is derisively called. The building, the length of four football fields, straddles a busy thoroughfare along the bank of the Seine.

Ruling over the fortress was Thierry Breton, a rare politician who had experience running large multinational companies before becoming finance minister. He had started his own IT firm, which he had sold before the dot-com crash. He had also run Orange, the former telecommunications monopoly he had helped privatize. And though his successes had been on a smaller scale than Ghosn's, he, too, had earned a reputation as a turnaround specialist.

With his quick, elegant smile and flowing white hair swept back, Breton had the smooth manner of the French ruling class. He also had a flair for the theatrical and liked to show that he hadn't been corrupted by power by driving a white Volkswagen Beetle.

After a brief exchange of pleasantries and some back-and-forth about the car industry and the Renault-Nissan Alliance, the finance minister started firing pointed questions.

He started with one that bordered on the existential.

"To whom am I talking?" he asked.

Ghosn was confused. "What do you mean, Mr. Minister?"

"The boss of Renault? The boss of Nissan? I just want to know: who am I speaking with?" Breton said.

Ghosn said he was there as the head of Renault but explained that he carefully partitioned his diary, starting the month at Renault and ending it at Nissan. Breton could see Ghosn's planner across the table. "Do you mind if I look at your agenda?" he asked, reaching for Ghosn's planner before receiving a response.

"Tokyo, Tokyo, Tokyo," Breton said as he riffled through the pages of Ghosn's agenda.

"Ah, Paris," he said. He motioned to his chief of staff and asked him to make a note of how many pages indicated days when Ghosn had actually been in France. After flipping through a few more, he remarked that the superstar CEO seemed to spend far less time at Renault than he had suggested a few minutes earlier. "I understand that things are always more complex in real life," he said.

Moving on from time management, the minister emphasized how important it was that he understand where Ghosn's economic interests lay; that is, how he was compensated.

"What is your salary at Renault? And what is your salary at Nissan?" Breton asked.

Ghosn shifted in his seat, then pointed out that his salary at Renault was public.

"Yes, but Nissan we don't know," Breton said. "This will stay between us, but I want to know: Whom am I talking to? Really. It's important to me."

Ghosn was flustered. But again he refused to answer.

"Okay, we have an issue," Breton said, sitting back. "Things don't work like this here."

Breton began to lecture Ghosn about the governance problems associated with running two companies. How could he trust Ghosn to have Renault's best interests at heart when he was also running not a partner or an ally but a *competitor*, a rival car company—and one that was probably paying him much more money than the French firm?

The situation between Renault and Nissan needed to be cleared up, he told Ghosn. With that out of the way, the minister took aim at the GM proposal. There were huge issues to sort out before Ghosn should think about expanding the Alliance, he concluded.

Stone-faced, Ghosn thanked him for his time and took his leave.

*   *   *

Soon after, the GM news broke in the papers. Breton immediately dialed his communication chief to find him a spot on one of France's many talk shows the following day. When he appeared on Sunday afternoon, the first question was about the GM news.

"We have to make sure that corporate governance rules are respected," Breton said, a polite nod to his conversation with Ghosn. But in the weeks that followed, he made it very clear that he was hostile to the deal. By that time, Ghosn had already been corresponding for months with the American billionaire Kirk Kerkorian, who had made a name for himself by strong-arming corporate boards and had built up a roughly 10 percent stake in the storied American carmaker. He believed that what GM needed was a hard charger like Ghosn and had already tried to convince Ghosn to ditch Renault and Nissan altogether. The idea had flattered Ghosn, but he was just a year into the dual-CEO job at Renault and didn't want to abandon Nissan.

His affection for Japan wasn't all business related. He appreciated the politeness, the punctuality, the gentility he found there. He had loved his first experience of cherry blossom season, which lasts for a week in the spring. He had discovered what he considered was a magical area of Tokyo, not far from his home: a small stream lined with cherry trees. Sitting there, tasting local dishes, taking in the delicate trees in bloom, Ghosn felt a warm affinity for his new home.

It also didn't hurt that he was considered Nissan's savior and was beloved throughout the country. You don't leave all that to go to GM, he thought. So Ghosn being Ghosn, he had taken the next logical step: to make GM come to him.

The talks to bring GM into the Alliance, however, were doomed to fail from the start. Ghosn had already been told that the French state, which was convinced that the Renault-Nissan partnership was barely working in its current state, was opposed to the addition of GM. It wasn't about to become the weakest member of a triumvirate.

More importantly, GM wasn't sold on the deal, either.

One of the biggest hurdles was GM's inability to understand how the Alliance worked. Without a transparent, functioning structure—one that could and would work in Ghosn's absence—being a part of the Alliance meant that a company would have to accept Ghosn as the unquestioned leader. But how would it actually work day to day? Who would be making the decisions? And on whose behalf at any given time? How would it be possible for any of the companies involved to have confidence that decisions were being made in its best interest?

The response was clearly that Ghosn would make all the decisions, while asking the three companies, each of which was governed by its own distinct ethos, and with its own board of directors, to just be willing to go along. Conflicts of interest aside, without him there, the whole system would collapse.

When Ghosn and GM CEO Rick Wagoner, a finance wizard whom Ghosn knew from his Michelin days, met in Paris in late September, the writing was on the wall. Talks had made little progress over the summer. "It's great for your shareholders, mediocre for us," Wagoner told Ghosn. Both men agreed to walk away.

To Ghosn, this served as confirmation that it was hard for outsiders to appreciate what the Alliance was about. It was like asking a happy couple about the virtues of marriage versus asking someone who had just gone through an ugly divorce. "It depends on motivation. If you are willing, you see many synergies. If not, you see few," he told the press.

Though he was disappointed with the outcome, the GM talks weren't all a waste. They had given Ghosn an inside look into the finances of a Detroit automaker. He had entertained the possibility that the Alliance would one day expand, but seeing a possible $10 billion in savings made it feel like an imperative. Ghosn started imagining what it would be like to run the world's largest carmaker. He stashed the report in a safe in his Tokyo apartment, where it could be dusted off when the timing was more opportune.

*   *   *

As years passed, Ghosn didn't relinquish either of his jobs. Patrick Pelata became increasingly worried about his boss. He had joined Ghosn in 1999 and worked at his side during the process of reviving the Japanese carmaker. But Pelata didn't quite recognize the executive Ghosn had become ever since he had started juggling two jobs. At Nissan, Ghosn was razor sharp. He knew everything that was going on, the intricate details of every project. He didn't make mistakes in those days. Back at Renault, mistakes were happening all the time. It bothered Pelata that Ghosn rarely showed up for HR committee meetings, where executives vetted high-profile hires and promotions. In Pelata's mind, putting the right people into the right jobs was one of the most important jobs for a CEO to do. The fact that Ghosn was delegating and deprioritizing the decisions was a huge red flag.

When Ghosn was present, Pelata sensed that people were misleading Ghosn. At Nissan, Ghosn would have seen right through it and called them on it. But at Renault, it was as though he was flying blind, paying little mind to where he might land.

The problem wasn't just at Renault; things appeared to be slipping at Nissan as well. In the early days under Ghosn, when Pelata had been working with his friend, decisions had been made lightning fast. Swiftly cutting through the bureaucracy of a large company was what had enabled Ghosn to fix Nissan so quickly. In his absence, however, meetings devolved into bickering among executives defending their individual fiefs.

Ghosn received any questioning of Nissan's performance with wry cynicism. Reporters, financial analysts, and investors started weighing in, suggesting that the Ghosn magic was wearing off, because—among a host of reasons—the operating profit margin had fallen. "I'm glad to see that the press thinks Nissan is struggling" with operating margins above 8 percent, he answered once. He often pointed to the fact that the figure was a very solid performance in the highly competitive auto industry. Still, it was becoming clear to people at Nissan that Ghosn wasn't as involved in the nitty-gritty details of car development.

At the time, one of Nissan's boldest projects, the Leaf electric car, was nearing completion. It was a gamble by Ghosn, intended to leap-frog over Toyota and take the lead in the automotive future. Toyota had been at the cutting edge of engine technology with its Prius hybrids, and Ghosn wanted Nissan to steal the thunder by jumping to fully electric vehicles, or EVs.

Though odd looking, the Leaf was one of the most ambitious attempts to date to win people over to EVs, despite long-held concerns regarding battery range, high costs, and a lack of charging infrastructure. But when Ghosn was headed to Dodger Stadium in Los Angeles to present the Leaf to America, he turned to one of the executives and asked, "What should I tell the media about this car?" The executive walked Ghosn through his comments, suggesting quips about the lack of a tailpipe. As he spoke, he wondered what had happened to his boss.

Ghosn had once cared enormously about every detail of his products and would engage in lively, well-informed conversations at every step of the development process. And at car shows, once the vehicles were launched, meticulous, dynamic presentations were his hallmark. Now it was as if he were looking over a car lot from the great distance of a private jet.

Pelata wanted to alert Ghosn that he was losing his Midas touch. The issue came to a head when the two executives were traveling from Tokyo to the Russian city of Togliatti, a one-industry town located five hundred miles southeast of Moscow. Renault had recently bought 25 percent of Lada manufacturer Avtovaz, and they were attending the first shareholder meeting since the deal had gone through.

After a short nap, Ghosn and Pelata had coffee on the Gulfstream while flying over the Volga, a river so wide that it looked more like a lake. Ghosn pulled up the draft of an article about his management style by a professor at the Stanford Graduate School of Business. The article was more than forty pages long, and the university had sent it to Ghosn before publication for his review. It was part of the deal the professor had brokered for access to the top brass at Renault and Nissan.

Ghosn loved most of the profile. It delved in great detail into how one man was able to run two Fortune 500 companies and how the diversity of the two companies had become a strength, thanks to Ghosn. The part of the article Ghosn didn't like was the quotes from Pelata.

Decision-making had slowed at both Nissan and Renault since Ghosn started running the two, Pelata had acknowledged. Ghosn no longer had time for factory floor visits, which hampered his ability to make decisions.

Ghosn wanted Pelata to retract the quote or at least add some favorable context. "By definition, you can't say I'm going to do the same job managing two companies. Obviously," Ghosn said. "I have less time to monitor; less time to check things. . . . The question is: Is it better for the two companies that one man manages them, even though he's doing it a different way? Or is it better that he goes one way and somebody else comes in? The objective is not being on the ground. It's what performance you can get from the two companies." His focus was still on his scorecard.

"Listen, Carlos," said Pelata, taking a liberty with Ghosn's first name that few others did. "Since you're head of both companies, you don't have time to visit the factory floor anymore. People are lying to you, no one dares to tell you the truth, and you don't have time to check things by yourself. Things aren't working as well as before, when you were just at Nissan."

Feeling unburdened, Pelata decided to be firm in airing his worries to his old classmate. "Your time is human time, and it doesn't work," he said. He refused to amend his quotes, despite sensing Ghosn's anger. "I truly believe what I said," he told him.

Ghosn rang the professor, who removed the bulk of Pelata's quotes and inserted some of Ghosn's arguments that the companies were better off despite his part-time role. In the end, all that remained of Pelata's criticisms was a couple of diminished points buried deep in the text.

A few months later, however, Ghosn called Pelata out of the blue to put him in charge of operations at Renault. He had been listening after all, Pelata thought. "He'd store it somewhere. And then it would come back."

By 2008, Ghosn looked down at the vast world from Nissan's private jet, feeling on top of it all. In addition to the strides he was taking within his profession, he was making friends and jockeying with the world's most powerful governments and heads of state.

From such a great height, he had the power to move the pieces around to his advantage however he saw fit. Or so he believed.

PART II

8

Swap Deals

Ghosn headed into the mid-aughts as the fine-dining, globe-trotting, lesson-imparting celebrity CEO of Nissan and Renault. The story of his rise was now the stuff of legend. It graced magazines, panels, and case studies around the world. He was beloved in Japan, feared if not loved in France, and respected worldwide. And for all his efforts he earned only what he felt he was entitled to: an enormous compensation package. Between his Nissan and Renault paychecks, he was making more than $18 million a year, with the Japanese company forking out an astonishing 80 percent of that total. In addition to his pay, Nissan covered a range of plush expenses and benefits, including his rent in Japan and France, which came to about half a million dollars a year. Then there was his "home leave" allowance, which reimbursed him for business- and first-class air tickets for his wife and children. The carmaker also picked up the tab for his children's education, first at private schools in Japan and France and then at Stanford University in California, where all four children went to college. Other perks included a company car, a bump in his pay to cover income taxes, and cash allowances whenever Ghosn was on the road and needed to refresh his wardrobe for a corporate event.

Given the steady stream of figures, balance sheets, and scorecards being tabulated in Ghosn's head, he always appreciated having a numbers guy on hand. Alain Dassas was just the type. Before bringing him to Japan, Ghosn had put him in charge of Renault's Formula One team and tasked him with ensuring that the program wasn't a financial black hole.

The accounting whiz was a year into his job at Nissan when the wheels of global finance seized up. The shocking collapse of Lehman Brothers in September 2008 shattered the bonds of trust that linked banks and corporations, pushing the world into a brutal economic recession. Consumers were afraid to buy cars, and banks were afraid to lend money. Vehicle sales collapsed, leaving carmakers in Detroit, Europe, and Asia scrambling to cut costs and fighting for survival.

Nissan didn't go unscathed. With plunging demand and soaring inventory, the company was burning through its cash reserves. There was no hope of raising money on the stock market; Nissan's share price was falling like a lead balloon.

In September, Dassas rang Ghosn in Paris with alarming news: "I'm not sure we are going to make it to the end of this year," he told his boss.

Ghosn first dismissed the concern as being overly dramatic, but twenty minutes later he called the Nissan finance chief back. Dassas told him that he had already started drawing up a list of assets Nissan could sell to raise cash. Ghosn instructed him to spread the word among management of how bad the situation was.

"I'm not going to let my work—ten years of work—be wasted," Ghosn said. "I will not let it happen."

Weeks later, Dassas learned that Ghosn was facing his own financial squeeze. Ghosn had an issue with Shinsei Bank, tracing back to his first Nissan contract, from 1999. Nissan had refused his request to be paid in dollars and instead paid him in yen, a highly volatile currency. To make his pay predictable in dollars, he had signed a currency protection agreement, often called a swap deal, with Shinsei Bank. But as the financial crisis raged on, he found himself on the wrong side of his dollar insurance policy. The yen was strengthening sharply against the dollar. The bank was buying dollars at an extremely unfavorable rate, leaving the burden on Ghosn to make up the difference with the market rate. Simultaneously, the value of the Nissan shares that Ghosn had provided as collateral was melting—in October, it was 80 percent off its peak—and the bank wanted additional guarantees from the Nissan chief.

Despite all his wealth, Ghosn's wallet was now $20 million short.

Ghosn asked Dassas to speak to someone at Shinsei to explore potential workarounds. But Dassas's contact told him that his hands were tied. Ghosn needed to deliver—cash was tight for the bank, too.

Quickly finding that kind of liquidity was a challenge in the thick of the financial crisis. With few options, Ghosn opted to transfer his financial liabilities from the swap agreement to Nissan. After all, he reasoned, it was the company's fault that he was facing this predicament; he had asked to be paid in dollars from the start. The bank agreed to the arrangement, on the condition that Nissan's board sign off on it.

When directors gathered on October 31, 2008, they had no idea that the point of one of the resolutions was to help Ghosn urgently fill a hole in his finances. Still, the resolution they approved contained a caveat: Nissan would guarantee these types of swap agreements for its CEO or other executives with banks, on a temporary basis, as long as it didn't cost the company any money. After the proposal had received the requisite signatures, the document was delivered to Shinsei.

Thanks to Nissan's help, Ghosn was off the hook for the $20 million.

*   *   *

With his personal financial crisis under control, Ghosn continued orbiting the planet like a satellite. Under a schedule prepared by three assistants located on three continents, he dedicated one week to Renault in Paris and one to Nissan in Yokohama. The rest of the time he was on the road, generally spending about a week in the United States, Nissan's largest market.

In November 2008, he happened to be in Manhattan, attending a fundraising evening at the Mandarin Oriental, a luxury hotel overlooking Central Park. Organized by alumni of his old school in Beirut, Collège Notre-Dame de Jamhour, more than two hundred guests attended, lured in part by the prospect of hearing a speech by its most famous graduate.

Ghosn had become a skilled, compelling public speaker, and he used the event to eloquently reprise two of his favorite themes: diversity and globalization. He never tired of proselytizing for the idea that diversity gave rise to new ideas, which in turn fed success in business. He spoke without notes, opening with the acknowledgment that promoting diversity was often challenging, because—as the bearer of three passports declared with a smile—"No one likes foreigners." But those who could master diversity, he went on, "are going to become the winners of this century."

Carlos Ghosn felt that nothing proved his point better than Carlos Ghosn. His status as a self-proclaimed "citizen of the world," coupled with his reputation for turning around the fates of struggling businesses, made him the ideal CEO for an increasingly globalized market.

At the end of his impassioned speech, he received an extended standing ovation. He posed for photographs with his eldest daughter, Caroline, who shares her father's dark features and self-confident presence, and his wife, Rita, who wore a leopard-skin dress and appeared open and generous.

Among the many Ghosn admirers present that evening was Carole Nahas, a glamorous woman dressed in black, with layers of wispy blond hair and a subtle, alluring smile. She lived in New York but had grown up in the same neighborhood in Beirut as Ghosn. She was twelve years his junior, and the two had never met. She approached the powerful CEO to shake his hand and introduce herself. "My name is Carole. I'm the cousin of Fabienne, the wife of Elie, one of your former classmates," she said. After a brief, amicable exchange, she informed Ghosn that she had emailed him months earlier on behalf of a charitable cause she was championing, but the tycoon hadn't replied.

"Forgive me, Carole, I didn't see your message," Ghosn said earnestly. "I get dozens of messages every day for all sorts of reasons." Like most Lebanese nationals, especially alums of Notre-Dame de Jamhour, Carole admired Ghosn for his power and achievements. She had seen him on TV and read articles about the savvy businessman who had gone to Japan and rescued Nissan. They wished each other good night and parted ways.

She would be in touch.

*   *   *

Shortly after his return to Japan, just as the rocky year was nearing its close, Ghosn learned that the reprieve from his debt to Shinsei Bank was short lived. Japan's financial watchdog, the Securities and Exchange Surveillance Commission, had uncovered Ghosn's problematic swap deal. How would Nissan account for buying dollars at a loss? it asked. Nissan needed to address the potential conflict of interest right away.

Toshiyuki Shiga, Ghosn's number two at Nissan, told his boss about the issue on Christmas Eve. After pausing for a beat, Ghosn told Shiga that he would reverse the transaction. That left him just over one month to transfer the swap agreement back to his name and avoid leaving any embarrassing red stains in Nissan's books.

This time, Ghosn opted to solve the crisis by calling on two acquaintances for financial help: Suhail Bahwan and Khaled Juffali.

Bahwan was the billionaire who sold Nissan cars in Oman, and who had previously refused to leave Japan without shaking Ghosn's hand. His was the type of work trajectory Ghosn respected in others: Bahwan had gone from working at his father's small import business to helming a sprawling conglomerate spanning everything from IT outsourcing to Rolls-Royce distribution.

Juffali was a Saudi billionaire whom Ghosn had recently hired to help jump-start Nissan sales in the Gulf region. Ghosn knew the sheikh from his Michelin days, and the two men regularly met at the annual World Economic Forum in Davos, Switzerland. Though he didn't fall into the self-made category that Bahwan did (his predecessors formed the "Juffali Group" conglomerate in the 1970s, managing one of the largest corporate enterprises in Saudi Arabia), Ghosn respected the sheikh's ability to cultivate international connections. He trusted him as a businessman and occasionally sought his advice on matters involving the Gulf.

Ghosn's decision to discreetly tap those men to resolve his currency fix at Shinsei Bank would normally have been his own business. But their status as Nissan partners also tied this request to company business. Ghosn had hopped from one conflict of interest straight into another.

*   *   *

In early 2009, Alain Dassas was still at work slashing costs and abandoning nonessential investments, doing all he could to save as much cash as possible. Ghosn simultaneously had him working on another confidential assignment: putting together a takeover of its US rival Chrysler, one of Detroit's Big Three car companies. Dassas dutifully crafted what he saw as the perfect deal, with a plan to save the debt-ridden maker of the Jeep and Dodge brands without needing to use any cash.

"You have done a good job," remarked Ghosn, rarely one to dispense praise. Dassas didn't even have an instant to bask in the compliment, as Ghosn concluded that the situation was too uncertain: "But I'm not going to do the deal."

Another Ghosn request soon landed on Dassas's desk: Would Nissan—a carmaker—be able to quickly provide a multimillion-dollar loan to a business partner, either a company or an individual?

Dassas answered that Nissan couldn't simply transfer money, but he would look into it.

Before meeting Ghosn on January 19, under the subject line URGENT, Dassas fired off an email to a colleague asking for the exact corporate names of the entities that needed the loans. Several hours later, his colleague wrote back that the companies were Suhail Bahwan Automobiles in Oman and another called Al Dahana in Saudi Arabia, a company that was owned by Khaled Juffali.

Like other executives at Nissan, Dassas had no idea that Ghosn had tapped Juffali and Bahwan to help him solve his financial jam. One of Dassas's underlings drafted loan documents, writing that they were for "general business purposes and to support the commercial and financial development of Nissan."

But this wasn't sitting well with Dassas. He couldn't send money to Nissan's business partners without a strong justification.

Conflicted over what he was being asked to do, he sought out advice from Greg Kelly, the newly installed head of the CEO office. Kelly had been brought over to manage the administrative side, tending to matters large (relations with Renault) and relatively small (creating board agendas). After two decades with Nissan in the United States, spanning the before-and-after-Ghosn period, he possessed both institutional knowledge and an appreciation of the necessity of keeping Ghosn happy.

Dassas and Kelly were joined by another Nissan lawyer for a call on January 24, and they decided to scrap the loan for Juffali. Instead, the three men discussed paying the Saudi businessman to locate wealthy individuals or companies that would be willing to invest in Nissan. The automaker needed to raise money, and Juffali arguably boasted one of the region's best Rolodexes.

Still, that arrangement made Dassas nervous, and he shared his concerns with Kelly. Nissan usually hired large investment banks to find investments, and Juffali's company was tiny.

The next day, a Sunday, Kelly wrote to Ghosn, "Alain [Dassas] informed me that he was uncomfortable legally and for business reasons about providing money to one of Mr. Juffali's corporations in exchange for Mr. Juffali finding funding for Nissan." Ghosn never followed up with Dassas, leaving the finance chief to assume that the idea to send money directly to Juffali had been dropped.

But there was still the case of the Omani billionaire, Suhail Bahwan, whose job was to buy cars from Nissan and sell them to consumers in the Middle East. Dassas also ruled out the request for a loan on the grounds that Bahwan's company, Suhail Bahwan Automobiles

(SBA), carried too much debt. But he knew that Ghosn was desperate to grow business in the region, and Dassas wasn't trying to block every request.

Ghosn had told Dassas that he wanted to support SBA to the tune of 3 billion yen, so the finance chief worked out a solution: if Nissan authorized the Omani company to pay for cars within 200 days of their being shipped from Japan—and not within 180 days, as it had done previously—the company would be able to show roughly that amount, equivalent to about $20 million, as extra cash on hand.

It was an elegant financial solution. In late January, Dassas sent a draft proposal to his counterpart at SBA. Nissan's Middle East managers, copied on Dassas's draft, were alarmed that such generous conditions would dent their region's cash flow, but a Nissan treasury manager explained, "It's a direct order from Mr. Ghosn, so please understand our situation."

Dassas thought he was doing his job, bending over backward for SBA in Nissan's best interest. So he had every reason to be dismayed when, on January 31, SBA rejected his proposal; it had a counteroffer that was even more in its favor.

"This is clearly not possible," Dassas replied.

Yet a week and a half later, the Bahwan issue was back on Dassas's desk after Ghosn made it clear to him that supporting SBA was a priority. In a message to an executive at the Omani dealership, Dassas apologized for the miscommunication and outlined even better terms than the ones he had rejected ten days earlier.

An SBA executive wrote back that Suhail Bahwan had agreed.

*   *   *

Bahwan would now receive the help from Nissan that Ghosn had requested, but Juffali's case still needed a solution.

The answer came in the form of something Ghosn created in March 2009 called the CEO Reserve. It was a budget line that allowed him to release funds with alacrity for any number of reasons he saw fit. Designed to fast-track important payments and get around budget delays, the mechanism was strikingly simple: a regional chief would complete paper forms, one of which contained a small box to justify the extra funds. From there, it was a box-ticking exercise with just three more signatures required, including Ghosn's. *Et voilà*.

Ghosn began asking Nissan executives for their ideas on how to spend $40 million a year using the CEO Reserve budget line, and he himself had a few ideas. In May 2009, he told an aide that he wanted to send $3 million to Khaled Juffali, the businessman who had helped him out of a financial jam just weeks earlier. The payment application sped through Nissan's new approval process. The justification was that Juffali would be working on an electric vehicle project with the intention of eventually setting up a factory for Nissan in Saudi Arabia.

The payments to Juffali became annual requests. They didn't necessarily seem extravagant: $3 million for the first one, then $3.6 million, then $3.9 million. Though Nissan's Middle East chief did question what Juffali was doing to warrant the payments, he reasoned that the Saudi billionaire would hardly get out of bed for less.

Eventually, a number of other distributors in the Middle East, including Suhail Bahwan, would receive Nissan funds from that accounting line. Pleased by the efficiency of the system, Ghosn created the same one at Renault, which he also used to send bonuses to SBA.

In a matter of weeks amid the financial crisis, Nissan had forged sweetheart deals with two of its Middle Eastern partners. Bahwan had been granted exceptionally favorable payment terms, while Juffali had started to receive special bonuses from the Japanese carmaker.

*   *   *

The arrangements Ghosn had struck with Bahwan and Juffali at the start of 2009 to solve his currency-swap problem dovetailed nicely with efforts at Nissan to provide the billionaires' businesses with more support. With Bahwan, Ghosn had written on a blank sheet of paper, "We hereby recognise a loan of 3 billion yens [*sic*], extended to us by sheikh Suhail Bahwan on this day for a period of 2 years. We pledge to pay an annual interest rate of 1.9% and reimburse the loan at the latest on 1/20/2011." This happened to be the exact same amount that Nissan had provided to Bahwan by improving his payment terms.

Rita and Ghosn signed the handwritten document and dated it January 20, 2009. Ghosn filed it away in the safe in his Tokyo apartment.

That same month, the Saudi billionaire Khaled Juffali had provided Ghosn with a 3 billion–yen letter of credit. Between the bulk of Bahwan's loan and the letter of credit from Juffali, Ghosn had been able to convince Shinsei Bank that he had the funds to support the swap agreement. The debt was still on Nissan's books, but it needed to come off before the carmaker was required to buy dollars at a loss on behalf of its leader. It was transferred back to Ghosn on February 20.*

With these moves, Ghosn had plugged a hole in his own finances. But he had also blurred the line between what was good for Ghosn and good for his companies.

There would be ramifications.

---

* Ghosn denies that providing Bahwan's car distribution company with favorable payment terms and paying special bonuses to Juffali was a quid pro quo for the financial assistance he received from them. Ghosn, Bahwan, and Juffali say the support Nissan extended to its Middle East partners was for legitimate business reasons. Ghosn also denies that his receiving financial support from them amounted to a conflict of interest.

9

Spillovers

A year after Carole Nahas had chided Ghosn for failing to respond to her message, the two of them were enjoying their third meeting, this one for lunch at the Peninsula hotel in New York City, close to Central Park. Like Ghosn, Carole had moved around her whole life, living in Saudi Arabia, Greece, and now New York, where she resided with her Lebanese husband, a high-profile banker. The couple had two sons and a daughter. Unlike Ghosn, who apart from his passion for bridge dedicated almost all his spare time to his family, Carole was sociable and active and had a large group of friends.

At the end of their lunch at the Peninsula, Ghosn pulled out his diary. His precisely partitioned timetable had colored pages depending on which country he was expected to be in next. He wanted to see her again.

"How about ten a.m. in one month?" he said.

Carole laughed and accepted his offer.

In Paris, it didn't take long for Rita Ghosn to find out that her husband was having an affair. In truth, the relationship had been on the rocks for some time, to such an extent that Ghosn and Rita had effectively worked out an unspoken schedule that prevented them from ever having to see each other. When Ghosn was in France, Rita was in Japan. And when Ghosn was heading back to Japan, Rita was generally on a flight back to their home in France.

Things had started to go wrong during their time in Japan. Rita had her own ambitions, which extended beyond being Ghosn's house-wife. She had picked up some Japanese and launched her own projects, starting a small chain of restaurants called My Lebanon, into which she put all her heart and energy. But she felt that Ghosn had belittled her endeavor. She had published an autobiography in Japanese, sharing some of her secrets on how to keep a marriage strong and raise kids, then felt that Ghosn resented her for it. Whenever she received a com-pliment, her husband was quick to counter with a put-down. When Ghosn had praised the women in his life during an interview, he had offered the names of his mother, sisters, and daughters. Rita felt un-seen, as though she didn't exist.

Indeed, Ghosn harbored his own resentments. He felt that Rita was constantly trying to compete with him and would get angry when she fell short of his successes. By his perception, she deliber-ately turned up to fancy events in cheap dresses, purely to embarrass him. He determined that the difficulties experienced at the start of the relationship—incompatibilities that he had initially attributed to her youth and her distance from her parents—had never been overcome, despite their having shared international adventures and raised four children together.

The couple had had shouting matches over the years, but Rita never thought that Ghosn would cheat on her. Within weeks of finding out about Ghosn's affair with Carole, Rita left their apartment in Paris and went to Lebanon to be with her mother.

Ghosn had no shortage of headaches during this time. There was no refuge for him at home, where his children were angry at him for having an affair. There was no refuge at work, with customers still not buying cars and regular crises flaring up at both Renault and Nissan that required his full attention. On top of everything else, there was Ghosn's ongoing fixation with being paid appropriately for his titanic work. The swap deal debacle had been one thing, but it wouldn't com-pare with the headaches soon to be brought on by the crisis brewing at Nissan.

*   *   *

Ghosn's compensation at Nissan was the realm of Toshiaki Ohnuma, a man known at headquarters as the "Keeper of Secrets." On Ohnuma's first day as head of the secretariat, Ghosn had said that he needed two things: discretion and diligence. Ohnuma solemnly used Ghosn's two-pronged request as his code by which to live and work. Impeccably dressed, he had perfect posture that lent him the air of a well-trained butler, ever standing at attention, prepared to deliver.

Ohnuma was a perfectionist by nature, and his disposition was complicated by the fact that he could barely communicate in English. He had taken private lessons three times a week and disciplined himself to read the company's intranet correspondence in English. Whenever possible, his meetings with Ghosn were preceded by a prolonged rehearsal: Ohnuma would create entire scripts and repeat them until he knew his delivery by heart. And he would walk in with a memo that listed their discussion topics on a single page, which Ghosn would usually revise. But Ghosn relied on Ohnuma and valued his steadfast diligence, loyalty, and discretion.

The secretariat handled compensation not just for Ghosn but also for the nine other members of the board. Ohnuma would make a lump-sum request from Nissan's finance department, then process the salary payments according to the breakdown he received from Ghosn, which meant that Ghosn had the power to determine what he thought was suitable compensation for the board members (within the bounds of the overall cap set by shareholders). That included his own pay. Beyond Ohnuma, nobody knew how much Ghosn was paid, which was precisely how he liked it.

At the start of 2010, a dark storm cloud appeared before the CEO. Japanese authorities were going to overhaul rules on executive pay disclosure, requiring companies to report the income of any director who made more than 100 million yen (roughly $1 million) a year.

Ghosn's pay wasn't public, but it was well beyond the proposed disclosure threshold. The company had only recently emerged from having to declare paying its board members an average of $2.5 million annually per director. At Toyota, by comparison, the average director was making $500,000. Shareholders wanted justification for such gross extravagance. Greg Kelly, the head of the CEO office, sent Ghosn a short message informing him about the forthcoming executive pay disclosure. It would be retroactive, meaning that Ghosn's earnings for the year would have to be made public.

Soon after he pressed SEND on the message, his phone rang.

"We need to argue against this," Ghosn said. He told Kelly to have the Nissan executives with the closest ties to the government, especially his number two, Toshiyuki Shiga, start lobbying to at least delay the passage of the rule. But the Japanese government was resolute. Companies were insulating their top managers against the global financial crisis, even as high numbers of workers were losing their jobs or taking pay cuts. The country was still in recession, and the public was outraged, clamoring for a modicum of social justice.

Ghosn shifted to damage control, knowing he faced the unpalatable prospect of reporting an annual salary of nearly 1.6 billion yen, or around $17 million. The mammoth figure would cause a backlash in both Japan and France. How could he preach frugality and ruthless efficiency—the foundations of his celebrity in Japan—while collecting corporate Japan's largest paycheck?

Ghosn briefly contemplated simply not reporting his salary, but his advisers, including Kelly, warned him against thumbing his nose at regulators. So Ghosn sought a number from Ohnuma and other executives: what was the ceiling of what he could earn without sparking a riot that might destroy his credibility and reputation in Japan. What were the bounds?

They came up with a figure: 890 million yen, or around $9.6 million.

Ghosn instructed Ohnuma to adjust his pay down to that number ahead of the adoption of the new disclosure rules. The prospect of having to return nearly half his pay stung, especially after dealing with the Shinsei Bank mess, while staring down the barrel of a possible divorce settlement.

Ohnuma followed orders, extinguishing the immediate fire. But Ghosn wasn't just going to let the whole thing go. For a longer-term fix, he turned to Kelly. Was there any way—any *legal* way, he emphasized—that he might be paid back? Without disclosing it?

*   *   *

Greg Kelly had the American can-do, brass-tacks, capitalist sensibility that Ghosn desperately wanted to infuse Nissan and Renault with. He was there to keep Nissan's brightest talent happy, and he knew very well that the company's most important person, who must be kept happy at all costs, was Carlos Ghosn. That awareness, plus his devoted schedule—twelve-hour workdays during the week, nine hours on Saturday, and usually seven on Sunday—made him one of Ghosn's most trusted lieutenants.

Kelly was well aware that Ghosn was paid a lot of money, but that was irrelevant, as he also knew that there were numerous entities willing to pay the man more. Ghosn was constantly being courted by competitors. In the spring of 2009, Steven Rattner, the former investment banker brought in by President Obama to help save the US auto industry, had sounded him out in a private room of the Washington Four Seasons Hotel about becoming CEO of GM.

If the Japanese couldn't grasp that there was a market for elite managers with a global vision, Kelly perceived it as his duty to do everything within his power to prevent Nissan from letting its greatest asset slip through its fingers.

Kelly first consulted Nissan's top in-house lawyer at headquarters about accommodating the boss. The terse response he received made clear that he would have to go outside the rigid confines of Japan. He called his favorite legal adviser, Scott Becker, a no-nonsense, get-it-done Nissan lawyer based in Tennessee. The two men zeroed in on a promising way to get Ghosn more cash. Under Japanese law,

Ghosn would not have to disclose any pay received from an uncon-solidated subsidiary (a company that Nissan partially owned but was independently managed). But the payment detour was not a free pass, Becker warned. Ghosn would have to work for it.

Kelly had a subsidiary company in mind: Renault Nissan BV (known as RNBV), the Dutch entity set up by Ghosn and Schweitzer and that served as a sort of United Nations of Renault and Nissan. To Kelly, it made sense that Ghosn should be paid for the three posts he held, as head of Renault, Nissan, and RNBV. Under that rationale, even if reg-ulators or media caught wind of the sideline salary, they could counter that it was an earned paycheck. But there was no need to raise ques-tions unnecessarily. The arrangement would remain secret.

In March, Kelly forwarded a detailed memo on the mechanics of the payment system to Ohnuma, who would oversee the minutiae. Ghosn asked him to make sure it was bulletproof. In April, Kelly asked Becker and Mouna Sepehri, the Renault lawyer, to conduct another round of checks. "Earlier this week the CEO indicated he wanted to make sure that payment of part of his compensation by RNBV without publically [sic] disclosing the amount is legal," Kelly wrote to her. "Will there be criminal sanctions and if so what will those sanctions be?"

RNBV was not ideal, and Becker's words of caution rang in Kelly's ears: *The payment detour is not a free pass.* Kelly himself wasn't entirely convinced that the company could justify the whole difference in Ghosn's reduced pay, simply because the chief hadn't put in enough time with RNBV to merit $9 million.

For the moment, however, it was the best option.

*   *   *

In June 2010, Nissan disclosed to the public Ghosn's "official" com-pensation, revealing that Ghosn had received $9.6 million. However diminished, it still established Ghosn as the highest-paid executive in Japan. The public was enraged. Even the newly appointed Japanese prime minister, Naoto Kan, criticized the celebrity. "Why is Ghosn's salary so high?" he said. "Because he's good at firing people."

Ghosn used the annual shareholder meeting to defend himself, saying he was paid well below the industry average. "If you compare this pay to Japanese standard, you can say it's out of line," he conceded. "But if you compare them with global standards, there is nothing out of line. In fact, we are below standard."

In France, Renault's unions had a scathing reaction, calling Ghosn's pay a scandal.

Still, it could have been worse. After the initial response to the disclosure and the ensuing meetings, Kelly was relieved that the storm had not been more severe. The controversy over Ghosn's pay would subside with the next wave of global headlines, and the money transfers through RNBV were scheduled to start in September.

Before even one payment could be made, however, Kelly's plan collapsed under him. In August 2010, the French stock exchange regulator changed its rules governing disclosures, and Renault would now have to report on the subsidiaries over which it had "significant influence." Ghosn would no longer be able to be paid by RNBV without disclosing it in France, which meant everyone everywhere would know.

Kelly called Ghosn in Paris to deliver the bad news but left it to Sepehri, Ghosn's chief French legal adviser, to explain.

A short time later, she called back. "Boy, he was pissed," she told Kelly.

* * *

The RNBV attempt had shown that it would be very difficult, if not impossible, to pay Ghosn through a corporate structure involving Renault without disclosing the outlay. Still, using a Dutch-registered company tied to Nissan sounded promising, and an opportunity to do just that soon presented itself.

In the summer of 2010, Nissan executives were debating the idea of creating a special fund aimed at investing in innovative startups. Ghosn had expressed concerns that Nissan risked falling behind in the race to develop electric vehicles and self-driving cars if it didn't keep track of disruptive projects being thought up in places like Silicon Valley.

Ghosn wanted the idea of an internal venture capital fund to be put on a fast track. In September, he called Kelly and the company's chief financial officer into his office to outline a plan. Kelly was tasked with writing a proposal for approval by the executive committee. Ghosn figured that $50 million would be just enough to make Nissan a serious player.

After the meeting, Ghosn pulled Kelly aside.

"So," he asked Kelly, "do you think I can be paid by this company?"

Kelly promised to look into it.

At the executive committee meeting the following month, Kelly read out the proposal, omitting the fact that it might be used to pay the boss. Ghosn requested that a name be chosen for this new Dutch-based investment fund that had no reference to Nissan. It was dubbed Zi-A Capital. The name was coined by Hari Nada, a smooth-talking British lawyer who had recently moved to headquarters. "Zi-A" was a play on the Arabic word for "light": "A" stood for "automotive," "Z" was a subtle nod to Nissan's most famous vehicle, the Z sports coupe. The committee voted unanimously to pass the motion.

After the vote, Ghosn turned to his top executives. "I expect you all to come to me with ideas," he told them.

10

Figure Out a Way

Ghosn was in Brazil, visiting his mother and celebrating the New Year, when a huge—if somewhat bizarre—corporate scandal exploded at Renault in France.

By mid-January 2011, the situation in France was becoming untenable: Renault had fired three senior managers for allegedly selling industrial secrets to Chinese competitors, but hadn't explained what evidence it had. The three fired executives filed lawsuits for unfair dismissal. Beijing denied any involvement. The company and Ghosn were being hammered in the court of public opinion.

Ghosn remained out of the country for more than two weeks as the scandal mushroomed. When he finally returned to Paris, he decided to appear on the most-watched evening news TV program to silence the doubters and prove that he wasn't an absentee boss.

Under the harsh glare of the lights, the anchor got right to the point: Did Ghosn have concrete evidence to justify the firings?

Ghosn's eyebrows shot up. In his signature staccato, he assured her and 10 million viewers, "Listen, we have certainties. If we didn't have certitudes, we wouldn't be here."

"But this evidence," the journalist asked. "Is it financial? Are they allegations made by other employees? Do you have anything concrete?"

"We have multiple pieces of proof," Ghosn said with conviction.

That night, lawyers for the accused went on every news program that would accept them and urged Renault to make public Ghosn's supposed evidence.

Executives began to question the internal investigation that had led to the firings. What they found was alarming: all the accusations and security reports rested on the say-so of one single source, who had shared intel with a former military intelligence officer who had spent some €250,000 (provided by Renault) to buy information of supposed malfeasance. But none of that information amounted to proof, per se.

Was it real information? Reliable? Who was to say. The company's decision to fire the executives was not his problem.

By early March, French authorities received confirmation that none of the accounts referenced in the security report had ever existed. However monumental these findings were, the news was completely overshadowed by the Fukushima nuclear plant disaster on March 11, 2011. The damage caused by the earthquake and the subsequent tsunami was devastating. Though there were relatively few employees in the stricken area, Nissan was hit hard and forced to shut down several assembly plants. The country's entire auto supply chain, usually a marvel of efficiency, was crippled, as parts makers couldn't access their warehouses located there.

Just when Nissan needed its CEO to be present, Ghosn was conspicuously absent, as he had been for Renault during the initial fiasco with the fired employees. In this case, the Nissan chief said he couldn't fly back because private jets weren't able to land. "Then get on a commercial flight," one of Ghosn's top lieutenants at Nissan grumbled to himself. But Ghosn had unfinished business in France.

On March 14, Ghosn met with the three fired Renault executives to apologize for the company's rush to judgment. Then, in an act of penance, he chaired a board meeting during which he gave up his bonus of €2.3 million and stock options for the year. That night, he went back onto French TV. "I got this wrong, *we* got this wrong," he said. "It seems that we were tricked." The budget minister and government spokesman criticized the "unbelievable amateurism" that had been on display at Renault. Even Louis Schweitzer, who had recruited Ghosn fifteen years earlier, joined in the efforts of those trying to get him fired. The response wasn't much better in Japan, where, for the first time, Ghosn was openly contested.

A few days later, Ghosn went with Pelata to France's Ministry for the Economy and Finance. The finance minister, Christine Lagarde, received the two men in her office. In short order, the famously composed Lagarde lost her cool and gave the men a dressing-down. For all of Ghosn's posturing, the past few months had laid bare the challenges—if not the impossibility—of running two global corporations on separate continents.

*   *   *

The following week, Ghosn finally landed in Japan to take stock of the damage caused by the tsunami and ensuing nuclear disaster. At headquarters, however, Kelly, Ohnuma, and a couple of other executives had a second priority: It had now been a full year since Ghosn had taken a pay cut at Nissan, and finding a solution was becoming ever more urgent. The boss wasn't happy he'd just lost another $2 million (at least on paper) due to the Renault fiasco.

Shortly before Ghosn's arrival, Greg Kelly came to the conclusion that he was again at a dead end. He had been exploring the idea of paying Ghosn through the new venture fund Zi-A Capital, but it raised too many problems. "Zi-A has no substance," Kelly told Ghosn. It was an investment fund that had not made any investments. The CEO could get paid by Zi-A but would be breaking the law if he didn't disclose the amount to shareholders.

In addition to Greg Kelly's ceaseless efforts, a separate team of two Nissan executives, including Toshiyuki Shiga, was working on various other solutions to appease Ghosn. When presented with one option, Ghosn became unusually heated, standing up from the table and raising his voice. Ghosn had been promised a higher paycheck when he

joined the company, he told Shiga. The Japanese executive should figure out a way for him to receive extra cash without disclosing it.

At a meeting on April 23, Ghosn, Shiga, and another Japanese executive settled on doing so through "contribution rewards," a set amount to
be paid annually as a consulting fee after he retired. Essentially, it meant
Ghosn would no longer be out half his salary; he would just have to wait
until he retired to receive the money. The agreement split Ghosn's
pay into two categories: "paid remuneration" and "postponed remuneration." As of March 2011, the document said, Ghosn's post-retirement
consulting fee already stood at 1 billion yen, or $12.7 million—the ex-
act amount the CEO had foregone since taking a pay cut to avoid disclosing his full salary.

With everything agreed, Ohnuma strolled into Ghosn's office, a
cavernous space with a panoramic view of Yokohama Bay. The two
men signed the agreement, which Ohnuma then filed away in his own
office across the corridor.

*   *   *

In parallel to the agreement Ghosn had signed with Ohnuma, and after the failure of the plan to pay Ghosn through Zi-A Capital, Kelly
was still trying to figure out how to keep the boss around. He feared
that if Ghosn lost his job at Renault—something that he had been perilously close to doing after the spy scandal—he would likely be out at
Nissan as well, because the French company had the power to appoint
some of the top executives at its Japanese subsidiary. Ghosn's replacement might not be so willing to defend Nissan against a merger. Kelly
needed to ensure Ghosn stuck around, no matter what.

One idea Kelly was toying with was a special consultancy arrangement that would keep Ghosn in the boardroom for an extra decade of
service after he officially retired from Nissan. The agreement would
guarantee Ghosn $10 million per annum, or $100 million in total, and
ensure that he didn't go work for a competitor.

In the summer of 2011, however, it was Ghosn who contacted Kelly.

He had a question: Would it be possible for Nissan to confidentially provide him an office and places to stay in Brazil and Lebanon? he asked. He planned to spend more time in those countries working to grow Nissan's business.

"I'll look into it," Kelly said. The idea sounded legitimate. Ghosn believed in the potential of emerging markets, and had long pushed Nissan to expand there. Kelly also knew that Ghosn traveled to those places fairly frequently, and a number of Nissan executives worried about Ghosn's security when he was there.

Ghosn set his sights on an apartment in the Copacabana Beach neighborhood in Rio. It was in a discreet building with a beautiful view of the beach. He asked his sister Claudine to check it out, and she told him that she thought he would like it.

Having been assured that the plan was legal, Kelly turned his attention to figuring out how to purchase the properties quietly. The American had a perfect resource: Zi-A Capital. The venture fund still had a bundle of cash since it had yet to make any investments. Now it would do real estate. For Carlos Ghosn.

Kelly asked Nada, the Nissan lawyer who had come up with Zi-A's name, to finalize the purchase. "It is absolutely imperative that Nissan's involvement is kept completely confidential from the vendor and does not become a matter of public knowledge," Nada wrote to the real estate agent.

On November 21, 2011, Kelly presented Ghosn with the $10 million-a-year agreement he had been working on. In addition to the eye-watering paycheck, Kelly added a last-minute sweetener to the deal: Nissan would gift Ghosn properties in Brazil and Lebanon, as well as in Paris. Ghosn didn't sign the document—he had been told by Kelly that he couldn't—but it was signed by Kelly and Saikawa, and Ghosn filed it away in his safe.

Two weeks later, the deal for the house in Rio was completed. The seller included the furniture and some of the apartment's artwork to sweeten the purchase price of $5.8 million. Nada formed two Zi-A subsidiaries in the British Virgin Islands. They served to put sufficient distance between Nissan and the Rio apartment, ensuring that even senior executives at the carmaker would be kept unaware of who owned the property. Nada proceeded with the payment, using funds transferred from Zi-A. Ghosn would be able to spend Christmas there.

Meanwhile, for the property in Beirut, Ghosn opted for a historic $9.4 million property in need of extensive renovations. The price tag caused Kelly to swallow hard—a multimillion-dollar ruin wasn't what Kelly had imagined when Ghosn had told him to find corporate housing in Lebanon—but he passed the details to Nada, who set up the companies necessary to make that purchase as well.

Kelly could finally exhale, comfortable in his belief that he had done the company a great service. Nissan would keep its captain.

*   *   *

Ghosn's professional life was back under control—for now. His private life, however, was still a mess. Ghosn and Rita had by now agreed to divorce. That was the easy part. The question was where. To Rita, it was simple. They had sealed their union in France, under a regime that made her entitled to half of the couple's assets.

Ghosn preferred to divorce in Lebanon. In 2005, the couple had signed a declaration transferring their matrimonial pact to that country, where the law stated that each spouse would hold on to the assets in their name. Ghosn had told Rita it would be advantageous for tax reasons and his personal lawyer had drawn up the paperwork.

At the time, the arrangement had made sense to Rita, but a divorce in Lebanon now meant she could claim ownership of nothing, other than a $400,000 Beirut building Ghosn had bought and registered in her name. All other assets, from the wine estate in Lebanon to the millions of dollars in savings, were in his name.

Divorce negotiations with Rita were at an impasse when a banker friend of Ghosn said he knew someone who might be able to help him, a Lebanese lawyer named Carlos Abou Jaoude. The banker told Ghosn a story: He described an impenetrable wall that several burly men had tried and failed to break down. Then a small lizard came along and started to look for the tiniest crack. He tried a first crack, then a second. Eventually, the lizard found a crack that led to a structural weakness. Pretty quickly, the wall came tumbling down. Ghosn's friend told him: the lizard was Abou Jaoude.

Abou Jaoude was one of the most prominent lawyers in the Middle East. He had a number of expensive cars and a cellar full of the finest French wines. He wasn't a divorce lawyer, but he had a legendary work ethic and an agile mind. The man known as Mr. 7-Eleven in Japan had found his ideal lawyer, and Abou Jaoude made an immediate impact on the talks with Rita. He was able to pry open her Beirut door, sit down with her, and set negotiations in motion again. "She made me understand that her deepest desire was to see the agreement come into force as quickly as possible," Abou Jaoude emailed Ghosn and other lawyers on the case in June 2012.

Following a number of concessions from Ghosn, Rita relented and agreed to divorce in Lebanon. The two signed the divorce agreement in Beirut on October 12, 2012. The settlement provided for a cash payment to Rita of $30 million. She would also receive an annual payment of around $2 million from Ghosn for the next fifteen years, with the promise of a bank guarantee in case the auto chief didn't pay. The agreement also stipulated that Carlos Ghosn would pay for the upbringing of their four children as well as their studies until they had stable jobs.

The closure, after years of acrimony, called for a toast.

*   *   *

Wearing a dark blue suit and an open-collared light-colored shirt, Ghosn took the microphone to welcome his guests at his Lebanese vineyard nestled into the mountains, overlooking the Mediterranean Sea. A day after signing his divorce agreement with Rita, he hosted a party with Carole, the new woman in his life, by his side. Guests included the cream of Beirut, from ambassadors to businessmen to fashion designers. Wine specialists were on hand to share their knowledge and tell the guests about Ghosn's latest vintage. A Lebanese magazine ran a photo spread of the event, claiming that all the Beirut jet set had been in attendance.

Ghosn had been through the wringer in the past few years, but that evening he was a happy man. Ghosn found Carole elegant, sweet, and empathetic. His friends often talked about how much in love he was. With her keen interest in art, design, and architecture, Carole had taught Ghosn to appreciate the finer things in life. Taking her fashion advice, he had even changed the way he dressed. His pants were tighter, his shirts crisper, his suits well tailored.

In fact, it was Carole who had chosen the house in Beirut that Nissan eventually bought for Ghosn. It was a decaying building on a corner lot in Ashrafieh, a historic neighborhood close to one of Ghosn's childhood homes. The walls were a dun gray, and there was no electricity or running water. Still, Ghosn had trusted Carole's taste so completely that he had asked Nissan to buy it without ever seeing it himself.

More profound than the tailored suits or enhanced aesthetic sensibility, their love was helping Ghosn to enjoy the present moment, rather than constantly making plans for the following year or the one after that. It was an impressive feat. She had even made the famously punctual Ghosn gracefully accept her tendency to be late. Until then, the only person he had tolerated making him wait was Vladimir Putin.

Carlos Ghosn had been fighting, chasing, and building ever since he had left Beirut as a teenager. He surveyed his estate, his jet-setting friends, and the beautiful woman on his arm.

He had earned all of it—and more.

11

Hall of Mirrors

Ghosn could hardly hide his pride as Dieter Zetsche sat next to him for a joint press conference during the Paris Motor Show. In the pantheon of carmakers, German brands were in the front row. Known widely as Dr. Z, the bespeckled Zetsche was the CEO of Daimler, the parent company of Mercedes.

The German executive was recounting how he had toured Renault's main research facility the day before and had been impressed by what he had seen: French and German engineers working in symbiosis. The Renault-Nissan Alliance and Daimler had agreed to extend a series of partnerships to jointly develop and produce critical car parts, from engines to gearboxes, in a bid to save on costs.

When reporters were given the floor, the first question was whether this collaborative work was the prelude to a merger.

"Can I answer?" Ghosn said. As Zetsche acquiesced through his bushy mustache, the Renault-Nissan chief explained how the philosophy of the partnership with Daimler was to maximize efficiency for both partners without encroaching on each other's independence. "You can be happy with the flirt without being happy with the marriage," Ghosn said.

On that day in September 2012, Daimler's decision to double down on its cooperation with Renault and Nissan, after an initial test in 2010, was a strong vote of confidence for the Alliance and its captain.

Through similar partnerships, Ghosn had managed to expand in challenging markets such as Russia and China, and in the process had transformed the Alliance into one of the world's top carmakers, alongside GM, Toyota, and VW. Behind these apparent successes, however, Ghosn knew that the Alliance had grown into an unwieldy beast. Nothing had made that more obvious than the financial crisis. The economic turmoil brought plenty of companies—auto and otherwise—to their knees, and the Alliance was far from immune. Renault had to rely on a multibillion-euro bailout from the French government. Nissan had been days away from running out of cash.

Despite flirting for well over a decade, Renault and Nissan still shared little more than their CEO and a common second home, RNBV, which was nestled in a boxy building on the outskirts of Amsterdam. When they had paired up in 1999, Renault and Nissan had plenty of reasons to work together. The Japanese firm needed Renault to avert looming bankruptcy, and the French needed Nissan to conquer new markets. But as the years passed, motivation waned.

Renault and Nissan functioned as separate entities. They had maintained parallel structures for everything from finance to research, design to production. Their cars shared less than 5 percent of identical components. The companies' much-touted electric vehicles—the Renault Zoe and the Nissan LEAF—had been developed by competing teams that had selected competing battery technologies. The Zoe and the LEAF themselves shared little more than the door handles. It wasn't just Ghosn's two briefcases that separated the companies. It was proving an ineffective model of operations in an era of efficiency and competitiveness.

When Renault and Nissan did collaborate, it was an uphill struggle. Since 2009, an Iranian-born lawyer named Mouna Sepehri had been working on measuring and boosting cooperation. A former skateboarding champion who had started her career as a mergers and acquisitions lawyer in New York, Sepehri kept running into engineers who harbored a strong patriotic allegiance, particularly on the Nissan side, that was extremely hard to overcome.

Each time Renault and Nissan sat down to agree on a common part, things quickly turned into trench warfare. It had taken months of heated discussions to agree on a common light switch and air-conditioning system for future small vehicles that they intended to develop together. Internal surveys of French and Japanese managers showed a persistent cultural gap. "When a Japanese person says yes, it means they've understood, not that they've agreed," one Renault engineer lamented. "By contrast, if we don't respond immediately, they consider that we agree, which is unfair."

On the other side, a Japanese executive who had started to work for Renault had responded that "something basic" was missing in Renault's approach that made it difficult to reach Nissan's level of success: people weren't involved in the decision-making process. "They cannot understand the way Nissan works," he said.

Sepehri eventually reached the conclusion that by far the best way to achieve significant cost savings was to merge Renault and Nissan into a single company. To those who pointed out this would entail steep job cuts, she would counter that all the jobs would be at risk if Renault and Nissan failed to streamline their operations.

Ghosn fundamentally agreed. A merger would help boost efficiency within the Alliance, but he was trapped in an impossible situation. While Renault's largest shareholder, the French state, wanted a Renault-led merger, the executives at Nissan argued that they should be in charge. Ghosn had been exploring all kinds of scenarios to extricate himself from this deadlock. One of them, concocted secretly with Greg Kelly and a US law firm, aimed at emancipating the Alliance from French government influence, possibly by pulling off a Nissan-led merger.

One Nissan executive involved in the plot had dubbed the idea "project Kali," after the Hindu goddess of destruction. It called for the Japanese company to use its Ghosn-restored financial heft to steamroll Renault and forcibly acquire what it saw as the real junior partner in the pair.

Ghosn quickly shelved the Kali idea, but staying put wasn't an option, either. Investors were dubious about the prospects for the Alliance. On the Paris stock exchange, Renault was worth some €10 billion, less than the value of its 43 percent interest in Nissan. In other words, excluding its Nissan stake, Renault was a stack of liabilities. Its depressed share price reflected the fact that its main market, Europe, was in the throes of the euro-debt crisis—but it was also a measure of how little faith investors had in the Alliance's life expectancy. If Ghosn left, there were few assurances that the partnership would survive.

In a bid to give the Alliance new impetus, Ghosn decided to hold Renault's October 2012 board meeting in RNBV's Amsterdam offices, where the vast majority of directors had never set foot.

Ghosn had invited several managers to feed the board on the status of the Alliance. Those presentations described a bottle that was both half-full and half-empty. Sepehri the Renault executive told the board how management was aiming to increase common parts in Renault and Nissan vehicles to a minimum of 28 percent by 2015. She said the plan was inspired by Volkswagen, which had created the industry's new benchmark by forcing its many brands to make cars with the same underpinnings.

When the time came for questions, the French state's senior representative said that Renault's low stock market value showed how investors believed that the Alliance had gone as far as it could in its current form. What did Ghosn think about "changing the structure"? he asked.

Ghosn knew that was a euphemism. The French official wanted an update on the prospect of merging the companies. He gave a familiar answer: the history of the automotive industry was littered with failed partnerships, Ghosn said. Recently, the collaboration between Daimler and Mitsubishi had been a catastrophe, even though on paper it should have worked. Over the past decade, several failed marriages had similarly dissolved, from Ford and Mazda to GM and Fiat, and Daimler's even bigger debacle, DaimlerChrysler.

Ghosn agreed the Alliance needed to generate more cost savings for the two companies and pledged to double those savings to €4 billion each year. He argued that achieving any more than that would require a full-blown merger, and that was too risky. "We have to be careful," Ghosn said.

After the meeting, Ghosn asked his top lieutenants in Paris and Tokyo to come up with ideas to make the Alliance operate more like a single company—a tacit acknowledgment by Ghosn that the reality didn't match his own rhetoric.

When he met with two of them several months later, Sepehri again proposed a merger, saying it was the most efficient way to combine the two companies. Hiroto Saikawa, Nissan's representative on the Renault board, demurred.

"Okay, nice try," Ghosn told Sepehri. "Propose me something else."

Ghosn already had something in mind: rather than make Renault and Nissan converge by starting from the top of the two companies, which is generally the process in traditional mergers, he wanted to make them converge from the base.

"Instead of doing top-down, please propose me bottom-up," he said.

The option that Ghosn chose involved naming a series of new vice presidents who would attempt to run portions of both Renault's and Nissan's businesses at the same time (including new chiefs for research and development, manufacturing, and purchasing).

Sepehri foresaw massive issues in the day-to-day running of things. Combining functions from the bottom up would require the kind of hopping back and forth between Europe and Japan that had become second nature to the CEO. But even if they succeeded in enduring the jet lag, it was unclear whether Ghosn's proposal would give the Alliance managers enough authority to impose decisions on Renault and Nissan. She told Ghosn that it would have to be a temporary solution. It was obvious that relying on a group of mini-Ghosns wouldn't be viable in the long run.

"Mr. Ghosn, everybody doesn't have your plane," she told the boss. "People are going to die!"

Ghosn instructed his lieutenants to get cracking. However odd, the bottom-up approach was the only plan both companies could stomach. It was the best he could do.

*   *   *

Ghosn's efforts to push Renault and Nissan together since 1999 resulted only in small steps forward. Success has a way of papering over the cracks, however, and Renault and Nissan had an abundance of success. The whole auto industry was growing at a rapid rate as the world recovered, and the companies were growing in both size and profitability.

As profits soared, the critics of the Alliance became harder to hear. Even without corrective surgery, Ghosn's Alliance seemed ever more alluring—and his legend only continued to grow. Business schools published studies about what Ghosn was attempting to do, to create the corporate equivalent of the European Union, where parties worked together out of mutual self-interest, setting aside petty self-interest for the sake of mutual prosperity.

Merger? Conglomerate? The old vocabulary didn't fit.

He had taken to showing investors a chart of the ten biggest tie-ups in automobile history, drawn up by one of the large consultancy firms. It made plain how his Alliance was the only one that had actually created value for shareholders.

This was worth celebrating.

In June 2013, Ghosn pored over a PowerPoint presentation made by his public relations chief that outlined some key events on his calendar for the following year. Added to the list—which included Cannes and major sporting events such as the World Cup and the French Open—was a lavish event at the Palace of Versailles to celebrate the Alliance's fifteenth anniversary. He wanted as many as two hundred people there. The budget was €300,000.

Ghosn thought that an invitation to Versailles would ensure that people actually turned up for the party. The dinner was meant to be a celebration of the Alliance and its foreign partners. While he worked the mechanics of the merger from the bottom up, he wanted to reinforce a sense of unified—and inevitable—power from the top down.

The affair was never meant for the employees of Renault and Nissan. Instead, the guest list included politicians from Japan and the United States, as well as heads of state from Brazil to Bhutan and Nigeria to South Korea. He also included the heads of major Japanese corporations as well as former bureaucrats and businessmen with whom Ghosn had negotiated deals in China and Russia.

In late January, these guests received a save-the-date by email. Mr. Carlos Ghosn "cordially invites you and your guest to attend a dinner in honour of our partners who have supported the Renault-Nissan Alliance," the message read. Dinner would be catered by the Michelin-starred chef Alain Ducasse. And in the sort of serendipity that only happens when you're one of the most powerful men in the world, the dinner coincided with Ghosn's sixtieth birthday.

In the weeks that followed, however, it became clear that almost none of the marquee guests would be able to make it. Some were too busy. Others didn't fancy flying to France just for dinner, even if it was being held at Versailles. All the Chinese guests had declined, something Ghosn attributed to an order from Beijing. The Russians also couldn't make it, probably because of travel restrictions stemming from US and European sanctions, Ghosn figured.

Ghosn had gotten himself into a bit of a jam. He'd signed a contract for a dinner party for up to two hundred people. The price would be the same with two hundred people as with twenty, but twenty people at Versailles would be a downer, to say the least. Rescheduling was pointless because there was no way of counting on busy people's future schedules. Canceling would also be rude for the few people who had confirmed their attendance.

As the head of two carmaking giants, for a party celebrating their partnership, Ghosn had plenty of options to fill the vacant seats. But

Ghosn simply did not want to invite current or former executives from Renault and Nissan, or really any or many of the thousands of available people who had helped to build the Alliance. People like Louis Schweitzer, Patrick Pelata, and Toshiyuki Shiga weren't candidates for Versailles. It was the corporate equivalent of a wedding, and he didn't want to deal with the politics of who got the invite and who didn't. He also had an aversion to the idea of paying for employees in Japan or elsewhere around the world to fly to a party in France. But this party was happening. Ghosn had spent the money and, come hell or high water, he needed to fill as many seats as possible.

*   *   *

At 7:30 p.m., on March 9, 2014, the cavalcade of black cars began pulling up to the golden gates of Louis XIV's 2,300-room home for a celebration of Nissan-Renault and Carlos Ghosn's work.

Dressed in black tie and evening gowns, some 150 guests strode across the cobbled courtyard toward the main entrance, past dozens of paid actors in tricorn hats and silk stockings as a means of re-creating how courtiers would have entered in the eighteenth century.

They found Ghosn in a gregarious mood, more Louis XIV than XVI. After cocktails, he invited guests to stroll through the royal apartments that surrounded the Hall of Mirrors as others might show off a finished basement. In each new antechamber, the guests were greeted by more musicians and dressed-up courtiers hired to channel the palace's legacy of giddy debauchery.

Once everybody was seated for dinner, Ghosn stepped onto a podium and greeted his guests. Assembled around the single long table were a handful of businessmen and politicians who had worked with the Alliance. Among them was Cherie Blair, wife of the former UK prime minister Tony Blair, who had represented the constituency where Nissan had a factory. Across from her was Trent Lott, a former US senator from Mississippi, where Nissan had built a plant in 2003.

None made Ghosn smile more widely than the blond woman opposite him at the center of the long table—his girlfriend, Carole. She was in a floor-length Elie Saab dress covered in black sequins. Also dotted around the table were Ghosn's children and his elder sister, Claudine.

Standing rod-straight in front of a white marble bust, his chin slightly up, Ghosn dialed back to the start of his journey trying to marry two carmakers. "As some of you know, this month marks the fifteenth anniversary of the Renault-Nissan Alliance," he said. "Some questioned how combining two second-tier automakers, one French and the other Japanese and near bankruptcy, would create an entity that together would become globally competitive," he went on, his left hand clenched into a fist. "Nobody had tried this kind of partnership before, there was absolutely no template."

Scanning the audience assembled in the Gallery of Battles, Ghosn said the tie-up was "the longest-lasting cross-cultural alliance" not just in the auto industry, but in any industry.

"So, we have gathered you here tonight, in this majestic and historic venue, to express our sincere thanks for all you have done to support, encourage and enrich the Alliance and its leaders," he concluded.

After the speech, the opulent meal, and the even more opulent dessert—featuring towers of macarons and profiteroles—Carole led guests back to the Hall of Mirrors, escorted by a master of ceremony in a powdered wig and feathered cap. They then guided the party to the seventeen archways that overlooked the vast manicured lawns of the palace grounds. Fireworks exploded into the sky, reflecting off the mirrors, the diamonds, and the Champagne glasses—the picture-perfect conclusion to end an evening fit for a king.

* * *

In the days that followed the event, there was no coverage in the French and Japanese media. The only article recounting the event was a diary item in a Lebanese French-language newspaper. Titled "The King of Auto in Versailles," the article described "Carlos Ghosn's Renault and Nissan evening" in lavish terms, including how guests had been greeted by halberdiers at the entrance of Versailles, the dinner by Alain Ducasse, and the "fabulous fireworks"—the apotheosis of the evening. Among the guests that Sunday were Cherie Blair and some American senators, the journalist wrote, "but also numerous Lebanese friends."

The journalist listed more than thirty of them, including Mario Saradar, the CEO of a bank in which Ghosn held a sizable stake. Etienne Debbane, who was a co-owner in Ghosn's wine business, was also there. Also in attendance was Father Salim Daccache, the rector of Saint Joseph University in Beirut, where the Carlos Ghosn Library for Economy and Medicine was due to open the following year. Omitted from the Lebanese report were Carole's children, Daniel, Anthony, and Tara; her parents, Greta and Arfan Malas; and her brother, Alain.

Indeed, the evening had turned into a kind of birthday party with a corporate gloss. Most of the guests had only a vague connection to the Alliance. Many could only point to a friendship or personal business relationship with Ghosn, or were relatives of Ghosn and his girlfriend. Carole had even suggested working a "Happy Birthday" song for Ghosn into the event, although that suggestion was rejected.

When the tab trickled through, it totaled more than €530,000. The dinner had been the largest expense. The catering came to €115,000, almost a third of which went directly to the celebrity chef. The bills were sent to Toshiaki Ohnuma, and the keeper of secrets was to pay the costs from the bank account of RNBV.

The numbers behind the party were well obscured from the ranks of Renault and Nissan, but the buzz around them was impossible to contain. There were hurt feelings across the executive floors of both companies' headquarters.

Dominique Thormann, Renault's finance chief, didn't know there had been an event until after the fact. When he arrived at Renault's office on Monday morning, one of his underlings in the finance department asked whether he had heard about the big party at Versailles.

"What party?" Thormann asked.

12

Money Canals

Carlos Ghosn kept almost everyone at arm's length. His tiny inner circle included Carole, his close relatives, and a handful of school friends. Among the latter group was Fady Gebran, a discreet lawyer who had moved the registration of Ghosn's marriage with Rita from France to Lebanon. Ghosn and Gebran had known each other since they were small children, having attended Collège Notre-Dame de Jamhour in Lebanon together. They had remained friends after graduation, with both opting to go to France for their higher education.

After the Lebanese civil war had ended, Gebran had happily returned to the homeland to set up his law firm. He rented a modest office on the first floor of a building near the city's main courthouse, with only one associate and one assistant. He rarely spoke about his work to his wife or three children. His passion in life was learning languages; he could converse in Russian, Japanese, and Hebrew, as well as in French, English, and Arabic.

Despite the physical distance between them in their professional years, Ghosn and Gebran remained closely entangled, due to the lawyer's specialization in a narrow, albeit globe-spanning, field of expertise: tax havens. At a business seminar near Paris in 2011, he had extolled the virtues of offshore companies over traditional corporations, praising Lebanon's decision not to ban them. Lebanon was enforcing a strict version of banking secrecy, allowing for huge amounts to crisscross its financial system anonymously. Offshore companies were charged a fixed annual tax of a few hundred dollars per year, no matter how much money transited through their accounts. On top of that, Lebanese banks were basically begging their wealthy expatriates to park their money in the country, offering double-digit interest rates. The prevailing wisdom was that if you stuck your money in Lebanon, you would become rich.

Gebran's knowledge of the country's lax regulations, coupled with his discretion, had allowed him to build up a small but loyal clientele consisting mostly of wealthy Lebanese who trusted him to manage their assets. The cornerstone of such a business was trust, which was particularly essential because Gebran was the official owner of many of the entities he created for his clients. The benefit to his clients was obvious: their ownership was anonymous, with their secrets stored in the practically inviolable vault of Gebran's head. Gebran relied on only one person to help manage his clients' web of offshore assets: his assistant, Amal Abou Jaoude (unrelated to Carlos Abou Jaoude), whom he often added as a director of the companies.

Ghosn, by far Gebran's most prestigious client, was counted among those who placed full confidence in the Lebanese lawyer. Ghosn kept Gebran on retainer as a legal adviser for both Renault and Nissan and had introduced him to some of his Middle Eastern business friends. In addition to professional concerns, Ghosn called on Gebran to handle personal matters, such as setting up his wine business.

The main task that Ghosn gave Gebran, however, was moving money in secret. In July 2013, Ghosn sent the trusted lawyer an email asking if he had received any "roses." Gebran had just put the finishing touches on one of his arcane money lines, and, indeed, €2 million in cash was moving through it. The Lebanese lawyer responded that "2000k Europeans" were on the way.

The source of such an extravagant bouquet was Ghosn's old friend Suhail Bahwan, the Omani billionaire who had lent Ghosn 3 billion yen, or roughly $20 million, during the financial crisis, a loan that the Nissan chief still hadn't paid back.

Bahwan's new tranche of money landed in an offshore company called Brasilensis, created by Gebran. Ghosn didn't feature in official documents, but his elder sister, Claudine, was the financial beneficiary.

The company had an ostensible purpose. In the first half of 2013, Gebran and Bahwan had exchanged paperwork stipulating that Brasilensis would help the Omanis find and purchase properties in Europe. One document contained a rather curious provision, however: even if the real estate deals fell through, Brasilensis would keep the money from the Bahwans.

In July, a few weeks after the brokerage agreement was signed, Gebran sent details about a house in Lamorlaye, a tony suburb in a forest north of Paris, and asked Bahwan to transfer €2 million to make the down payment for its purchase.

Soon after, the Bahwans delivered their first batch of roses.

Over a period of several months, Gebran sent three more messages to the Bahwans, listing a number of potential properties and requesting corresponding payments in dollars and euros to be transferred. Without delay, they sent cash to two Lebanese bank accounts tied to Brasilensis.

Yet in December, Gebran wrote to inform the Bahwans that, after all that, the deals were off—all of them. Due to market conditions, he wrote, none of the properties had been purchased. As stipulated, however, the money would stay in Brasilensis's bank accounts. "We shall stay in touch to follow the progress of the discussed investments," he concluded.

In a matter of months, the Bahwans sent $9 million to Brasilensis.

*   *   *

That pile of cash in Lebanon was just a start. In 2015, Gebran set up a new company called Good Faith Investments. Again, it was based in Beirut. And again, Ghosn's name didn't appear in corporate documents. This time, however, the sender wouldn't be Bahwan himself. Rather, it would be the general manager of his car distribution company, an Indian-born executive named Divyendu Kumar, who was also listed as the chairman of Good Faith Investments, and for whom Gebran created a Lebanese bank. It was strange enough that Kumar would, by all appearances, be sending money to himself from his bank account in Switzerland to Lebanon; yet these documents also contained a curious provision of their own: while Kumar was the beneficiary of the account, the Good Faith account, it was his in name only, and the real owner of the funds was another person.

In essence, the arrangement was similar to the one with Brasilensis, but without the real estate listings, and without the now unnecessary step of Ghosn involving his sister.

At times, Kumar was unsure how much cash he needed to send to Good Faith Investments. In those instances, Gebran would turn to Ghosn.

"Cher Carlos," the Lebanese lawyer wrote in an August 2016 email to his childhood friend. "Could I confidentially send you Divyendu's calculations to this email address? You can check if there is an error in his calculations."

Ghosn wrote back, asking whether they could discuss the calculation on the phone. After that conversation, Gebran emailed Kumar, who agreed to send €3 million.

Over a three-year period, Kumar sent tens of millions of dollars to Good Faith Investments.

Once the money arrived in Lebanon, Gebran had control of where to send it next—and Ghosn was in the background with a few ideas.

*   *   *

It is hard to fathom what Ghosn wanted for at this point in his life, or why he might need tens of millions of fresh dollars; but, lo and behold, there was a prize that only a few people on earth compete over every year. Who has the newest, best boat. Carlos Ghosn did not have a yacht.

It turns out that, short of going to space, owning a yacht may be among the most conspicuous ways to consume money and to make evident that one has more funds than necessary. It is also an expense that, due to the cost of upkeep alone, only a select few can afford. Ghosn, used to measuring success by the black ink of quarterly earnings on his scorecards, was learning to measure success in feet.

He homed in on a Navetta, a top-of-the-line yacht made by the Ferretti Group in Italy. The vessel served as a floating mansion, allowing all the comforts of home as one cruised around, saluting the world's fellow megarich. The brochure assured a sleek hull and a "poetic soul," one lyrical enough to justify a €13 million price tag. Ghosn was given a sizable discount but splurged on nearly €2 million of custom features, including queen-size beds and televisions in all the staterooms. The vessel had four decks including the rooftop and boasted teak flooring and a jacuzzi. In Ghosn's master suite, there were an additional four bedrooms for the seven crew. In total, there were thirteen bathrooms.

The shipyard provisionally called it the Navetta 36, but as it was 121.6 feet long, a Beirut-based yacht broker, Alain Maaraoui, lobbied to name her Navetta 37, to reflect the fact that she was thirty-seven meters long. In December 2014, Maaraoui fired off an email to Ghosn: "I am pleased to inform you that finally the board of the Ferretti Group have been convinced and accepted my request to change the name," he wrote. "In fact, she is a 37-meter yacht."

The broker was also in touch with Gebran, who was engineering the ship's purchase. Would the buyer like to appear in the contract? No, Gebran told Maaraoui. The client wished to remain anonymous.

When the first yacht payment, roughly 10 percent of the agreed price, was due, Gebran emailed Ghosn to let him know he had consolidated the money from the two Brasilensis accounts into a single account at the Near East Commercial Bank (NECB).

In February 2015, Gebran emailed Ghosn's elder sister because he needed her to sign some fund-transfer papers. "Ma chère Claudine," the lawyer wrote. He asked how she was doing, and also for her address in Rio.

"Salut Fadi!" she responded familiarly, having known him for decades. "I'm doing very well," Claudine wrote. "I'm preparing for Carnival, which starts today." If Gebran was in a hurry, she suggested, he should use an express courier service because the state postal service would be slow during the weeklong festivities.

By March 5, Gebran had the papers back from Claudine. He sent a note to NECB, asking it to make a transfer for the Navetta 37.

In the same message, the lawyer requested a $7.5 million transfer from Brasilensis's recently consolidated single account at NECB to Ghosn's personal account at the same bank. The size of the transfer raised a red flag, and a banker emailed Gebran six days later, saying that the bank's control commission had asked for more information. Gebran wrote back immediately that the funds had come from Ghosn's sister. NECB executed the transactions.

The yacht was under construction. But for the rest of the money that had amassed in Lebanon—and there was a lot of it—Ghosn had other ideas.

*   *   *

A continent away, in the United States, Anthony Ghosn was entering his final year at Stanford. His course of study was called Symbolic Systems, or SymSys, which aimed to create leaders who could do "practically anything."

By 2015, Carlos Ghosn's youngest child was also working as chief of staff for Joe Lonsdale, one of the most high-profile investors in Silicon Valley. When Anthony told his father about the sky-high returns Lonsdale and other venture capitalists were making, Ghosn was amazed. He soon had a proposition: Anthony would identify the most promising startups in the Valley, and Ghosn would provide the funding. They called their venture capital fund Shogun Investments LLC. Anthony shared his father's obsession with history, in particular military and political leaders. He also had a great love for Japan, and he was intrigued by the military warlord shoguns from the country's historical lore. (Shogun is also an almost-anagram of Ghosn.)

In October 2015, Ghosn contacted Gebran, and this time asked him to send $5.5 million from Good Faith Investments "into a fund that invests in start-ups in Silicon Valley." He provided bank details for a Wells Fargo account held by Shogun Investments. The following day, Gebran asked the account manager at NECB to make the transfer, explaining that Good Faith Investments wanted to "diversify its investments."

With the funds, the younger Ghosn was able to back his bets on dozens of startups, including his own.

"Good morning Tantoum," Ghosn emailed Anthony in one of their exchanges. "Following our phone conversation, I ordered a transfer of 3 million dollars to Shogun Investments (2 million for grabtaxis and 1 million for the company of your friend that you think will do very well)."

In 2016, the younger Ghosn was interviewed by the *Breakout List*, a publication that covers companies on the rise. When asked whom he admired most, Anthony answered that it was his dad, citing a number of reasons: "He's just really managed to discipline himself and accomplish a lot and make great contributions to society. I really credit him. He created opportunities for his family."

Unbeknownst to Anthony—who had assumed he was being entrusted with his father's hard-earned cash—the money he was receiving was traveling from Kumar's account in Switzerland, via Beirut, before reaching California.

Thanks to the offshore companies set up by Ghosn's trusted Lebanese lawyer, all told around $50 million traveled from the Bahwans and their deputy Kumar into entities controlled by Ghosn.

An obvious question was begging: why were these businessmen in Oman showing such generosity to the Renault and Nissan chief?

*   *   *

At Renault and Nissan, where nobody knew about Gebran's money canals, executives had long puzzled over a mirror question: Why were the two carmakers showing such generosity toward the Bahwans' company, SBA? They knew that the elder Bahwan was close to Ghosn, but that couldn't justify the hefty payments that the distributor was receiving through the companies' CEO Reserve mechanisms, especially at times when SBA's performance was lackluster. (At Renault, the Omani company was the only distributor to receive payments through the French carmaker's CEO Reserve.)

A few years later, prosecutors would allege that the answer to both questions was simple: the bonus payments to SBA and the cash transfers into Good Faith Investments formed a single money line. According to Japanese and French prosecutors, Ghosn was using the Omani distributor to route company funds into his own pocket.

The timing and amount of some money transfers certainly raised eyebrows upon review.

Even after the yacht had been purchased and Anthony Ghosn's venture propped up, the money continued to flow. In the first eight months of 2017, SBA collected three CEO Reserve payments from Ghosn's companies—two from Renault and one from Nissan.

During that time, the Omani distributor made three transfers out of the dealership's accounts and into the Bahwans', two marked "Reno" and one marked "Nissan." The payments totaled almost $4.4 million.

Shortly after SBA made those transfers, Kumar deposited precisely that amount in euros into Good Faith Investments in Lebanon from his UBS account in Switzerland.

As soon as Kumar transferred the cash into Good Faith Investments, Gebran informed Ghosn, using the thinly veiled code of "europeans" for euros. Gebran also alerted his friend that he would convert all the euros into dollars and lock the cash in a savings account for two years to accrue interest. "Finally, everybody will be American for two years," he wrote.

Ghosn replied, acknowledging the news, "Merci!"*

---

* Ghosn denied receiving company funds through the dealership in Oman. He said the payments to the Omani distributor were legitimate incentives and boosted car sales in the region. A lawyer for Suhail Bahwan, Christophe Ingrain, said his client categorically denied taking part in an alleged scheme to pay Ghosn with money received from Renault and Nissan. The lawyer added that he had handed over evidence to French judicial authorities demonstrating Bahwan's innocence.

13

Double Vote

Hiroto Saikawa spoke so rarely in the Renault boardroom, some directors joked that they didn't know the sound of his voice. Others said that if he did speak, his sentences invariably began with "Mr. Ghosn said."

In most cases, Saikawa was simply struggling to follow the mélange of English and French, with a translator speaking through his earpiece. But after nearly ten years on the French company's board, the Nissan executive had grown familiar with the unspoken signals of local corporate culture. He could translate the insincere smiles, the dagger looks, and the sort of clan warfare that would play out when Renault directors gathered at headquarters. The recurrent tussle, and the one Saikawa followed most attentively, pitted the French government (which named directors to the board, reflecting the state's 15 percent interest) against Carlos Ghosn.

Like many at Nissan, Saikawa initially regarded Ghosn as a real-life Superman. As far back as 2002, as a young manager, Saikawa had witnessed the French side's efforts to coax Nissan into merging with Renault. Much to Saikawa's admiration, Ghosn persisted in putting his foot down. Whenever a director asked questions about Nissan, Ghosn would deftly change the subject, leaving Saikawa with full confidence in Ghosn's loyalty to Nissan's interest, as well as his capacity to keep the Renault board—and the French government—in check. When Louis Schweitzer and others at Renault had been pushing so hard for a merger, Ghosn consistently—and successfully—fought to keep Nissan independent.

As the years passed, Saikawa became less confident in the man he had once considered Japan's greatest defender. One after the other, his superhero took body blows and made subsequent concessions to France. In 2011, the Japanese executive had seen how close Ghosn had come to being fired after the spy scandal debacle. Saikawa knew that Ghosn had saved his job in exchange for a promise to tie the French and Japanese companies more closely together. In 2013, Ghosn had announced that he would move the production of Nissan's Micra hatchback from India, where the company had recently built a factory, to a Renault plant in France, despite the higher labor costs there. He justified the move by saying it would free up plant capacity in India. But Nissan managers had questioned the business logic, and their engineers complained that Renault factory workers couldn't be trusted to build their cars.

Decision by decision, under a scrutiny motivated by adulation, then curiosity, then skepticism, Saikawa observed the changing tide of tolerance—or lack thereof—for his boss. The quiet, capable manager had grown increasingly aware that Ghosn didn't have the sway at Renault that he enjoyed in Japan.

By 2014, Saikawa was seriously concerned. That year, a law was enacted in France that sought to address what Paris saw as a growing threat: short-term foreign investors buying up French companies and hollowing their industrial operations. The law was nicknamed "Florange," after a town in France where the government had faced off against a steel tycoon who wanted to close two blast furnaces.

Red flags sprang up as the alarmed Saikawa learned about a section of the new law stating that shareholders who held on to their stakes in a company for more than two years would be rewarded with double voting rights. Within two years, the French state's 15 percent stake would carry even more voting rights. The French government would have more say at Renault and therefore more say at Nissan. If Renault again tried to launch a takeover, would Ghosn prevent it from happening?

Saikawa and the rest of Nissan saw a reason for hope with the appointment of the new French finance minister, who took office in the summer of 2014. The media-savvy Emmanuel Macron was a former investment banker, and Nissan executives believed he might start liquidating the state's holdings in a bunch of private companies, including Renault. That would make the Florange law irrelevant. But the more opponents predicted that the thirty-seven-year-old minister would implement laissez-faire policies, the more Macron appeared eager to pick fights with CEOs, including Carlos Ghosn.

Ghosn saw no reason to worry. He had met with Macron at the Elysée Palace, when Macron worked as a presidential adviser, and the young man had made a good impression. Instead of giving Ghosn a lecture on how to make a car, he had humbly asked what he could do to help Renault. He was a straight shooter, clear and efficient. As for the Florange law, it contained an opt-out clause: a company could decide not to apply the double voting rights rule as long as it received the approval of its shareholders. That was exactly what Ghosn intended to do. He was sure that the issue would be resolved at the next meeting.

Within weeks of the new minister's appointment, however, Ghosn was in Macron's crosshairs. Macron was deeply concerned with the lack of progress on Ghosn's succession plan at Renault and at the helm of the Alliance. Two potential deputies had left Ghosn's inner circle, and there was no clear successor.

Macron felt that the Alliance was a house of cards held together almost entirely by Ghosn. Without Ghosn the Japanese might decide that they didn't need the French. So French officials routinely, relentlessly asked Ghosn about succession and also about ways to tie the companies closer together. In those instances, Ghosn would agree and evade, and French officials would again press him for a plan. But the plan never came.

Exasperated by Ghosn's lip service, Macron decided to tighten his grip on what was within his purview: the French state's stake in Renault. He instructed Régis Turrini, who managed the French state's interests in corporate assets, to sound out Ghosn: Would Renault implement the double voting rights rule?

When Turrini and Ghosn met over lunch, the Renault CEO was direct: Nissan didn't want the Florange law to be applied at Renault, especially because its own stake in the company didn't carry voting rights. Turrini wasn't satisfied, and suspected that Ghosn had ulterior motives.

"But who is Nissan?" the French technocrat asked. "It's you, right?"

It's the board, Ghosn deflected. The Nissan directors were up in arms against the double voting rights rule, he explained. The Japanese directors feared that it would be the prelude to another attempt at a merger. Turrini didn't buy it. For years, Nissan had been Ghosn's perpetual excuse for shooting down any number of suggestions by Renault's largest shareholder. But to the best of his knowledge, Ghosn had total control over Nissan's board, which was composed entirely of executives who reported to him. Turrini believed that it was Ghosn who feared French control, for a simple reason: he didn't want the French state to have a bigger say on the future of the Alliance, on his succession, or on his pay.

As the months went by, with the calendar turning over to 2015, Turrini and other French officials struggled to reach Ghosn to discuss the double-voting rule. "Where is Mr. Ghosn?" Turrini would ask. His subordinates never seemed to know. And in March, Renault published its proposed resolutions for the annual meeting—including one to reject the double voting rights rule.

That was tantamount to a declaration of war, Turrini thought. He refused to sit by and watch the CEO of Renault humiliate the French government. Turrini hatched a plan to secretly bump up the French state's share in Renault, which would deprive Ghosn of the shareholder support he needed to prevent the Florange law's application at Renault. That would require buying stock in a big hurry, with as little noise as possible.

The first few banks Turrini tried wouldn't touch the deal. One lender had the requisite pirate reputation to do the job: Deutsche Bank.

Its executives were enthusiastic, with the head of investment banking even expressing amusement at the audacity of the proposal. As the next step, the ministry needed to mobilize as much as €1 billion of taxpayers' money. Macron was on board. By April 7, the government and Deutsche Bank had signed an agreement. The German bank would buy Renault shares and transfer them to the French government over a ten-day period.

Macron would inform Ghosn.

Shortly after 8:00 p.m. that night, Macron ducked out of the French Senate and dialed Ghosn. The minister was blunt, as is his way: He told Ghosn that the French state had increased its stake in Renault and would be announcing it to the stock market authorities in the morning. The French president, François Hollande, was aware of the plan, he said. Their call lasted no more than three minutes.

Ghosn sat in a rare state of utter shock and silence. He hadn't anticipated that. The government had opened the public coffers to defeat him. He was particularly upset because the opt-out clause he was planning to use was included in the French state's law, yet it was *still* intent on imposing its will on him. The government could have made the new rule mandatory in the first place.

It was very illogical and totally unfair, Ghosn decided.

Worse, the Alliance was on a perilous course. Turrini was half right; Carlos Ghosn was, in many ways, Nissan. But he wasn't all of it. And he had been genuine when telling the French that the Japanese would not be happy. There was no way they would take the blow without responding.

The following week, Renault directors gathered for a board meeting presided over by Ghosn. At the U-shaped table were Turrini, who represented the government, and Saikawa, who represented Nissan.

A slide went up, showing all the shareholdings in the company. Ghosn turned to face the screen and told the directors what it meant. Unless something changed, the government would have enough power to reject the opt-out resolution, and the state would get its double votes.

Ghosn called on the usually circumspect Saikawa to describe Nissan's stance. The Japanese executive briefly composed himself and began reading from prepared remarks written by Nissan's chief legal strategist, Hari Nada, and the law firm Latham & Watkins.

Nissan took the move by the French state "very seriously" because it "put the future of the Alliance at risk," he said. If the French state followed through with the plan, Nissan "should take all the measures that would allow it, through its shareholding in Renault, to reach the same level of voting rights as all other shareholders."

The other directors around the table froze as the dire implications of the statement settled in. Saikawa had all but announced that Nissan stood ready to void RAMA, the nonaggression pact signed in 2002, and possibly launch a hostile move to increase its stake in Renault. For all of Ghosn's emollient-soaked speeches about a friendly partnership held together by mutual self-interest, the Japanese were clearly prepared to shatter the Alliance.

The faces around the table turned to Turrini. What was the French government trying to achieve? "Since when is the government capable of moving so fast?" asked one director. Another hinted that the government was motivated by its opposition to Ghosn: "Is the government buying shares in other companies, or is Renault a special case?"

Turrini found it implausible that Nissan's reaction and Saikawa's letter had not been dictated by Ghosn. He had never had to sit through such a pummeling, but he held his ground nevertheless. The government had every right to defend its interests in a company in which it had been a shareholder for decades. "We've been here forever," he thought. "The other shareholders will get over it."

At the Renault shareholder meeting on April 30, the motion to opt out of the Florange law was voted down.

As far as the French government was concerned, it had prevailed over Ghosn. That day, Macron was in Rome, meeting with his Italian counterpart. After learning about the positive outcome, he sat down with a reporter at the French embassy. The discussions turned to French CEOs in general and Ghosn in particular. The problem with

Ghosn, Macron said, was his loyalty. "He's Japanese," Macron said. "With Ghosn, it's simple: In Yokohama he's the emperor, and he's paid 10 million euros. In France, he's a manager, and he's paid 1.5 million euros."

*   *   *

Despite the French government's seeming victory, Saikawa's threat on behalf of the Japanese still hung over the Alliance. The Renault and Nissan partnership was in disarray. The atmosphere was poisonous. In the weeks that followed, Turrini left his post in the French government for a job in the private sector. He was replaced by Martin Vial, who launched a new round of talks to put an end to the standoff. Ghosn recused himself from the conversations, due to his conflict as the head of both companies. He sent Saikawa in his stead and placed him in charge of negotiating on Nissan's behalf, with Greg Kelly and Hari Nada acting as advisers.

Saikawa took a commercial flight to Paris and checked into his regular hotel, Le Méridien Etoile, on the western edge of the city. The talks began at Renault's office, where the tall, lanky Saikawa, with his distinctive buzz cut, was easily spotted going in and out. As the press sought any hint of a breakthrough or collapse in the negotiations, which could spell the end of Ghosn's Alliance, the teams opted to meet in less predictable locations, in assorted rented conference rooms throughout the city.

Vial asked Saikawa what could be done to reassure Nissan. Saikawa was prepared with a compromise that cut through the clutter. He outlined Nissan's position clearly: Renault owned nearly half of Nissan, which meant that the French company could force decisions on its Japanese counterpart. If Renault wanted to reassure Nissan, Saikawa said, it should surrender its voting powers at the Japanese company. That would mean that there was no way that Renault could hold sway over its Alliance partner.

And that was the central concern: France exerting control over Japan.

Vial had no issues with the proposition. The French state had little interest in running a Japanese carmaker. If limiting Renault's influence on Nissan would reassure it, he was happy to go along with it. Nothing was going to change with Ghosn acting as chief executive officer and chairman of both companies. With him on both sides of the negotiating table, Renault had never voted against a Nissan board proposal. If a situation arose when Renault needed those votes, it could tear up the agreement and go to war, Vial reasoned.

The two sides drew up an amendment to the Alliance agreement, the RAMA, which gave Nissan the power to buy a bigger stake in Renault—and even launch a hostile takeover of the French company—should Renault be found to be meddling in the Japanese company's business. The new agreement, if it went through, gave Nissan a stronger and more assured defense than Ghosn could ever muster against French influence.

The final hurdles to the deal were cleared at a Renault board meeting on December 11. To the Nissan negotiators, the agreement represented a huge victory. Before the amendment, Nissan had basically been a subsidiary of Renault, albeit one shielded by Ghosn from the harsher realities of that status, namely, that decisions were being made with Renault's interests in mind. After the vote, Renault had almost no influence over the Japanese company's affairs, except through Ghosn. There was a sense of elation at Nissan headquarters in Japan, where executives and lawyers had remained well past 10:00 p.m. to learn of the outcome of the vote by Renault directors. The deal basically assured their independence from Renault.

From his perch atop the Alliance, Ghosn surveyed the damage. The tracks he had laid to work toward more convergence between the companies had been obliterated in a matter of months. It would take years to rebuild trust, most notably on the Japanese side, as they felt wronged by the secrecy of Macron's raid. The seemingly invincible Ghosn had always assured them protection, but what they had just witnessed came perilously close to a disaster. In the end, it was Nissan, and not Ghosn, who had cleared up the mess.

Within Nissan HQ, a hitherto unthinkable question began to be asked: Did they even need Carlos Ghosn?

*   *   *

In France, people weren't altogether thrilled with him, either. Both within the boardroom and as a public figure, Ghosn's behavior was that of a man who not only operated outside their establishment—he actively dismissed it. His fiancée could also be out of sync, at least with the French preference for understated wealth. In February 2016, Carole went to the Palace of Versailles accompanied by two friends. She was on a scouting mission, looking for a venue in which to hold her fiftieth birthday party in the autumn. The Alliance had used the illustrious venue for its fifteen-year celebration in 2014, and she was hoping for something similar: classy, with a bit of flair and some dancing to keep the guests entertained. Instead of the château's main building, she trained her sights on the Grand Trianon, which Louis XIV had used as a getaway when he wanted a break from the royal court.

Ghosn set the budget at €250,000 for 120 guests. The use of the Grand Trianon would be provided for free, part of a sponsorship agreement that Renault had signed with the château to fund renovation work.

In the summer, Ghosn's chief of staff, Frédérique Le Grèves, whose job spanned both his work and personal commitments, reached out to the event organizers to settle some issues: "Anouchka, we caught up with Mrs. Ghosn to really understand what she wants. . . . In a few words, she wants a simple dinner that is chic and elegant and she is counting a great deal on this soirée." Among the lengthy list of requests were a very opulent dessert table and specifics on everything from the timing of the musical genre to the antique crystal glasses to the proportions of Moët & Chandon and millésime Champagne. "For the red carpet at the entrance," she specified, "thank you for doing a red carpet and not a fuchsia."

To make the evening extra festive, Carole and her event planner opted for an elaborate Marie Antoinette–themed party—complete with no shortage of assorted cakes. Actors were hired to dress up as courtiers to complete the immersive, privilege-soaked scene.

On October 8, all the Beirut elite were there, as were Carole's friends from New York, London, and Hong Kong. Lebanese media reported on the essentials of the evening, including attire: "As the good Lebanese sheik that he is, Marwan Hamza made a prominent entrance in a silk abaya that was slipped over a Marc Jacobs suit, a ribbon passed under the collar of a black Hermès shirt, and he wore on his feet some stuffed moccasin mules made by Gucci."

"We wanted it to feel as if we were inviting guests into our home—nothing too studied," Carole later told *Town & Country* magazine, the social chronicler of the rich and famous.

Ghosn made a short speech, saying that he had wanted to honor the person who now brightened his life and whom he had married a few months before. "That's why we wanted to host this party in this magnificent location," he said.

Ghosn was no longer untouchable after his disastrous fight with the French state that almost destroyed the Alliance, but the second Versailles party—and the fact it was covered in the press—underscored how secure he felt in his position. Little did he know that the party would later prove to be a public relations disaster in France. The Japanese also took note of the festivities, with some Nissan executives wondering how Ghosn was funding such an extravagant bash. That was all the more dangerous because, while Saikawa had started to realize years earlier that Ghosn's power wasn't limitless, others at Nissan were now coming around to a new reality: Ghosn was no longer Superman.

14

Currents

Ziad Gebran was working in Paris when he received a panicked phone call from his older brother. Their father, Fady Gebran, had been hospitalized in Beirut. His days were numbered. But there was more. Over the past two decades, Gebran had created shell companies on behalf of wealthy customers, including Carlos Ghosn. Many of them were registered in the lawyer's name and work address, to provide anonymity for his clients. If their father died, Ziad and his brother might face the nightmare of seeing those dozens of companies ending up in their name. They had to get rid of them. Quickly.

Ziad took a leave of absence from the communications agency where he was a partner and flew to Lebanon. The twenty-nine-year-old landed in Beirut on July 26, 2017, and went immediately to his father's bedside. He was hoping to wrap up his business affairs swiftly, so he could spend the rest of that precious time with his father.

He soon realized that the situation with his dad's business was far more complicated than he'd imagined: there were no books of accounts, no registry from which to divine who was the rightful owner of which company. Gebran's assistant, Amal Abou Jaoude, could not offer much help. Lacking higher education, she had started working for the lawyer in the 1990s as a typist. Over the years, she had become more of a classic personal assistant, helping with scheduling and managing her boss's email. Gebran often used her name in corporate papers, but she didn't have intimate knowledge about the web of shell companies.

Everything was in his dad's head.

Ziad asked him to write down as much as he could remember. At first, Gebran didn't want to do so—not out of confidentiality concerns, Ziad felt, so much as because to do so would be an admission that it was the end. But Ziad insisted: his mother risked being left with nothing unless he was given a map to help navigate his father's labyrinth of companies.

Each day, Ziad arrived at the hospital around 9:00 a.m. He sat on a chair and, with his dad's help, made lists of who was the real owner of which company and what needed to be done with each of them. There was a stack of unpaid bills, and Ziad had no idea how much cash the business had on hand or how much his father owed to other people. On top of that, he needed to close the office and fire Amal, as well as another lawyer who worked with his dad.

After two days, Ziad brought up an increasingly urgent topic: his dad needed to call Carlos Ghosn, his old friend and most prestigious client. "You need to tell him that he needs to find someone else," Ziad told his dad. "You have to tell him that it's the end."

Gebran had told Ghosn that he had cancer but not how serious it was. He had been diagnosed with pancreatic cancer the year before, in 2016. He had received both radiotherapy and chemotherapy at a hospital in Beirut. When the cancer had continued to spread, he had flown to London three times for expensive laser treatments to try to control it. As a last option to prolong his life, he had signed up for an experimental treatment back in Beirut.

A few weeks later, Gebran had learned that the latest treatment had failed. Both he and the family realized that all they could do was wait for the inevitable. Yet he still hesitated to contact Ghosn. He didn't want to create problems for a man whom he had come to regard as being far more important than himself. Serving Carlos Ghosn had been an honor for Gebran. "But what will he think of me?" he asked his son. "I was supposed to have things under control, and now I . . . don't."

It took most of the day to discuss the matter, but finally Gebran came around to his son's arguments and contacted his old friend. Gebran was clear, and Ghosn was supportive. "We'll find a solution," Ghosn said. He asked for a list of the companies that Gebran managed on his behalf; making the call lifted a huge weight off Gebran's mind.

*   *   *

Ghosn's Nissan corporate jet, the Gulfstream G650 with the tail number N155AN, landed at Milas-Bodrum Airport on the Turkish Riviera on July 29. He was going to be joined by Carole and some of his children for a family vacation.

This year's vacation would be special. A month earlier, the shipyard had finally completed the construction of the Navetta 37. It had been christened *Shachou*, the Japanese word for "CEO." A smaller boat—a tender—and a pair of jet skis had been loaded on board, adding more than $140,000 to the sizable overall bill. The yacht would spend three weeks floating up and down a beautiful stretch of Turkey's coast before island-hopping in Greece.

The day *Shachou* pushed off from the Yalıkavak Marina in Bodrum, Ziad Gebran and Amal Abou Jaoude were going over the list of companies that Ghosn had requested. The list had been checked by Gebran to ensure that it was complete and without errors. Even at the end of his life, the lawyer wanted to ensure that his priority client was taken care of properly.

On August 1, as *Shachou* floated through picture-postcard coves along the coast of Turkey, Amal Abou Jaoude forwarded the list of companies that Gebran owned on behalf of Ghosn, using the lawyer's email account. "Further to our telephone conversation last Friday, and upon your request please find here below the list and details of the companies you have asked for," she wrote. Including Brasilensis and

Good Faith Investments, the list included nine companies. One had been used to manage Ghosn's ill-fated currency swap arrangement in Japan. Another was being used to manage the mansion in central Beirut, which was still being renovated.

Ghosn knew that time was short for Gebran, and he was business-like in his emails with Amal Abou Jaoude. On August 2, Ghosn emailed her to ask about a transfer he had requested:

Dear Amal,

Last friday. I asked Fady to order a transfer of 3.5 million dollars from goodfaith investments holdings to shogun investments LLC in the US.

He said he would do it. The money did not land yet at shogun investments.

Could you please check if everything has been done from your side and from Saradarbank side?

Thank you,
Carlos Ghosn

Amal Abou Jaoude panicked. "I had no idea about carlos's demand!" she wrote to Gebran's son. "Can you ask your father about it?"

"Mmmm . . . I will try to ask Papa," Ziad Gebran replied.

Gebran didn't want to sign any more paperwork that day. He was in pain, and his end was near. He was still thinking clearly, but he was tired and needed to rest.

A few hours later, another email arrived in Gebran's inbox while he was on his deathbed, this one from—of all people—*Shachou*'s captain. It was an invoice for the six crew members' July salaries, which came to more than $22,000. There was also a ledger of spending from the petty cash account on the vessel for mooring fees and other incidental expenses.

Amal Abou Jaoude emailed Gebran's sons Ziad and Joe to ask for advice. The bills needed to be paid by Beauty Yachts, and doing so would require Gebran's signature. Ziad said he would do what he could and asked whether he and Joe could transfer signing authority to her to handle such matters in the future.

The next morning, Amal Abou Jaoude was at her wit's end. She was struggling to make sense of the web of companies and bank accounts that paid the expenses. "Yesterday I spent around one hour looking for a transfer that Fady did 3 months ago for buying cups to [sic] the boat," she wrote to the lawyer's sons.

After spending hours sifting through paperwork and old bills, Amal Abou Jaoude said she finally grasped some of the money flows. She understood that the yacht payments came out of a bank account owned by Beauty Yachts, located in the British Virgin Islands. When that company needed money, she had to move it from another company, called Phoinos. And when the Phoinos account was depleted, it was necessary to contact Divyendu Kumar, who, she assumed, worked for Nissan, to collect fresh funding.

On August 7, Ghosn received a message from Fady Gebran's email address to say that the transfer to Shogun Investments was done. "Thank you!" replied Ghosn. "Looking forward to see you soon in Beirut."

On August 11, Gebran became unconscious. Four days later, he passed away.

The day Gebran died, Ghosn received an email from Alain Maaraoui, a yacht broker with Sea Pros in Beirut. *Shachou* was near the end of its journey. It had stopped off in Rhodes and Pserimos in the Aegean Sea and was back cruising along the coastline of Turkey. Maaraoui told Ghosn that he still had not received the transfer of ownership for Beauty Yachts.

Ghosn forwarded the email to Amal, who was grieving the death of her boss, asking her to check that Gebran had signed the necessary documents. "Thank you in advance for your cooperation and looking gorward [sic] to see you in Beirut next monday!" he wrote.

Normally, Amal Abou Jaoude responded to Ghosn's emails immediately. That time, she did not. She would eventually, a few days later, on August 20. That day, Ghosn would be flying back to Beirut from Turkey, aboard a private jet paid for by Nissan, accompanied by three of his children, Nadine, Maya, and Anthony.

Before answering Ghosn, Amal Abou Jaoude needed to go to the office. It was familiar, the place where she had spent the majority of her waking hours for the past two decades. Now it felt empty without Gebran, who had been a father figure to her. For twenty years, he had told her about the history of Lebanon and encouraged her to travel and to generally broaden her horizons. "The office is so sad and melancholic. Couldn't come alone but I had to because I was sure that Carlos wanted to know about the Company Beauty Yachts that owns his boat," she wrote in an email to Ziad. "I miss him like hell."

She then typed a message to Ghosn from Gebran's email account. Gebran had indeed signed all the necessary documents, she wrote. That wasn't completely accurate. The documents had been backdated to August 11, before Gebran's death, and been signed using his electronic signature. But Amal Abou Jaoude did not want to cause Ghosn any headaches. By the end of the month, Beauty Yachts—and thus the Navetta 37—was in Carlos Ghosn's name.*

*   *   *

In the weeks that followed, Ziad and his brother succeeded in paying off the bills and closing the office permanently. Ghosn hired Amal Abou Jaoude as his secretary in Lebanon. She took over some of Gebran's tasks, namely, overseeing cash transfers from Divyendu Kumar, the SBA general manager in Oman, to Shogun Investments in the United States and Beauty Yachts in the British Virgin Islands.

---

* Ghosn's counsel said no money changed hands when the yacht was transferred to his client's name because the company that owned the yacht had debt and was therefore of negligible value.

Though Fady Gebran had died, his intricate system of monies kept flowing, as designed by their creator.

Now paid by Nissan, Amal Abou Jaoude resettled in the premises of the Japanese carmaker's main distributor in Lebanon, where she moved into a third-floor office with a desktop computer. When she did so, she took with her many files from Fady Gebran's office.

15

Global Motors

Being chief of staff to Carlos Ghosn meant you didn't really have a home—or a life that looked like anyone else's.

Ghosn had warned his chief of staff, Frédérique Le Grèves, that taking the job would require the discipline and devotion of a nun. Her days routinely started long before sunrise, and she could never schedule a social engagement during the week. She followed the globe-trotter practically everywhere. Flying commercial airlines—she viewed the Nissan corporate jet as one of Ghosn's many homes—she always tried to arrive before him and depart after he had left.

In the spring of 2017, Le Grèves was hard at work on an annual chore: organizing Ghosn's agenda for the entire following year. She was used to sifting through the multitude of events he would have to attend, from shareholder meetings to motor shows. But this year, she was trying to accommodate an unusual request from Ghosn: the workaholic boss wanted time off.

Ghosn was well into his sixties and had been working tirelessly for four decades. He was ready to slow down and spend time at his mansion in Beirut, where the renovations were almost complete, and aboard his yacht. He wanted to give himself the opportunity to pursue activities he truly enjoyed, such as teaching. Carole and his children had been telling him for years that it was time for him to take a step back from his work and start enjoying life.

Le Grèves dutifully added several breaks into Ghosn's 2018 time-table: an extended weekend here, a full week off there.

Creating spare time was a challenge, particularly since Ghosn had recently added a third cap: chairman of Mitsubishi Motors. The previous fall, Nissan had bought a 34 percent stake in its Japanese competitor, and Ghosn was in the midst of trying to turn around the beleaguered carmaker. Mitsubishi had asked him for help after an embarrassing admission that it had cheated on fuel economy tests.

Ghosn reprised a well-worn playbook. He set up cross-company teams and benchmarked Mitsubishi's costs against Nissan's and Renault's, finding easy savings in procurement. Mitsubishi sold fewer than 1 million vehicles per year and plugging the company into the Alliance helped with its lack of scale. Ghosn set clearer targets for employees, including monthly goals for each unit, and aligned compensation with reaching those targets.

Within months, Mitsubishi was on a sounder footing, and its share price had risen sharply. For Ghosn, the whole thing was proving to be a walk in the park.

The addition of Mitsubishi, however, wasn't without challenges for the Alliance, where it disrupted the delicate balance of power within the Alliance. At Nissan, there was hope that adding another Japanese company would provide leverage in disputes with Renault. At the French company, there was fear that the addition of Mitsubishi would further dilute Renault's diminished influence at Nissan.

Still, Ghosn regarded the enlargement of the Alliance as a golden opportunity for it to become a juggernaut to rival GM or Toyota. Renault and Nissan were posting spectacular record sales, reflected in their soaring share prices.

This called for a monument.

*　　*　　*

On June 22, 2017, inside Nissan's Yokohama headquarters, Ghosn beamed as a huge white sheet slid off the sixteen-foot-high sculpture that he'd commissioned.

The piece comprised five steel wheels of different diameters assembled like a vertical Olympic logo. Standing by the towering piece of art, Ghosn explained to the employees, journalists, and photographers gathered around that the five wheels represented the five elements that had powered the carmaker since he had begun leading it: diversity, sustainability, competition, globalization, and Nissan's alliance with Renault. "Good art, whether it's a vehicle or a sculpture, has a way of reminding us of where we have been and opens our imagination to what is possible," he said.

Ghosn reveled in the ceremony: the camera flashes, the accolades, the recognition. Hiroto Saikawa, whom Ghosn had recently chosen to succeed him as CEO of Nissan, praised his chairman and thanked him for his years of leadership. Shedding the normally dour, humorless expression he wore in the office, Saikawa smiled as he posed for photos in front of the glistening mass of metal.

It was all a charade.

Saikawa willed himself to bury his growing annoyance with Ghosn. He had been told about the morning unveiling only shortly before it happened, as though his invitation had been an afterthought. The business teams still went to Ghosn for approval; the PR teams still devoted their attention to Ghosn's image. Saikawa was technically in charge, but he was still very much in Ghosn's shadow.

Indeed, it was Ghosn who had come up with the idea of planting a milestone in the Nissan hallway to commemorate how far the company had come during his prolonged tenure. He had commissioned the sculpture from a Lebanese artist, Nadim Karam. It had cost the Japanese carmaker nearly $900,000.

Still buzzing that evening, Ghosn pulled up in his black Nissan sedan with tinted windows to Honmura An, one of his favorite restaurants in Tokyo. As he strode confidently to his table, people recognized him and turned their heads. Ghosn was dining with two French journalists. He was generally strict with his diet and drank very little alcohol, particularly on weekdays. The two reporters had interviewed Ghosn many times over the years and had gotten used to the cold, professional demeanor of the Nissan chief, who managed his schedule like a bullet train timetable. That night, however, Ghosn was cheerful and relaxed. As he sat down at the table, he ordered a round of sake straight off the bat. He invited his French guests to raise their glasses.

"At the end of the month, we will be number one," he told the reporters, who had flown over from Paris for the interview and had been promised a scoop.

"That's it, we can write it?" one of the reporters asked.

It wasn't official yet, but Ghosn had access to data showing that Renault, Nissan, and Mitsubishi had sold more than 5 million vehicles in the first half of 2017—more than Toyota, Volkswagen, and General Motors. Industry experts would argue that Ghosn was stretching reality by adding up sales by three midsize automakers and mashing them into one, but he had grown used to bypassing critics.

Over small plates of wagyu beef, octopus, and sea urchin, Ghosn was ecstatic. Since his arriving at Nissan in 1999 and taking the helm of Renault in 2005, he had endured critics and doubters. He had a perfect recollection of his detractors' predictions, because he had kept all the articles, he told the reporters. But now the Renault-Nissan tandem was number one, and those doomsayers would have to keep quiet.

"It's game over," he said. "It's impossible to argue anymore. With the Alliance, we've created something special."

Ghosn, who always sat ramrod straight, was slouched in his seat by the end of dinner. The reporters asked him about his pay, which they thought hovered around $18 million between his salaries at Renault, Nissan, and Mitsubishi. Ghosn asked to go off the record. The reporters acquiesced: they wouldn't publish his answer. He explained that in a company as large as the three-way alliance he had assembled, with

$200 billion in revenue and $10 billion in profit, a few million dollars spent to have "a good boss" was a drop in the ocean.

"This might shock you, but since we're off the record," Ghosn said matter of factly, "me, I'm not very well paid."

*　　*　　*

Beating Toyota, Volkswagen, and GM to the top of the automotive leaderboard was just the start. In September, Ghosn told the world that the Alliance wasn't content to sell 10 million cars a year; it wanted to sell 14 million. Ghosn reasoned that with the advent of electric vehicles and self-driving cars, only the biggest companies would have the cash to survive and prosper. If the Alliance could gain an edge in the early chase for breakthroughs, Ghosn thought, the gap would only continue to widen. He set targets for Renault, Mitsubishi, and Nissan to hit those sales numbers by 2022.

Saikawa was uneasy about Ghosn's aggressive sales targets, fearing they would further erode the profit margin at Nissan, which had already missed its sales targets a few months earlier. "We're going to have slow-and-steady growth," Saikawa had told reporters.

There was an increasing distance between Ghosn and his handpicked successor as Nissan CEO. Saikawa felt that, despite all its successes, Ghosn's growing empire was unwieldy. Both Nissan's and Renault's sales had risen by 40 percent since 2011, as Ghosn had pushed them to expand into new regions of the world. They had spent billions of dollars on new factories in rapidly growing countries, such as India and Brazil, acting on Ghosn's belief that those nations were poised to create a billion new members of the middle class, eager to buy their first car. But many of the factories sat underused, as the expected boom had yet to materialize.

That fall, an additional weight had been placed on Saikawa's shoulders. Government officials had toured a Nissan factory and found a problem: final vehicle tests on steering, brakes, and other essential functions weren't being performed by the proper staff members. It was an antiquated regulation, given that technology had rendered the manual tests obsolete. But in Japan, rules are rules. Nissan had to recall more than a million cars at a cost of over $200 million, because the right person wasn't moving the steering wheel and applying the brakes.

Saikawa addressed reporters, bowing for the cameras. When delivering the findings of an internal study to the government, he bowed again; taking all the heat, leading some at Nissan to wonder whether Ghosn had lost interest in their company.

*   *   *

In January 2018, Greg Kelly, who was at home in Tennessee, got a call from Frédérique Le Grèves, telling him that Ghosn was in New York and wanted to see him the next day. Kelly couldn't get a flight, as the airports were closed because of the "bomb cyclone" that was dumping snow on the East Coast. So he drove twenty hours to get there in the blizzard.

An exhausted Kelly met Ghosn near the Alliance office near Central Park. Skipping the pleasantries, Ghosn told Kelly that he was seriously considering leaving the companies. Ghosn's CEO mandate at Renault would be up in 2018, and Renault's largest shareholder (the French state) was making two demands if he stayed: he would need to take a pay cut, and, more important, he would need to finally merge the French carmaker and Nissan. Ghosn told Kelly that he was tired of fighting. He had been having the same arguments for so many years. The last time Kelly had seen Ghosn look this discouraged and depressed had been in 2011, when he had been juggling his divorce and the spy scandal at Renault that had almost cost him his job.

"Well, Mr. Ghosn, we'd really like you to stay. I believe we can still make it worth your while," Kelly said. The postretirement payday that Kelly had been working on since 2010 had gone through several iterations, and was still evolving.

"I'm thinking of just leaving it all behind," Ghosn said.

The meeting wrapped up soon thereafter. It was a long way to drive to hear your boss tell you he was thinking of quitting.

By the start of February, however, Ghosn decided to stay and accept the French government's terms, including the pay cut.

With his mind unencumbered, Ghosn flew to Rio de Janeiro on February 8, 2018, to watch the Carnival.

Nissan supported one of the teams and had invited eighteen people on behalf of "Mr. and Mrs. Ghosn." The list included Khalil Daoud, who ran the post service in Lebanon and had unveiled a postage stamp in Ghosn's honor four months prior; the head of a Lebanese bank in which Ghosn was a shareholder; and an alumnus from Ghosn's high school, Collège Notre-Dame de Jamhour.

The first float began rolling down Rio de Janeiro's three-hundred-yard-long venue, marking the start of the Carnival's official competition, in which teams jostled with extravagant costumes and heart-pounding samba beats. From their luxury suite, Ghosn and his guests watched the Nissan-sponsored float, on which dancers with giant wheels performed in front of a spinning model of Jupiter. Another float featured dragons, giant lotus flowers, and a kung fu panda in a tribute to the travels of Marco Polo through China in the thirteenth century.

Ghosn, who attended Carnival every year, said the 2018 edition was one of the best. Soon after, Nissan received a €209,500 bill for the guests' expenses in Rio covering their hotel stay, restaurants, and cultural visits.

* * *

After landing back in Paris from Rio, Ghosn addressed financial analysts on February 16, giving them an update on his plans for the future of the Alliance. He said that he was committed to bringing Renault and Nissan closer together and convincing investors that the two companies would stay that way. "We all agree on the irreversibility of the Alliance," he said. "Now the question is, how do you do that?"

The answer wasn't easy, and Ghosn knew he needed to tread carefully to avoid igniting a rebellion at Nissan, where the top management was firmly opposed to any arrangement that would reduce their autonomy or cause job cuts. But Ghosn was sure that he could pull it off, and he even had a name in mind for his future company: Global Motors, or GLM.

That same day, Renault officially announced that Ghosn had agreed to a 30 percent pay cut as CEO, while his mandate was extended for another four years, pending approval by shareholders.

Any pain Ghosn might have felt from the looming pay cut was assuaged by the good news he'd received from Nissan. Nada had finished setting up the paperwork necessary to secretly pay Ghosn around €8 million in cash. Funds had already been sent from Nissan and Mitsubishi to NMBV, a Dutch subsidiary set up to manage cooperation between the two Japanese carmakers. All Ghosn needed to do was sign an employment contract with the Dutch company.

After years of gritting his teeth at what he thought was a diminutive salary, money was now flowing in from multiple channels.

A few days later, Ghosn flew to Tokyo, where he signed his lucrative Dutch contract with NMBV. Although he had worked for Nissan since 1999, the pay arrangement included a signing bonus of nearly €2 million in addition to an annual salary of almost €6 million as the managing director of the new Dutch joint venture.

The €8 million Ghosn was preparing to receive from NMBV was the exact sum of his 30 percent pay cut at Renault, plus the pay cut he had taken at Nissan when he had bequeathed the CEO job to Saikawa—and very few people would know about it.

*　　*　　*

By spring, Ghosn was talking about the merger openly and with great excitement with those closest to him. He went to the sprawling flea market on the northern border of Paris with his close friend Carlos Abou Jaoude, and their wives. After lunch at Ma Cocotte, a restaurant decorated in "industrial baroque" style, the two women walked around the stalls admiring baubles and antiques for their respective homes. Meantime, his eyes shining, Ghosn buoyantly described to his friend his vision for the Renault-Nissan merger. He talked about the value that would be created—tens of billions of dollars! And if he managed to add another carmaker such as Fiat Chrysler, he could take his rightful seat atop the biggest auto company in the world, dwarfing the likes of Toyota and VW.

As he talked, he was so consumed by his vision that he barely acknowledged the people who were nodding their heads and saying hello. "You know, you can smile back at them," Abou Jaoude said to him during a rare break in Ghosn's narration.

With cost savings in the billions, a merger was also likely to yield a massive payday for Renault and Nissan shareholders, including Ghosn. He felt confident that the value of Nissan and Renault shares would rise significantly.

As Ghosn chaired the boards of both Renault and Nissan, however, he would have to recuse himself from directly participating in the negotiations. Nada led the talks on the Nissan side. Martin Vial, who oversaw the state's industrial assets, would represent the French side.

The French government asked Ghosn to announce a comprehensive timeline for a merger with Nissan at Renault's shareholder meeting in mid-June, but the two sides could hardly have been further apart in their thinking. The French wanted a merger, but Nissan was pushing for more independence. When the day came, Ghosn's statement was a study in diplomatic language. "My responsibility is to propose and take the necessary measures on organization and integration, so that there can be no more reasonable doubts about the lasting nature of the Alliance," he said.

Ghosn used words that were close enough to what the French state had wanted. Saikawa and the rest of the Nissan management team were also pleased, because nothing in the speech could be read as a firm commitment to a merger from the Nissan side.

*   *   *

Ghosn was well distracted by his travel schedule that summer. On June 29, he went to Naples, Italy, where *Shachou,* the yacht, was waiting in the marina. Less than a week later he was on the small island of Naoshima in Japan, where his eldest daughter was getting married.

On July 13, Ghosn's jet touched down in Italy once more before *Shachou* embarked on a tour of some picturesque volcanic islands off the coast of Sicily. After a brief stop in Paris to deliver the good news of Renault's record earnings to analysts and the press, Ghosn then took the whole month of August off, boarding his yacht with his children to anchor in coves next to the famed beaches of eastern Spain.

Ghosn's daughter Nadine posted a photo of herself on Instagram aboard a jet ski on August 11 with the caption "Royally soaked."

The merger talks had made no substantial headway during the summer, but Ghosn was nonetheless confident that his plans were coming together. At his request, Saikawa had been trying to structure a merger that would allow Nissan to continue operating as it always had: independently. One idea favored by Ghosn was to transfer all headquarters functions to a holding company while keeping the operational departments local. That would allow him to tell the French that he was delivering a merger—investors would now be able to buy shares in a single entity—and tell the Japanese that he had protected their independence because some of their operations would continue to be separate.

In September, Saikawa wrote to Ghosn that he was working to make a "scenario acceptable for both sides." If all went well, Ghosn would announce the tie-up in 2019, coinciding with the twenty-year anniversary of the Alliance.

*   *   *

When Ghosn landed in Morocco in mid-October, he had logged some 140,000 miles so far that year on company jets, the equivalent of circumnavigating the globe five times. In addition to Rio and Cannes, he had also touched down in Maldonado on the coast of Uruguay for some winter sun and visited Vancouver for a ski vacation. In the Nissan aircraft flight log, he almost always justified his use of the corporate jet with a single word: "Meeting."

On October 26, Ghosn's agenda listed a work meeting in Marrakech with Saikawa. Weeks before, the new Nissan CEO had booked a ninety-minute encounter to discuss the merger plan with the boss who was trying to pull it off. It was rare for any Ghosn subordinate, even someone as senior as Saikawa, to get so much time with the boss.

Ghosn left the meeting perplexed. Saikawa had flown more than three thousand miles from New Jersey after a tour of Nissan's US operations to meet with him. Still, during the hour and a half of their sit-down, he had said nothing substantial. It was bizarre.

The next day, Ghosn went to Rabat to attend the globalization forum. Ghosn recounted how he had devoted his career to cross-breeding Renault's and Nissan's cultures to build an industry champion. It was challenging, he told the audience, but the simple recipe was to be respectful and to talk straight.

"People are ready to cooperate if they have a common project that does not threaten their identities," he said.

* * *

In mid-November, Ghosn and Carole headed to Beirut, now the couple's favorite destination. After six years of intense work, the house that Nissan had bought for Ghosn was finally ready.

The protracted renovation had added about $10 million to the acquisition price. It had been worth the wait. In testament to the designer's deft skills and Carole's taste, the pink-walled house with baby blue shutters shone with understated elegance. The living room was bathed in light from the garden. At one end was a sitting area with a pair of leather chairs positioned at either end of a low marble table laden with greenery and orchids. During the day the windows could be flung open, letting in the breeze. At night a crystal chandelier lit up the space.

In one of the rooms, a large photo of the tycoon showed him from the back wearing a light gray suit and facing a dense wall of photographers. During the renovations, workers had discovered a pair of ancient sarcophagi. They were protected by thick glass flooring, in front of the wine cellar, and lit from within. Ghosn loved to take his guests down to that part of the house, where bottles were arrayed in racks the shape of a honeycomb along the wall. Cases of wine from Ghosn's vineyards were piled up in the climate-controlled room. The centerpiece of the entire place was an ancient olive tree with a broad, sinuous trunk that stood in the garden. After years of globe-trotting, Ghosn finally had a home. It would be the perfect retreat when he finally stepped back from day-to-day operations, overseeing his empire from Beirut.

On November 18, 2018, he had lunch with Carole and his in-laws at Em Sherif, one of Beirut's finest restaurants, before heading to the Beirut airport for his 11:00 p.m. flight to Tokyo. Before departing, Ghosn sent a message to the family WhatsApp group, which they had named "Game of Ghosns"—a tongue-in-cheek reference to his favorite TV show: "On my way to Tokyo! Love you guys!"

Ghosn was looking forward to conclusive meetings with Nissan management in Japan. He was confident that they would now come on board to consolidate the Alliance with at least something approaching a merger. "They have understood that they need to play their role," he assured a Renault director.

The merger would be Ghosn's crowning professional achievement, but it also would yield a significant personal goal, a sort of finish line that he had been calculating and working toward for years.

On his iPhone, Ghosn kept all sorts of notes, from his favorite dining places to things he needed to buy, and gym exercises to improve his flexibility. Earlier that year, he had written down a quote by the

British writer C. S. Lewis: "Humility is not thinking less of yourself, it is thinking of yourself less."

He also compiled notes about his assets. One listed the estimated value of his real estate properties in Brazil, France, and Lebanon. In another, he kept track of his share options at Renault, Nissan, and Mitsubishi.

All this wealth was summed up in yet another note. Under a section titled "Sygma," the Greek letter used to denote a sum in mathematics, Ghosn figured that he had between $820 million and $900 million in assets.

The last line of the note read, in French shorthand, "Completer par fus a 1000."

Top up to one billion with merger.

PART III

16

Terminal Velocity

In the summer of 2017, Hidetoshi Imazu was probing an obscure investment company that Nissan had created a few years prior. Little was known apart from its name, Zi-A Capital, and the fact that it was incorporated in the Netherlands. Imazu had heard from his predecessor that there was something fishy about it, and the company was late in filing its annual accounts. He had paid a visit to Amsterdam to take a closer look but had found nothing particularly enlightening.

Imazu was one of Nissan's *kansayaku*, a special supervisor tasked with checking the books and monitoring the conduct of board members at Japanese corporations. Over the course of four decades at the company, the affable and soft-spoken Imazu had developed a reputation for quiet competence, rarely speaking more than a handful of words in the numerous management meetings he sat through. Executives called him "the Boy Scout." His straitlaced nickname came from his reputation for having strong, rigid principles.

Back at headquarters, Imazu had learned that Zi-A was tied to the purchase of properties in Lebanon and Brazil for Carlos Ghosn. That was highly unusual, but the chairman was a high-flying executive, a living corporate legend who was presiding over three global carmakers.

Imazu, who noted everything in his pristine handwriting, would have to tread carefully.

The first person Imazu confided in was Hitoshi Kawaguchi, who ran

Nissan's government and external affairs department, especially the company's relations with the powerful Ministry of Economy, Trade, and Industry, or METI. The pair met regularly at the Nissan cafeteria reserved for executives, and Imazu knew that Kawaguchi would lend a sympathetic ear, especially if the topic was Ghosn. Like others at Nissan, Kawaguchi had developed a litany of concerns about the boss.

Imazu briefed Kawaguchi on his findings about Zi-A Capital but said that he wasn't sure how to gather more information. The two men needed an insider, someone who was close enough to Ghosn to be in the know but who wouldn't immediately alert the chief that he was under watch.

Kawaguchi knew who fit the bill: the Nissan lawyer Hari Nada.

Nada wasn't Japanese; he was born in Malaysia, of Indian descent, and raised in the south of England. But he had begun working for Nissan long before Renault had arrived. Both Imazu and Kawaguchi had worked with him when they had been stationed in Europe.

Nada was meticulous, almost obsessive, by nature. He was always impeccably dressed in a three-piece suit, with his salt-and-pepper hair carefully brushed back. In one meeting, he attacked a bowl of candy, downing piece after piece, seemingly unaware of his consumption. Outside of meetings, he was a chain smoker in between attempts to quit cold turkey. People gossiped about his spending. How could he afford those flashy suits or an expensive vacation at the company-owned nature reserve in South Africa? Still, the gossips treaded carefully; Nada was known for his ferocity toward his rivals.

Despite those quirks, Nada was a brilliant lawyer and a manic worker.

Kawaguchi often confided in Nada, and the two regularly spoke about a potential merger with Renault—a topic of constant speculation both inside and outside the company. In January 2018, the two men were becoming increasingly concerned that Ghosn would finally relent to pressure from the French. Ghosn's contract at Renault was coming up for renewal, giving the French government a trump card. The government said it would only back his nomination if Ghosn pledged to make genuine progress toward a merger. Kawaguchi and Nada shared the view that combining the companies would spell disaster for Nissan, marking the end of the proud Japanese automaker that they had known.

That same month, Kawaguchi approached Nada and told him that Imazu was compiling a dossier on Ghosn for alleged misconduct. Nada did not react in horror, nor did he run screaming down the hall to Ghosn's office. In fact, he was more than willing to help his two colleagues, especially since he knew where the skeletons were.

Still, he had a problem: his fingerprints were also all over the place. He needed to think about how much help he wanted to provide.

* * *

In mid-February 2018, Ghosn accepted the French government's terms to keep the CEO job at Renault, saying he would "take decisive steps to make the alliance irreversible"—a promise included in a Renault news release and repeated on a call with financial analysts. In Japan, alarm bells started ringing more loudly still. Ghosn had always protected Nissan from a merger with the French, but suddenly his loyalty seemed to have shifted.

The French state wanted to open negotiations with Nissan as soon as possible. As CEO of Renault and chairman of Nissan, Ghosn was conflicted. Nada, who was head of the CEO office at Nissan as well as head of the legal department, was put in charge of negotiations on the Japanese side.

The atmosphere was glacial. The French were excited at the prospect of a combination of the two carmakers, but Nada was digging in his heels—he wanted the companies to stay separate and for Renault to sell down part of its ownership in Nissan. "I said that Nissan would like to stay faithful to the principle of autonomous companies," he wrote to Ghosn after one meeting with the French side.

At the same time, Nada started planning for a potential post-Ghosn future.

In late March, a small group of lawyers met in Nada's office on the twenty-first floor of Nissan's headquarters in Yokohama for what he said was a top secret discussion. He kicked off the meeting by swearing everyone to secrecy, saying that what he was about to discuss could be considered treason. "We'll all lose our jobs if it's found out what we're doing," he said. "Ghosn's like a wolf."

Nada instructed them to work on a range of theoretical scenarios: What should Nissan do if Ghosn were ousted from his position at Renault? Or what if Ghosn suddenly left? And how about if he faced criminal charges? The group produced sprawling flowcharts laying out timelines and options in which they tried to anticipate every possible move.

Nada had another concern, one that made his secret scenario planning all the more urgent. Greg Kelly was finalizing the latest plan to pay Ghosn in secret, and this one was predicated on the chairman officially retiring from Nissan the following year. Nada reasoned that Ghosn would want to remain atop the Alliance forever, and that the best way to achieve that after retiring from Nissan would be to merge the companies. Nada became increasingly convinced that the merger train was about to leave the station.

In May, Nada learned from Kawaguchi that Imazu had hit a wall; what they had dug up on Ghosn wasn't serious enough to justify his dismissal. They needed more.

Nada began to meet directly with Imazu. He told him about Ghosn's rent-free use of properties purchased by Zi-A but said he had much more to share if Imazu started a more formal probe. He recommended that Imazu hire Latham & Watkins, a firm that Nada had grown close to over the years after making them the company's main legal adviser. Latham had advised Nada on a number of plans to pay Ghosn secretly as well as on Nissan's relations with Renault. Nada told Imazu that only Latham could be trusted to keep everything completely confidential.

Around the same time, Nada issued a request for the general counsel, Ravinder Passi, to prepare a memo on the Japanese government's plan to introduce something resembling a US-style plea-bargaining system. If Nada, who had played an active and willing role in Ghosn's secret remuneration, was going to start a brush fire of an investigation, he wanted to make sure there was a way to save himself from being burned alive.

When he received the memo he had requested, he lit up as he began flipping through it. His plan was lining up perfectly: he would be protected, and the investigation would be handled by lawyers he knew and trusted.

*   *   *

In mid-June, the internal investigation into Carlos Ghosn shifted gears when Imazu turned up at the public prosecutors' office in central Tokyo. The Nissan executive had spent months amassing information, and he now had a straightforward question: did the rent-free houses constitute a crime? If authorities said they didn't, then everyone could move on. If that did, however, amount to illegal activity, then Imazu would have done the right thing by reporting a potential crime. One prosecutor listened to Imazu explain what he knew about Zi-A Capital and a couple of other issues that he had uncovered.

The prosecutor asked whether anyone else at Nissan knew of these suspicions. Imazu said that only he, Nada, and Kawaguchi were aware of the investigation.

Keep it that way, the prosecutor told him. If word got out, Ghosn might try to destroy paperwork and tamper with potential witnesses. Though dubious about their prospects, the public prosecutors were stirred by such a juicy target.

The prosecutor proposed a way forward: if Nissan passed evidence from its investigation to the prosecutors, they would pay close attention. That put Imazu in an awkward position. On the one hand, he reported to shareholders, so the results of any investigation he commissioned ought to be delivered to the board of directors. But he also had clear instructions from prosecutors to keep it secret.

A week later, Imazu briefed Kawaguchi and Nada on his meeting.

Nada had hoped that any contact with law enforcement would be limited until Nissan built a solid case against Ghosn. But in one motion, Imazu had boxed him in. As long as matters remained within the company, Nada had widespread access and influence. But as a government informant, he would have no wiggle room.

Nada was doubly nervous, because the law on plea bargaining had been adopted but had never been tested in a high-profile case. He still feared he could become a suspect. To prepare for the worst, Nada hired his own attorney—and sent the bills to Nissan.

*   *   *

On July 2, 2018, Imazu retained Latham to begin the internal investigation.

Nada opened up to the Latham lawyers. He explained that Ghosn's 2010 pay cut had been taken to avoid a public backlash and that Ghosn had searched for ways to make the lost money back. He described how he had helped arrange for Ghosn to receive a secret salary from NMBV, the Dutch company co-owned by Nissan and Mitsubishi.

But even as Nada was spilling the beans, new information kept landing on his desk. In late July, Kelly rang Nada from Paris with an update: Ghosn had agreed to abandon an earlier plan to collect $100 million in retirement and consulting fees in cash and would instead receive discounted Nissan shares, a less controversial option because the share award would be disclosed in a filing, so Ghosn would not be getting paid in secret. Yet Ghosn still hoped to collect a hefty bonus in 2019, after he officially retired from Nissan, without disclosing it. Kelly thought that not informing shareholders about the payment would be illegal, and he intended to talk Ghosn out of it.

Kelly had no qualms about sharing any of this with Nada. After all, this was the man he had handpicked to succeed him at the helm of the CEO's office. Unbeknownst to Kelly, Nada wrote up a summary of their conversation and sent it to Kawaguchi and Imazu, as well as to a Latham lawyer.

*   *   *

Three months after Imazu's visit to the prosecutors' office in central Tokyo, it was Nada's turn to walk up to the monolithic structure composed of gray stone and glass. Nada recounted what was now a familiar spiel, laying out the story of Zi-A Capital and the houses Nissan had bought for Ghosn. When the discussions turned to Ghosn's 2010 pay cut and the machinations to pay him secretly, the prosecutors showed a particularly keen interest.

Nada told them what he knew, which was that Ghosn had taken a pay cut and that he and Kelly had drafted a number of contracts to pay Ghosn but none had materialized. He told them that there was one person who knew much more: Toshiaki Ohnuma, the keeper of secrets. The collection of documents that he had access to was the closest thing to a complete picture of Ghosn's compensation.

Shortly thereafter, Nada was asked whether he could get Ohnuma's laptop.

The authorities were asking a lot. Nada would have to reveal the existence of a secret investigation to Ohnuma, who was known for his loyalty to Ghosn.

In early September, Nada walked into Ohnuma's office and told him that Nissan was conducting an internal investigation. Nada informed him that he had turned over his laptop to the investigators and now it was Ohnuma's turn. Ohnuma could have asked questions but simply handed over his computer. He also produced a list of all money transfers made from Zi-A Capital's account in Dubai.

The next month, Ohnuma was summoned to a meeting on the twentieth floor of Nissan headquarters, where Kawaguchi and Imazu took turns grilling him. They asked about the houses in Brazil and Lebanon. Ohnuma detailed everything he knew. Then came the revelation. After he finished talking, Imazu told him he should seek to cooperate with the prosecutors.

The prosecutors? Ohnuma asked. He had thought it was just an internal audit, where the worst possible outcome would be a humiliating firing and the loss of his pension. Now law enforcement was involved. And soon, he was hit with a stunning realization: Ohnuma wasn't a witness; he was a potential suspect in a criminal investigation.

And so was his boss.

*   *   *

Half a world away, the man officially tasked with the stewardship of Nissan, current Nissan CEO Hiroto Saikawa, was still in the dark. He had just finished delivering a talk at the Nissan Institute of Japanese Studies at Oxford University when Nada rang him in his hotel room to let him know there was an ongoing investigation at Nissan that could impact Ghosn. Saikawa, still fuzzy on the details, wasn't overly concerned, and took three days to get back to Yokohama.

Once he was home, Imazu explained to Saikawa that he had been investigating Ghosn in secret and had taken the matter to the authorities in the summer. Now prosecutors wanted to speak with him, too. Saikawa was outraged that Imazu had gone to law enforcement before telling his own CEO. He thought he would have been able to prepare, or at least try to limit the damage to the company. Imazu explained that he had been forbidden from speaking to anyone until now.

"You better have good evidence," Saikawa said. Then he paused. "Do you suspect me?" he asked.

Saikawa could only think of the destruction that could be wrought by a full-scale prosecution. He immediately called Christina Murray, Nissan's chief internal audit and global compliance officer, into his office. Imazu, he told her, would no longer be overseeing the investigation. She would now be in charge of it, with Latham & Watkins reporting to her. But Saikawa allowed Nada to stay involved. He was the sound legal mind at Nissan on whom Saikawa relied heavily for advice, especially when it came to dealing with Renault. It also helped that he, more than anyone, knew where the bodies were buried.

*   *   *

Nada's professional life now boiled down to two roles. One for Nissan, where he was still head of legal and a key adviser to Saikawa. The other was serving as an informant to Japanese authorities.

In October 2018, Nada flew to Brazil to interview Ghosn's local assistant, Vania Rufino, with the goal of making "a thorough record of our acquisition of the property, its use over recent years, and all works carried out to the property," as he put it in an email.

The meeting took place at 11:00 a.m. at the offices of the law firm Gouvêa Vieira. Rufino found it odd to have to sit in a formal conference room in order to meet with someone who worked for the same company. She didn't feel any more at ease when Nada placed an iPhone on the table to record her, as he claimed to have an injured hand that would prevent him from taking notes. Then she asked if Ghosn was aware of the meeting, only to be told, "Not yet." She asked Nada to send Ghosn an email, just to be on the safe side, and he obliged.

Rufino didn't understand why Nada was asking her questions about a property he had been closely involved in purchasing. She was sure that he knew everything already: he had even hired the real estate agent. Rufino herself had exchanged dozens of emails with Nada over the years, ever since the purchase in 2011. If anything, the man sitting across the table knew more than she did. After the two-and-a-half-hour meeting ended, Rufino called Ghosn to tell him how weird she had found it.

"His behavior is very strange. He asked me some bizarre questions about the property, the family, all details that he already had in the past. Has something happened, Mr. Ghosn?"

Ghosn trusted Nada and told her not to worry.

Nada's next stop was in Lebanon, where he interviewed Amal Abou Jaoude, Ghosn's assistant there who had worked for Ghosn's late lawyer, Fady Gebran. Nada again placed a voice recorder on the table and asked questions about the Beirut house, its six-year renovation, and about Phoinos, the Nissan subsidiary that owned it.

In Japan, prosecutors were now starting to get a fuller picture, and Nada was keen to ensure that he wouldn't be prosecuted alongside his boss. He had been involved in purchasing the houses in Lebanon and Brazil, and in a number of schemes to pay Ghosn secretly. In late October, he cut a deal: he would testify against Ghosn, in return for avoiding charges himself. Relieved about his own fate, he could now concentrate on the best way to help prosecutors.

He started preparing a raid on Ghosn's homes around the world to gather any potential evidence located outside Japan. He ordered the general counsel, Rav Passi, to put Nissan lawyers on standby to travel to Brazil and Lebanon. Passi, who would be dispatched to the United States, hated the whole plan. Send his lawyers to enter Ghosn's houses without warrants in potentially dangerous parts of the world? "This isn't *The A-Team*," he thought. But Nada was adamant. Those houses were Nissan property and the lawyers would be perfectly within their rights to search them.

There was one more item on Nada's to-do list: he needed to get Greg Kelly to Japan for questioning, without tipping him off.

Kelly trusted Nada. The American had been Nada's greatest cheerleader at Nissan when Kelly had stepped back in 2015. He had recommended that Ghosn take Nada on as a replacement, saying, "He will serve you better than I did"—and Ghosn had taken his advice. Kelly even felt that he had saved Nada's job on two separate occasions. The first was in 2011, when he defended him following Nada's decision to flee Japan in the wake of the tsunami that had caused fears of a meltdown, which many at the company felt was a dereliction of duty. The second time came after the 2015 negotiations with the French government and Renault that had cost the French company its voting power in Nissan. At Renault, some people had called for Nada's head. Kelly had flown to meet Ghosn to ensure that Nada wasn't canned.

For all the history between the two men, convincing the American to fly to Japan was made tougher because doctors had recently diagnosed Kelly with spinal stenosis. The condition had left him in constant pain and required surgery. Even sitting was excruciating.

Nada knew Kelly was seriously ill, so he was more than a little surprised to wake up to an email from Nada's secretary informing him that he was urgently needed in Japan for the November board meeting in a few weeks. "The corporate jet will be arranged if necessary," the secretary wrote. "Is it possible to come to Japan from November 19 through the 22nd?"

By the time Kelly saw the email, it was early evening in Japan. He sent a text to Nada: "Hari, please let me know when I can call you about an urgent matter."

It was nearly five hours and several texts later before Kelly was finally able to get a hold of Nada. He explained that his doctor was alarmed at the state of his spine and was advising urgent surgery to prevent permanent damage. What was so important that he couldn't attend the board meeting by videoconference? As far as Kelly knew, they would not be discussing anything controversial.

Nada said that the problem wasn't the meeting, it was Ghosn. He was worried that the boss would back out of a pressing deal unless Kelly was there to force the issue in person.

The matter at hand was the yearslong negotiation to have Ghosn purchase the Beirut and Rio de Janeiro residences from Nissan and get them off the company's books. Kelly had been trying to get Ghosn to purchase the homes ever since he had seen the bill from the multimillion-dollar renovation of the Beirut house. Ghosn had originally agreed to do so but hadn't yet. Nada's task was to get Ghosn to sign on the dotted line. The story seemed plausible to Kelly, because Nada regularly complained that he couldn't control Ghosn the way Kelly had. He needed his old boss standing by his side.

Besides, he said, if Kelly was in constant pain, what difference would it make if he was in pain in Japan or in Tennessee? It was just a quick trip to make sure that it all went smoothly. Kelly would be home in time for his surgery.

"We'll get you in and get you out," Nada said.

If it had been just the issue of the houses, Kelly might not have bothered to go. His family and his wife, Dee, were firmly opposed to his traveling. "What's so damn important that you can't do this by video?" Dee demanded. But Kelly was also concerned about another topic on the table: Ghosn's bonus, a massive cash payout linked to Nissan's share price, which Ohnuma believed didn't have to be disclosed if Ghosn officially retired from Nissan before it was paid. Ghosn seemed inclined to listen to Ohnuma, which worried Kelly. He knew it was going to be a potentially contentious discussion, which would be made much harder if it wasn't held face-to-face.

Kelly did not want his plan to come crashing down so close to the end. Not after all these years. Of course, he was unaware that he was being lured to Japan precisely because the plan was already in tatters. It took several more calls and a confirmation of Kelly's surgery date, but Nada finally won out over Kelly's family's objections.

On November 13, Kelly called Nada to say that he would be coming to Japan.

17

The Arrest

The Gulfstream G650 began to shudder as it approached Haneda Airport on the outskirts of Tokyo on November 19. There was always turbulence in the vicinity of the airport, due to the winds whipping around Mount Fuji. Ghosn barely looked up from the Nissan documents he was reviewing.

As Ghosn's plane descended toward Tokyo, another plane, carrying Greg Kelly, was nearing Japan. Unlike his boss, the American wasn't accustomed to flying in private jets. His aircraft had taken off from Tennessee, making an hour-long stop in Anchorage, Alaska, for refueling.

Despite his plush leather seat on the swanky jet, Kelly couldn't sleep. The pain and tingling in his limbs made it impossible to get comfortable. He sat back in the leather seat, pulled a yellow legal pad out of his bag, and started drafting a memo for his meeting with Ghosn. He had spent nearly a decade working on plan after plan to pay Ghosn more money. For Kelly, believing that his boss would be retiring as part of the proposed merger, those efforts had taken on a renewed sense of urgency.

At the top of his legal pad, he wrote the thing that he knew mattered most to Ghosn: the amount of pay he had forgone over the past eight years. Including pending stock options, the amount totaled around $120 million. After that, he wrote the amount he planned to offer Ghosn to sign a deal to stay on as board director after retirement. Between the stock options, the pension, and the postretirement deal Kelly was working on, it came to nearly $150 million. The pitch to Ghosn was simple: if you stick around at Nissan after retiring, you'll finally be paid what you're worth.

After eight years of dead ends, Kelly had managed to find a way to pay for the postretirement deal: dirt-cheap Nissan shares. Nissan would grant the shares for Ghosn to purchase for around 1 yen each; he would be buying at an enormous discount and would pocket the difference when he sold them, their value having inflated significantly by the burst from the merger.

*   *   *

While Ghosn and Kelly were on their way to Tokyo, Saikawa was preparing to deliver a speech about the Renault-Nissan Alliance to the French Chamber of Commerce and Industry in Japan. He had a sinking feeling all morning. He was sure that the prosecutors would grab Ghosn when he landed, because it would be the first time he had returned to Japan since September. Would they arrest him? Just question and release him?

He sat on a stool in front of eight hundred people, waiting for his turn to speak, staring hard at the back of Louis Schweitzer's head as the former Renault chief recounted the history of the Renault-Nissan Alliance. When Schweitzer finished speaking, Saikawa approached the lectern. The Alliance, Saikawa told the crowd, had succeeded because of the mutual trust and respect that had been built up between hundreds of people on both sides. He avoided mentioning Ghosn. In doing so, he hoped to send the message that the Alliance hadn't succeeded just because of Ghosn and could survive without him.

*   *   *

At 3:41 p.m., Ghosn's plane touched down at Haneda Airport.

He was greeted by a young lady from the travel agency that handled the ground services for his private flights. As usual, she filled out the arrival paperwork for his arrival and guided him to the immigration desk. Ghosn strode up and handed his passport over. After the man typed in his details, he paused. "There's something wrong," he told Ghosn and disappeared with the passport into a back office. Ghosn had flown into Japan hundreds of times in his nearly two decades at Nissan. This was the first time he had ever encountered an issue.

The man returned and asked Ghosn to follow him to the back office. In the room was another man, who was not introduced. After the immigration officer finished his paperwork, the unintroduced man stood up. "My name is Yoshitaka Seki, and I'm from the prosecutor's office in Tokyo," he said to Ghosn. "Please come with us."

Seki refused to explain why Ghosn was being detained, nor would he allow him to make a phone call. Ghosn wanted to call Nissan, particularly Hitoshi Kawaguchi. The head of government affairs would call the right people to fix whatever the hell was wrong.

He also asked to call his daughter Maya, who was waiting for him at his Tokyo apartment. She was in town to visit him and introduce him to her new boyfriend. The three of them were due to have dinner at 7:00 p.m. at Sukiyabashi Jiro, the legendary sushi restaurant. Seki also denied that request.

Ghosn was escorted out of the airport by a phalanx of prosecutors and ushered into a waiting car.

*   *   *

On the other side of Tokyo, the sun was setting as Kelly's plane landed at Narita International Airport. He was exhausted after the sleepless journey and was happy not to have to deal with the lines at immigration, thanks to his arrival on a private jet.

Kelly could barely recall how he got through the airport and into the waiting van that would take him to his hotel. He was half asleep as they traveled along the southern edge of Tokyo on the highway to Yokohama. He was jerked awake by the driver, who said he needed to pull over to make a phone call to his family.

After the driver navigated through the parking lot into an open space, Kelly looked over at a nearby vehicle as its doors opened and six men in dark suits piled out and walked with intent toward his vehicle. Kelly sat bolt upright as the men opened the doors and piled in. "What's going on?" he asked.

One of the men, who appeared to be in charge, started to speak in Japanese while another translated. "We're from the Tokyo prosecutors office," said the English speaker.

"Okay, so what?" Kelly said. "Why are you in my car?"

The explanation would come later. Three of them climbed into the rear of the vehicle, and two sat on each side of Kelly, who was in the center. The last suited man got into the front seat with the driver. The van, which had seemed comfortably spacious a minute ago, now made him feel claustrophobic.

*   *   *

The vehicle carrying Ghosn navigated the outskirts of Tokyo, bound for a holding facility in the far northeast of the city, near Kosuge Station. The car entered through an underground parking area, where Ghosn got out and jail officials unloaded his luggage. Once inside, his suitcase was opened; its contents were cataloged, then seized.

The prison guards obviously knew who he was and conducted their business in a cool and professional manner. No one spoke English, but Ghosn managed to understand their curt directions.

Ghosn stripped fully naked and was searched. He lifted his arms and legs one at a time and finally bent over in front of the guards. His clothes were confiscated and he was given a prison uniform— essentially medical scrubs in a dull teal shade but made of a rougher, scratchier fabric. For shoes, he was handed hard translucent plastic clogs, then escorted through the prison to his cell, a small room with a straw mat on the floor.

The heavy steel door shut on Ghosn.

*   *   *

At around 5:00 p.m. the *Asahi* newspaper, one of Japan's largest, broke the news that Ghosn had been detained for questioning. Its website posted footage of dark-suited prosecutors boarding Ghosn's private jet.

Across the world, phones began buzzing with the headlines.

As Kelly's van was speeding down the highway, he received a text from Dominique Thormann, the former Renault finance chief, whom he had worked alongside for years. It was a link to an article saying that Ghosn had been arrested. Kelly struggled to process the information in his sleep-deprived state. The prosecutor to Kelly's left saw the message, and quickly confiscated his phone.

Soon after Ghosn's arrival, the van carrying Kelly pulled into the same underground car park. His briefcase was confiscated, and prosecutors took his documents, including the yellow legal pad on which he had just been writing.

Kelly stripped naked, surrounded by twenty guards, after which he changed into the harsh prison uniform. He was led to an interrogation room, where prosecutors questioned him. Kelly felt a little like a character in *The Deer Hunter*: one second he was Robert De Niro at a wedding, the next scene captured and being interrogated in Vietnam. He was sleep deprived, stiff with pain, and utterly bewildered. The prosecutor read out the accusation against Kelly, saying that he had helped Ghosn underreport his compensation. Questions swirled in Kelly's mind. But he signed the document anyway, put his fingerprint on the designated spot, and was led to his cell.

*   *   *

With Ghosn and Kelly detained, a convoy of vans carrying a small army of prosecutors pulled up to Nissan's headquarters. Dressed in dark suits, they marched single file into the building. It was near the end of the workday, and employees were in meetings or leaving conference rooms. Several prosecutors walked purposefully toward certain rooms, which they sealed with yellow tape. They knew exactly whom they wanted to speak with, and Nissan security personnel grabbed these people and took them to conference rooms to be interrogated.

One person on the executive floor watched the scene in disbelief. Suddenly prosecutors were everywhere, and they were moving fast. It was like a Tokyo train at rush hour, he thought—busy but eerily silent.

In parallel, Nada was coordinating a raid of Ghosn's properties around the world to ensure that any potential evidence ended up in Japan.

To that end, the British lawyer reached out to Amal Abou Jaoude, the former assistant to Ghosn's late Lebanese lawyer. She now worked for Nissan, and was responsible for the Beirut house. He informed her over email that her boss had been arrested, and asked her to immediately go to her office.

"I realize that this matter must make you feel conflicted and awkward and I'm sorry about that," Nada wrote. "However, I have always found you to be straightforward, honest and professional [. . .] and I know that you will do the right thing."

Amal responded to Nada's email within five minutes. She was on her way and would follow instructions, she told Nada.

When she arrived, she found Nissan's regional general counsel, Fabien Lesort, and four other men waiting for her, drinking coffee. The group made its way to Amal's office, where Ghosn's assistant sat at her desk as the five men took files down from her shelves and packed them into boxes. Some of the files pertained to a company called Phoinos, which owned the Beirut house. Others were marked "Brasilensis," a company the men had never heard of. Lesort also asked Amal to hand over her company laptop and cell phone, and they took her desktop computer.

The search took about thirty minutes. Once they were done, Lesort asked Amal to take them to the pink house where Ghosn stayed when he was in Lebanon, so she got into one of their cars and directed them there. When they arrived, she asked a member of the house staff to open the door. The men took notes as they strolled through the home, going into the gym and the wine cellar and looking out into the court-yard with its centuries-old olive tree.

A similar scene took place across the world in Brazil, where Ghosn's local assistant was interrogated by Nissan's regional head of compli-ance, then ordered to hand over her phone and laptop. Once the ques-tioning was over, she went with members of Nissan's investigation team to the residence in Copacabana used by the Ghosns.

As they had done in Lebanon, they made their way through the house, taking notes.

*   *   *

Meanwhile, at Ghosn's apartment in Tokyo, men from the local pros-ecutors' office presented Ghosn's daughter Maya with a search war-rant. Maya was extremely concerned about her father's health, and asked where he was and what was going on. She was refused a detailed response; the prosecutors would only confirm that he was not in the hospital. For a number of hours, prosecutors turned the apartment up-side down. The couch cushions were flipped up and opened. They scru-tinized everything: birthday cards from Ghosn's children; their school report cards. At one point, one of the men asked if Maya knew the code to the safe in an office. She didn't. While searching the rooms, one of the prosecutors answered a phone call and headed to the safe. At the airport, prosecutors had confiscated Ghosn's cell phone, on which was a document that contained all the codes to his safes around the world.

The prosecutor punched in the code: 29211109. Inside were a num-ber of documents, including the handwritten loan contract with Suhail Bahwan, signed when Ghosn had taken out a 3 billion–yen loan from the Omani billionaire. Also in Ghosn's study were records of bonus payments Renault had made to Bahwan's company.

*   *   *

Around 10:00 p.m. that night, Nissan CEO Hiroto Saikawa entered the fifth-floor conference room dressed in a charcoal suit and magenta tie. He broke with Japanese tradition for these sorts of events by sitting down rather than standing up to make his speech. It was going to be a long night of questions from the press.

Saikawa pulled out the speech he had written only an hour or two before. As prosecutors had prowled the halls, he had locked himself in his office to decide what he would tell the world. He had found it difficult to keep his rage in check. The selfishness of Ghosn's actions angered him the most. As he examined the draft, Saikawa struck out any language that might get him started on that chain of thought; if he started expressing the many ways he felt betrayed, he might not be able to stop.

"Ladies and gentlemen, I'm sorry to invite you so late at night," he said. "According to the internal investigation, we discovered significant misconduct led by Mr. Ghosn himself," he continued as the gathered press corps typed furiously on their laptops. He then laid out the allegations against his mentor and former idol: Ghosn had understated his pay in securities filings and misappropriated company assets.

"I don't know how to put it," Saikawa said. He pulled his lips tight and his eyes took on an intensity that belied his emotional state. He delivered his next words slowly, with notable, labored precision. "I feel great disappointment and frustration and despair and indignation."

In France, a small group of Renault executives and directors watched Saikawa's press conference from their own conference room at headquarters. Their reactions were a mixture of disbelief at Ghosn's sudden arrest and shock at Saikawa's condemnation. There was an overwhelming consensus that there had to be some ulterior motive for this series of events. Could it be tied to the fear of a merger that many at Nissan didn't want?

One director interpreted the arrest as an attack on Renault. *"Putain,"* he cursed as he watched Saikawa. Instead of playing nice, he suggested, Renault should buy a stake in Nissan and forcibly merge the two companies.

Saikawa wrapped up his press conference after over an hour of questions and got up from the table. He gave only the briefest of bows. That was a loaded message in Japan. When you need to apologize, the expectation is that the bow will match the severity of the transgression. Saikawa wasn't going to apologize tonight, certainly not on Ghosn's behalf.

*   *   *

In Beirut, Fabien Lesort, the Nissan lawyer, returned to his hotel. He extracted the hard drive from Amal Abou Jaoude's desktop computer and packed it in his suitcase along with her laptop, her phone, and the pile of documents that he had collected earlier in the day. He then headed to the airport for a 7:00 p.m. flight out of Lebanon. Lesort's boss had been worried about the assignment: Beirut isn't the safest city, and Ghosn had a lot of friends there. But everything was going to plan.

Nine hours after Ghosn's arrest was made official, Lesort was sitting on a plane with the precious cargo next to him. As the aircraft took off, little did Lesort realize that the hard drive he was carrying—which contained hundreds of emails belonging to Ghosn's late lawyer, Fady Gebran—would become the central plank in the prosecution's case against Ghosn.

18

Boxed In

The call to wake up sounded at 7:00 a.m., late in the day for Ghosn. The guard barked orders in Japanese for the prisoner to get up and clear away his futon bedding quickly. Roll call and room inspection would be at 7:15.

It had been a restless night for Ghosn, not to mention a rude awakening to Japan's harsh detention system. The lights in the cell had remained on all night. Their fluorescent glare had been dimmed slightly, but they had never gone out. The sleeping arrangement was also foreign, a traditional cotton-padded futon. Like the pillow, it was rock hard, and the thin blanket—an antisuicide measure in the prison—was a far cry from the plush duvets to which he was accustomed.

Ghosn folded away his bedding and presented himself to the guards. Then came breakfast: a few Japanese pickles, a bowl of rice, and a bowl of soup.

Ghosn's first visitor was Laurent Pic, the French ambassador to Japan. The previous evening, Ghosn had asked that the French, Lebanese, and Brazilian ambassadors be made aware of his detention and provide him with consular protection.

Most of all, he wanted to get word to Nissan as quickly as possible.

Having arrived first, the French diplomat was saddled with breaking the bad news: Nissan was his accuser.

"You have to be careful," Pic said. "Nissan is against you."

Ghosn looked as though he'd taken a body blow. He had endured his first night at the spartan Tokyo Detention Center in Kosuge—a meteoric fall for the high-flying auto titan—in the hope that his detention had been a mere misunderstanding.

After lunch, he was taken to a meeting room. Yoshitaka Seki, the prosecutor he had met at the airport the previous day, sat opposite him with a translator and an official in charge of monitoring the proceedings. Ghosn wasn't allowed to take notes. The ambassador had been correct; it wasn't a mistake. Seki accused him of concealing millions of dollars in pay.

The accusation made no sense to Ghosn, who denied misreporting his compensation. Even if he had, that was essentially a paperwork violation, nothing that would justify treating him like a criminal. Hopefully, the prosecutors would give him a chance to clear up any confusion and he would be released soon. The first full day of interrogations ended minutes before 9:00 p.m., allowing Ghosn to return to his cell just before the mandatory bedtime.

Before anything else, Ghosn needed to put a legal team into place. Since Nissan had turned foe, he went to Renault, which recommended Motonari Otsuru. A former prosecutor, Otsuru had made a name for himself by handling the last big white-collar crime case involving the CEO of a Japanese firm, Takafumi Horie, in 2006. He had a reputation for being ruthless, once having penned an essay titled "Fighting Against the Darkness of Injustice." Ghosn wasn't sure what to make of him. Bespectacled and slightly disheveled, he looked more like a university professor than a sharp defense attorney. And his government career had ended abruptly, in a cloud of scandal, after prosecutors had fabricated a confession under his watch. Still, he had one qualification that Ghosn hoped would matter more than others: he used to run the prosecution office that was after Ghosn, so he knew its tactics. He had also been Seki's boss. Ghosn decided to hire him.

Outside the correctional center's walls, the Ghosn family was in angst. A week after the arrest, Carole flew to Beirut from New York, where she had been visiting her children. But when she arrived at the pink house, she was prevented from entering by guards she didn't know. Nissan had changed the locks. Ghosn's lawyer would challenge the carmaker's right to do that in a Lebanese court, but a decision would take time. Scattered around the globe and barred from having any direct contact with Ghosn, close relatives gathered for daily calls in a WhatsApp group to support one another and see how they could contribute to his defense. His sister Claudine and eldest daughter, Caroline, were in Brazil. His children Anthony and Maya were in the United States. His daughter Nadine was in the United Kingdom. For many, the calls took place in the middle of the night.

Anthony quickly took on a leading role. In the days that followed the arrest, he received an intriguing proposal: a person at Nissan offered to steal the emails of the group of people who had secretly investigated his dad: Nada, Kawaguchi, and others. The idea was that through the correspondence, Ghosn's family might be able to obtain evidence that would help prove that he had been the victim of a setup aimed at disrupting his plan to merge Renault and Nissan. Evidently more careful than his father, Anthony declined, saying that they had a plan and his father would be out soon.

For now, however, Ghosn was stuck in a Tokyo jailhouse. The priority, Ghosn told his newly recruited lawyer, was to arrange for bail and get him out of his cell. Otsuru countered that he needed to be realistic; in Japan, granting bail before trial is the exception, not the norm. Ghosn's best shot, Otsuru said, was to be forthcoming. Ghosn promised that he would try to be accommodating.

The prosecutors were relentless, arriving at the detention center every day, seven days a week. They arrived early in the afternoon and pelted Ghosn with questions for hours, often until 9:00 p.m., sometimes even later. They brought in towering piles of papers, so high that Ghosn thought it must be a stunt aimed at revving up the pressure on him, an intimidation tactic that they thought might break him.

Ghosn was being held under a pretrial detention system, where a judge grants prosecutors the power to hold a suspect for questioning before filing charges. A suspect can be held for an initial period of up to three days, and with approval from a judge, that period can be extended to twenty-three days. In practice, prosecutors can go well beyond that limit by bringing fresh charges to reset the clock on the detention period, dangling the prospect of freedom if a suspect confesses. Defense lawyers are banned from attending interrogations. Critics call the system "hostage justice," saying it is designed to crush suspects into submission.

For the first time in many years, possibly decades, Ghosn wasn't in the driver's seat; Seki was. And his version of the good-cop/bad-cop interrogation technique was upsetting Ghosn. One day, Seki sought to bond with Ghosn, asking him about his taste in music. Ghosn was perplexed. At work, people knew not to waste his time with small talk. "Does this sucker think I'm going to get into that kind of relationship?" he wondered.

Another day, when Ghosn balked at answering questions, Seki shifted gears, suggesting that refusing to admit his crimes was going to create more problems. "You know how much suffering you are creating for your family by not confessing?"

At times, the prosecutor would go on tangents during their long conversations.

"Apparently Nissan's buying your suits," Seki said one day, referring to an article in the press.

"Of course," Ghosn said. He was the face of the company.

"When I go to a prosecutor conference, I don't have my suits paid for," Seki said. Ghosn was desperate to regain the initiative, but Seki had a plan and was barreling ahead with it.

On December 10, Tokyo prosecutors filed charges against Ghosn, claiming that he had conspired to report only half of his actual compensation over a five-year period ending in March 2015. He should have reported income of $87 million, the indictment said. At the same time that the prosecutors filed those charges, they rearrested him on suspicion of doing exactly the same thing for a three-year period up to 2018, giving them another ten-day period to interrogate Ghosn. Now they had until December 20.

Ghosn was furious with Otsuru. He felt misled by his lawyer, who had told him that the prosecutors would go easy on him if he answered questions. Instead, he was being run through the grinder, with charges being split up for the sole purpose of keeping him in jail for as long as possible. Ghosn felt that as a former chief prosecutor, Otsuru had known exactly how things were likely to go but hadn't told him. Worse, he had no strategy to fight the system.

December 20 arrived, offering Ghosn a ray of hope that he might get out of jail soon. The judge denied a request by the prosecutors to grant a second ten-day period to interrogate Ghosn for the latest charges they had filed. That gave him a shot at bail. Ghosn was fixated on being released by Christmas. His lawyers were confident enough about his release to buy a plane ticket for him to fly to Paris. They argued that he posed no flight risk, as escaping would ruin his reputation.

Ghosn's hopes were shattered the next day, when he was arrested again. This time the charge was aggravated breach of trust, one of the most serious white-collar criminal charges in Japan. The charges related to Ghosn's relationship with Khaled Juffali, the Saudi Arabian businessman who had bailed Ghosn out of a financial jam during the financial crisis of 2008. The prosecutors alleged that Ghosn had paid back his debt to Juffali through business deals with Nissan. Ghosn's lawyers hoped that Juffali would issue a public statement confirming that he had performed legitimate work for Nissan, but the Saudi billionaire initially kept silent, worried about being dragged into the case.

Ghosn confronted his lawyer: Where was the plan to get him out of jail? Unfortunately, Otsuru's responses sounded like a broken record: he had urged Ghosn to cooperate because he feared that the prosecutors would escalate charges to breach of trust. That was the case now, and in his experience, it meant that bail would be impossible.

"If you want to get out, you need to confess," Otsuru told Ghosn. After he got out, Ghosn could try to retract his confession at trial, saying he had confessed only to get bail. The idea seemed idiotic to Ghosn. If he confessed, everyone would assume that he was guilty, and he would be finished as a businessman. Also, if he was willing to lie about a confession, why would the judge believe him when he said he was innocent? But most of all, doing so would mean surrendering. For a man like Ghosn, it was akin to putting one knee on the ground, handing his enemy his sword, and saying, "Do whatever you want with me."

And so Ghosn celebrated Christmas alone. By then, he had been moved to a room near the infirmary that was slightly more spacious and had a Western-style bed. He still had no view of the outside world and found the cell both claustrophobic and mind-numbingly dull.

Ghosn was allowed out of his cell for a thirty-minute period on weekdays at 8:00 a.m. The outdoor exercise area was on the roof of the prison, with a chain-link fence overhead. The inmates were allowed to pace back and forth in a concrete area roughly the size of their cell, but at least they got a view of the sky. On weekends and holidays, he was locked in his cell all day. When it rained, he also stayed indoors, as he had nothing to cover his head and was worried about getting sick.

Banned from talking to his relatives, Ghosn received information through old-fashioned letters, most of which were carried by the diplomats. "You are my ray of sunshine, my light, my balance, my pillar," Carole wrote in a December 27 letter to her husband. "I want you to stay strong because I need you and I can't live without you." Ghosn wasn't even allowed to hold the letters. He could only read them through the glass against which the diplomats held them.

Without a watch, Ghosn lost track of time. He couldn't tell if it was 6:00 p.m. or 9:00 p.m. For him, that deprivation was a form of torture. He had lived a life with a schedule packed full with back-to-back engagements; he had always been on the move. To pass the time, his family sent him books by Dan Brown and Harlan Coben. He didn't want any of the more intellectual history books he was used to reading. His family also sent him books of sudoku puzzles.

From the confines of his cell, Ghosn wondered if this was the end. He didn't see how he was going to convince the prosecutors that he was innocent, and the odds against a not-guilty verdict were so long, they might as well be infinite. Ghosn had always prided himself on rational thinking, and a rational man would say that he was likely to spend a considerable chunk of time behind bars.

But confessing, surrendering, or yielding to an outcome—that was not him, he thought. That was not his family, either. Ghosns had endured worse places on earth—including other jails. There was always a way out. He would just have to find it. He also knew, from the ambassador, that his family was trying to marshal support for him, and that gave him strength.

In the media, however, Ghosn was being ripped to shreds. The public image of the savvy executive that he had carefully crafted and curated over the years was gone. In addition to the criminal charges, the press covered the multimillion-dollar residences Nissan had bought for Ghosn in Rio and Beirut, how the auto titan had used the Nissan jet to fly to places where Nissan had little business, and the tens of thousands of dollars that Nissan had paid Ghosn's sister each year for her supposed advice for the past decade and a half, despite the Japanese carmaker's finding no evidence that she had done any work.[*]

The end-of-year holiday in the detention center was terrible. Staff was reduced, which meant that inmates couldn't take their thirty-minute walk on the roof in the morning. Meals were served through a hatch in the door. Visits were banned. As December turned into January, Ghosn fell ill with a high fever. His lawyers arrived at the jail to visit him but were turned away. His daily interrogations were suspended.

A French diplomat called Carole in the middle of the night to tell her about his condition. She panicked. She had never known Ghosn to be ill. Immediately she feared the worst. Carlos was going to die, and

---

[*] Ghosn said these reports were part of a campaign to sully his reputation. He said the houses in Rio and Beirut were provided by Nissan out of concerns for his security, and that all the people who needed to know at the company were informed. He said he didn't use company jets differently from other CEOs and that the money his sister received from Nissan was commensurate with the work she performed for the company.

nobody cared. She, too, developed a high fever, but to her great relief, Ghosn quickly recovered.

On the morning of January 8, Ghosn was taken to court to make his first public statement after almost fifty days in jail. He had pushed his lawyers to get him the opportunity. The hearing was a rare procedural move in Japan, where the accused asserts his constitutional right to hear the reasons for his detention. The right is rarely exercised because it almost never results in the release of the accused. But it allows the accused to make a public statement, and that was what was important to Ghosn.

The news that Ghosn would be speaking caused a stir. More than a thousand people entered a lottery for a shot at sitting in one of the fourteen seats available to the public. When he showed up in the courtroom at 10:30 that morning, Ghosn's appearance shocked the crowd. He looked like an old man, a shadow of his former self. He had lost weight; his suit hung loosely on him. Ghosn, whose grooming and attire were always impeccable, looked unkempt. His hair was noticeably grayer than it had been when he had been arrested. He arrived handcuffed, with a rope tied about his waist and plastic slippers on his feet.

In a brief speech, he provided a defense against the charges against him. Yes, the Saudi businessman, Juffali, had bailed him out of a financial jam, and yes, the Saudi had been in business with Nissan, but there was no connection between the two, he said. Juffali, Ghosn added, had performed legitimate work that had greatly benefited the Japanese carmaker.* On his allegedly underreported pay, he said that the prosecutors had misinterpreted his retirement papers. No amount had been agreed upon, and nothing had been paid. To hammer home his argu-

---

* In a statement on January 8, 2019, Juffali's company said bonus payments from Nissan were for legitimate business purposes and listed a number of services the company performed to support the Japanese carmaker in Saudi Arabia.

ment, he said that if he passed away tomorrow, Nissan would owe his family no additional cash.

"Your Honor, I am innocent," he said. "I have been wrongly accused and unfairly detained based on meritless and unsubstantiated accusations." The judge, Yuichi Tada, did not grant him bail. He ruled that Ghosn had been appropriately detained because he was a flight risk and could destroy evidence if he was released.

Carole was in Paris when she learned that his application for bail had been rejected. During the fifty days that her husband had already been in jail, she had kept a low profile, following Otsuru's instruction not to talk to the press or cause any stir. But it was clear that the lawyer's strategy wasn't working. Perhaps France could come to the rescue. After all, contrary to Nissan and Mitsubishi, which had stripped Ghosn of all his corporate titles immediately after the arrest, Renault still listed her husband as its chairman and CEO. And several French officials had stressed that he was presumed innocent until proven guilty.

On January 10, two days after Ghosn's appearance in court, Carole walked up to the doors of the Elysée Palace, located on the famed Rue du Faubourg Saint-Honoré, dotted with fashion stores. It was a bitterly cold Thursday morning. She handed over her passport to a guard, saying that she was there to deliver a personal letter to President Macron about the situation of her husband, Carlos Ghosn. The guard asked her to wait, then disappeared to make some phone calls. Carole waited for more than an hour in the cold. When he returned, he took her letter and promised he would deliver it safely to the secretariat of the president.

The letter elicited no response. By then, the French authorities were focused on Renault, not on Ghosn. One of France's biggest companies would not be run from a Japanese jail cell. Renault directors soon decided that it was time to part with Ghosn. The question was how to proceed.

At retirement, Ghosn was due more than €30 million between his pension, performance bonuses, and noncompete agreement. The last thing the French government wanted to do was sign off on an eight-figure check to a guy sitting in jail. Renault board members and executives huddled to discuss which one of them would go to Tokyo. The acting CEO, Thierry Bolloré, raised his hand. But what if, for any reason, the Japanese also arrested him? The company could not send its acting CEO.

They eventually agreed on Claudine Pons. The businesswoman ran a PR agency that had done sensitive work for Renault. She knew Ghosn well.

Pons flew to Japan. At the jailhouse she was taken to the same room where the ambassadors had met with Ghosn. The man she admired was on the other side of the thick glass partition. Their communication was formal and to the point. Ghosn was dressed in an elegant sweater and sat with his back straight. He still appeared to be the same executive she had known.

His eyes, however, jumped out at her. They were filled with darkness.

*　　*　　*

The World Economic Forum kicked off in Davos on January 22, 2019. Heads of state, economic pundits, and financial market luminaries congregated in the resort town surrounded by snowcapped mountains to discuss the state of the world and attempt to adjust the trajectory of human affairs. As it had been every year since 1971, the idea was for the participants to leave behind their earthly worries and gain some perspective in the rarefied heights of the Alpine retreat.

This year, however, the man who had come to symbolize globalization and incarnated the Davos spirit more than any other corporate leader was notably absent. For the first time in two decades, Carlos Ghosn was unable to attend.

Ahead of the forum, Ghosn's family had tried to rally support from the WEF founder, Klaus Schwab, and some other high-flying participants, but nothing had come of it. The snub had left Ghosn bitter. Despite his absence, he dominated the news from Davos on January 24.

On that day, at the crack of dawn, French finance minister Bruno Le Maire gave an outdoor interview to Bloomberg, shielded from the biting cold by a gray cashmere scarf. After answering questions on climate change, Le Maire announced that Ghosn had stepped down as chairman and CEO of Renault the night before.

After Pons's visit to the Kosuge jailhouse, Ghosn had signed his resignation letter. He had been careful to use language prepared by his lawyers and aimed at protecting his rights to his pension and performance-linked payments. It wasn't clear whether Renault would have to pay Ghosn part of the €30 million in the future, but the French government wanted to turn the page.

"The key is to move on," Le Maire said.

19

Scorched Earth

When the call came from the Elysée Palace, Jean-Dominique Senard couldn't refuse. The president of France wanted him to replace Carlos Ghosn as chairman of Renault. Senard wasn't looking for a job and the pay wasn't alluring. Capped at an annual €450,000, it amounted to a fraction of what he was making running Michelin, the tire maker.

Still, Senard felt a patriotic obligation to accept the assignment, a reflexive sensibility born out of his childhood as the son of a dutiful diplomat. The French government was deeply concerned. For years, Ghosn had said that he was the only one capable of running the odd pairing formed by Renault and Nissan. Since his arrest, joint projects had ground to a halt. Worse, the companies were at each other's throat. Nissan held Renault responsible for allowing Ghosn to amass so much power within the Alliance until his arrest. Renault accused Nissan of bloodlust in trying to find evidence against their former executive. The acrimonious path risked dire consequences for Renault. As much as their distaste for Ghosn had grown over the years, he kept the company relevant. Alone, the emblematic French company would be dwarfed in a global industry dominated by German, Asian, and US giants.

The French presidency gave Senard a twofold order of mission: "First pacify and then strengthen the Renault-Nissan Alliance."

On January 24, 2019, hours after Ghosn's resignation, Senard arrived at Renault's head office near Paris. His style was in sharp contrast to the taste for luxury and lofty manners that had evolved in his predecessor. He was going to be a man of the people and kill with relative kindness.

A week into his new job, Senard went to Amsterdam for his first Alliance meeting.

He watched as Renault and Nissan executives robotically went through PowerPoint presentations. Something was wrong. There was no interaction, no decisions were being made. Senard couldn't understand the presentations. Worse, it seemed as if even the people presenting had no idea what they were talking about, either.

That evening, Senard went for dinner with Hiroto Saikawa, the CEO of Nissan. The conversation moved to strategy, and the Frenchman candidly brought up the issue of merging their companies. The project had been put on standby by Ghosn's arrest. How about relaunching it at some point in the future? That would be one possible solution, Saikawa said. But pushing for one could also end up shattering the relationship entirely. Be careful, he warned.

Ten days later, Senard boarded an Air France flight for his first trip to Japan. Before he managed to disembark from the aircraft, he was mobbed by Japanese reporters asking whether he would be Nissan chairman. As chairman of Renault and under the terms of the Alliance, Senard was entitled to claim Nissan's chairmanship. Senard decided to pick his battles. He would play the long game and try to build trust with the Japanese.

In the weeks that followed, he announced a number of concessions.

First, he would settle for the title of vice-chairman at Nissan.

Second, Senard would scrap RNBV, the Dutch company that managed the Alliance. The structure had become toxic. Nissan's internal investigation had uncovered how RNBV's budget had been used by Ghosn to fund a number of extravagances and charitable flourishes.

To replace RNBV, Senard announced the creation of an operational Alliance board. The new steering committee would include four members: him and the CEOs of Renault, Nissan, and Mitsubishi. Decisions would be made unanimously. That new structure—and the fact everything was to be done by consensus—meant that Renault gave up the

casting vote it had held until now at RNBV. The Japanese side hailed
the new setup. "This is a big step forward for Nissan," Saikawa said.
"RNBV traditionally has had something more of a biased balance.
[. . .] This is a true partnership on equal footing."

Senard deflected any questions from the press regarding a merger.
This wasn't the right time to discuss this, he said.

Little by little, the ice thawed. Renault and Nissan executives began
talking to one another again, and some joint projects resumed.

But progress was very slow, and Senard was preoccupied with what
lay ahead. As Michelin chief, he had seen how Chinese companies had
muscled in on the tire market, doubling their share of sales in Europe
in just a few years. Chinese cars were now first rate, and the Frenchman feared the looming competitive threat. On top of that, keeping
up in the race to develop electric vehicles and self-driving technology
required gigantic wherewithal. Senard was convinced that if Renault
and Nissan remained two separate, midsize carmakers, they would fall
behind.

There was something else: Nissan's financial performance had hit a
rough patch. Their executives blamed Ghosn's strategy of aggressively
pursuing more sales, particularly in the United States. Regardless of
the reason behind it, the situation was worsening by the month. Contrary to what Senard had said at the press conference in Japan, he now
felt that Renault and Nissan should at least consider the option of a
merger as one possible solution to their woes.

On April 11, Senard hosted Saikawa in Paris to toast the twentieth
anniversary of the Alliance. Ghosn had commissioned a book and a
documentary to commemorate the event, but the projects had been
abandoned in the wake of his arrest. A running joke inside Renault
had been that they should hold the party at Versailles. Instead, Senard chose somewhere more modest: the Renault showroom on the
Champs-Elysées. It was a confidential affair, with big boards propped
up against the ground-floor windows to prevent reporters from looking in.

The next day, still in Paris, Senard broached the topic of a merger with Saikawa. By this stage, Senard's relationship with Saikawa had blossomed. "Jean-Dominique, you're like my older brother," Saikawa had told the Frenchman during one of their many conversations. In Senard's view, the conversation was merely a continuation of their January discussion in Amsterdam. The new company, Senard explained, would be evenly split between shareholders of Renault and Nissan, with a roughly equal number of directors from each side. The Nissan chief listened politely.

Later in April, Nissan said it would miss its profit target for the second time in as many months, with executives again blaming Ghosn's strategy. Shortly thereafter, several media reported on the merger overture made by Senard. At Nissan, the Frenchman was portrayed as a liar, because he had said in March that merger talks were not on the agenda. Senard was flummoxed. The only conclusion he could see was that people at Nissan were leaking to the press to make him look like a liar. He felt they were trying to kill the Alliance by playing on Nissan's fear of a merger.

He rang up Saikawa and accused the Nissan CEO of sacrificing him to the Japanese and global press to deflect attention from the company's poor financial performance—and kill any chance of a merger.

"Listen, I know exactly what you've done," Senard told the Nissan chief. "That's not fair."

For the Frenchman, the incident confirmed what he increasingly suspected: Saikawa wasn't fully in command at Nissan. He was sure that the leak had come from a group of Nissan executives around him who opposed the Alliance, including Hari Nada.

*   *   *

Senard found himself in an untenable position. Not only was Renault not recognized as the dominant partner in the Alliance, despite owning nearly half of Nissan, it wasn't even treated as an equal.

So when a call came in May from Fiat Chrysler's chairman, John Elkann, Senard leaped at a golden opportunity. Elkann wanted to know if

Renault would be interested in a tie-up. The Alliance and Fiat Chrysler had discussed one during Ghosn's time. Why not revive those talks
now? Senard was interested. By combining Renault and Fiat Chrysler,
Senard had an opportunity to create a behemoth that would dwarf the
Japanese leg of the Alliance. With Fiat Chrysler by its side, Renault
might be able to shoehorn Nissan into a single company. The French
government, which had suggested exploring this exact deal when
he'd taken the job several months earlier, would almost certainly be
supportive.

It was the kind of poker move that could solve many of his problems.

Senard agreed to open talks. Renault's annual shareholder meeting
was about a month away and the two men got to work with the hope
of announcing a deal by that date. The Frenchman decided not to tell
Nissan, where recent events had underscored that any sensitive documents would find their way into the press. Nissan could be invited to
join the conversation later, once the deal was announced. The two sides
hired lawyers and bankers and negotiations progressed quickly. Elkann and Senard met half a dozen times in Paris and Turin for working meetings. They kept up a constant dialogue on WhatsApp.

On May 24, with an agreement almost in place, Senard made the
short trip over to Bercy to inform the French government. Finance
Minister Bruno Le Maire told the Renault chairman that he would
look at the deal when it arrived on his desk. But, he added, any deal
would have to be endorsed by Nissan. The French government had
learned during its fight with Nissan in 2015 that you surprised the
Japanese at your own peril.

The following day, reports appeared in the press that Renault and
Fiat Chrysler were discussing a tie-up. Nissan was blindsided and Japanese executives were dumbfounded. Could this be true? The idea that
you would negotiate a merger without speaking to your partner of
twenty years? It seemed outrageous. On the evening of May 26, however, Fiat Chrysler officially proposed merging with Renault, and Senard informed Nissan executives that what they had read in the press
was true.

A few days later, Senard flew to Japan to explain his vision of the proposed merger with Fiat Chrysler to Saikawa. Over dinner, he said the merger could help Nissan in the United States—where Chrysler was performing strongly—without threatening its dominant position in Asia. Why not join the deal?

Saikawa didn't give a response that evening. It came instead on June 3, just as Renault directors were preparing to sign off on the merger agreement. Spurred by Nada and other executives who remained hostile to the Alliance, the Japanese CEO waved a big red flag, saying that the proposal being discussed by Renault and Fiat Chrysler would require a fundamental review of the existing relationship between Nissan and Renault. The implied threat was that if Renault wanted a new partner, Nissan might want a divorce. Saikawa's statement had a chilling effect on the French government, whose support Senard needed to push through the deal. The Renault chairman opted to postpone the vote on Fiat Chrysler's merger offer for another twenty-four hours.

Elkann's offer for Renault had been open for two weeks now and the young financier was losing patience. When Senard finally convened his board, he asked for a show of hands to see who supported the deal. Nissan representatives said they needed more time to review the proposal and would abstain. The director representing the French state, Martin Vial, left the room to confer with his boss, the French finance minister, about what to do. During the break, some directors ordered sushi and pizza. When Vial finally came back in, more than an hour later, he looked somber. The minister was due to travel to Japan the following day and had asked for a five-day delay so that he could talk about the deal with his Japanese counterpart, Vial told directors. The finance minister had made it clear that he wanted Renault to have the support of Nissan, and it just didn't look like they had it, at least not explicitly.

Senard was furious. He couldn't possibly put the deal to a vote with his two biggest shareholders, the French government and Nissan, refusing to back it. He asked Vial whether he had thought through the consequences of the state's actions. "We're taking a huge risk," he told

him. For Senard, the French state's decision was akin to putting Renault's future in the hands of the Japanese carmaker. As Senard weighed
his next move, he received a message from Elkann. Fiat Chrysler had
withdrawn its offer. The deal was off.

In the days that followed, Senard considered resigning. He conferred with Renault's directors, suppliers, and high-ranking French
officials. But after two days of contemplation, Senard decided to stay.
The Alliance was a mess and he needed to sort it out.

*   *   *

A juiced-up Senard got back to the job he had been brought in to do
initially: restore peace within the Alliance. There were problems in
both camps. At Renault, Senard felt that the CEO, Thierry Bolloré,
and some of his underlings had an unhealthy obsession with opposing
the so-called nationalists at Nissan. At Nissan, the group led by Nada
was similarly focused on waging a war for control of the Alliance.
What's more, a number of top managers at the Japanese company were
far more focused on managing the fallout from the Ghosn investigation than on running the company.

In June, Kelly gave his first interview since being arrested to *Bungei
Shunju*, a highbrow Japanese monthly magazine. His comments were
explosive. "If Saikawa wasn't arrested, I shouldn't be arrested," the
American said. The magazine printed a copy of one of the agreements to pay Ghosn in secret with Saikawa's signature alongside Kelly's. Kelly also told the magazine that Saikawa had known about the
houses purchased for Ghosn in Brazil and Lebanon. Not only that, but
in 2013 Saikawa had requested Nissan's assistance to buy a property
of his own. He wanted to buy an apartment in central Tokyo, but he
was short on cash. Kelly said that Nissan had adjusted the date when
Saikawa cashed in his stock appreciation rights, a bonus linked to Nissan's stock price. By moving the date by a week, Saikawa had collected
an extra $430,000 and bought his apartment soon after receiving the

money. The interview had a devastating impact on Nissan. The company was pointing the finger at Ghosn, saying he had treated the company as his personal ATM.

Now Saikawa, his successor in the CEO's seat, was being painted with the same brush.

Senard was losing patience. The financial performance of the companies was abysmal, and he had made no progress on the mandate given to him by the French government. Shareholders and government officials were telling him that he was taking too much time to pacify the alliance. Some rare good news was that the Japanese carmaker was preparing to overhaul its corporate bylaws to create a new board structure. The Nissan board was still dominated by directors who also held executive positions and were therefore loath to criticize themselves. Replacing them with independent directors, Senard hoped, would help create a genuine board capable of holding management to account and focusing their attention on the company.

In late June, Senard flew to Japan to attend the Nissan shareholder meeting, at which the board composition change would be voted on. It was another gnarly experience. When it was time to head to the venue, Senard strode through the lobby of his hotel and into a waiting black van. When he arrived at Nissan's HQ and stepped out of the vehicle, he realized to his horror that he had traveled in a Toyota, Nissan's biggest rival. He made sure the mistake wouldn't be repeated for the return journey, but it was too late. The press had already seized on the embarrassing moment, again making him look like an enemy of Nissan.

At the meeting, things only got worse. One after the other, Nissan shareholders lambasted the Frenchman with withering remarks, accusing him of trying to subjugate the Japanese company. "French people have a smile on their face," one shareholder said. "But they have hidden intentions. They are really sly. Mr. Senard, can you behave as a Nissan director rather than as the Renault chairman? That's my question. Can you do that? Can you be fair as a Nissan director?"

Senard bristled. "I would like to remind you that since I arrived,

I did everything I can to smooth the relationship of an Alliance that I found in a much worse state than I thought," he said. "I have done everything I could."

Although he had no proof, Senard suspected that the Toyota incident was a trap to further discredit him. Some people in Japan clearly wanted him to fail and appeared ready to resort to anything to bring him down.

But despite the avalanche of scorn at the shareholder meeting and the Toyota snafu, Senard was relieved. After prolonged debates, shareholders approved the resolution aimed at revamping the board and giving it more clout.

As June turned to July, Senard became convinced that he had to do something radical. The leadership at Nissan and Renault—who were thwarting all his proposals and making his life a misery—would have to go.

In Nissan's new board, he would have a powerful new ally to regain the initiative.

*   *   *

After returning from his summer vacation, Senard sprang into action. Discredited by Kelly's revelations, weakened by Nissan's poor financial results, and deprived of support from the rank and file, it was clear Saikawa had to go.

On September 9, Nissan directors gathered in the cavernous boardroom on the twenty-first floor, dubbed the Wheel for its circular layout. Senard, Saikawa, and the other directors took their seats at the oval table. Surrounding them at desks laid out like a university lecture hall were a phalanx of executives and administrative personnel. Saikawa was told to step out while other directors decided his fate. Some directors proposed giving him a grace period, but Senard argued that the CEO should be shown the door now. When Saikawa returned, the directors delivered their verdict and demanded his immediate resignation. Saikawa accepted.

In a further blow, directors slashed his retirement payout from $15 million down to $3 million.

The board wasn't done. Over the course of September, Senard and other directors received a series of anonymous letters containing serious accusations against the Japanese executive class. According to the whistleblowers, Nada and other Nissan executives had played an active role in arranging Ghosn's controversial remunerations. Yet Nada continued to influence Nissan's investigation into those events, the letter said. In addition, some press reports described how Nada had allegedly collected $300,000 thanks to the same date-change trick used by Saikawa for his stock options. Nada, according to some reports, had also sought to redact his name from several sections of Nissan's investigation report in a bid to minimize his role in Ghosn's alleged wrongdoing. He had also refused to submit to interviews with an outside law firm investigating the extra funds that he and Saikawa had pocketed.

The set of letters and the press reports criticized the Nissan probe, which was being run by Nissan employees, assisted by Nissan's longtime law firm, in a trial in which Nissan was also a defendant. Also denounced was Nissan's notable selectivity of the targets. It was open season on Ghosn and Kelly, but people who had looked the other way—or even cooperated—seemed to be protected.

On October 8, the Nissan board convened to choose a successor to Saikawa. Minutes into the meeting, Thierry Bolloré, the Renault CEO, who reported directly to Senard, said that he wished to read a declaration. Bolloré recounted the various accusations contained in the anonymous letters and press reports. The message was clear to all the directors present: Nada and his like-minded acolytes had to go. The board decided to limit Nada's responsibilities but keep him as a special adviser ahead of Ghosn's trial. Because of his role assisting Tokyo prosecutors, Nada couldn't be evicted. His demotion was the best Senard and some of the other directors could achieve.

Back in France, Senard trained his sights on Bolloré himself. He felt that the Renault CEO was also culpable for the cross-continental air of persistent acrimony. When Bolloré refused to resign, Senard decided to convene Renault's board and put the CEO's ouster to a vote. "The brutality and the totally unexpected character of what is happening are stupefying," Bolloré told a French newspaper ahead of the vote. His departure was confirmed. Senard told the press that he regretted having to fire Bolloré, but he had little choice. "The Alliance needs a bit of fresh air," the chairman said. "It's nothing personal."

As 2019 drew to an end, Senard contemplated the scorched earth around him. He had arrived thinking the Alliance was a troubled but ultimately friendly partnership between two carmakers that wanted to work together. What he had found was nothing but palace intrigue and plots, twisted loyalties and tensions. He had intended to rule with a benevolent disposition, but the state of affairs made that impossible.

Senard had finally managed to bring back a semblance of peace within the Alliance but at enormous human cost. Over the past month, the CEOs of both Nissan and Renault had been fired. Also gone since Senard's arrival were numerous senior executives such as Hitoshi Kawaguchi at Nissan and Mouna Sepehri at Renault. Of the top ten managers with senior roles at RNBV, eight had now left the company.

Anyone who had worked closely with Ghosn had been disappeared.

20

Inside Out

Early in 2019, a Nissan employee with unusual sympathy for Ghosn's predicament went to speak frankly with Carole at her Paris apartment. He was vehement that Ghosn had made poor choices of lawyers.

"This has to stop now, or Carlos will be in prison forever," he said.

"What do you suggest?" Carole asked, exhausted and desperate.

"Carlos needs to switch to Junichiro Hironaka, who is the right person." The Nissan employee, who was very much in Ghosn's corner, had already spoken to the lawyer, who had agreed.

"Okay," Carole said. "I'm going to Lebanon tomorrow, and I want to have a remote meeting with Hironaka if Carlos's lawyer in Lebanon approves."

A call was organized between Hironaka and Carole. Swiftly, Carole introduced him to Ghosn; Ghosn asked to meet him in person and made a decision instantly to go with him. Otsuru had been the worst possible choice, and the switch brought a welcome breath of fresh air, or at least hope. Hironaka was the sort of defense lawyer you might see on TV, the closest thing Japan had to the famed O. J. Simpson attorney Johnnie Cochran. Hironaka even had a made-for-TV nickname, "The Razor," for his ability to slice apart the prosecution's case in the courtroom.

Hironaka was in his seventies, and told Ghosn that by the time the legal process ended—in around five years' time—he might be too old to properly defend him. Two other lawyers were brought on board to assist him, and their first piece of advice to Ghosn amounted to an about-face in advice after the obliging Otsuru. "Don't open your mouth," they told their new client. Japan's laws give the authorities wide berth to detain and question people suspected of crimes. There was little the new lawyers could do about that. But Ghosn was under no obligation to answer any of the prosecutors' questions. Ghosn had signed dozens of affidavits that were written in Japanese during the first round of questioning. There would be no more of that.

One member of the new team was a US-trained criminal defense lawyer named Takashi Takano, who sported a full beard and flat caps. He came across as a bit of a hippie, but Ghosn was reassured by Takano's self-confidence. "I'll get you out, but you have to work with me," Takano said. For the first time, Ghosn felt as though he was dealing with professional defense lawyers who had a plan to win and who wanted to fight the system instead of cozying up to the authorities.

The mood in the Ghosn camp was improving. A Lebanese court had ordered Nissan to hand the keys of the pink house to the Ghosns. Carole could once again take up residence there. Meanwhile, Anthony was taking steps to gather bail funds. To that end, he transferred €4.8 million from one of his dad's bank accounts in New York to another one in Lebanon. Though it had been a mere mirage in the time of Otsuru, bail now seemed a possibility, and the family wanted to be ready.

The new team's work quickly began to pay off. At the end of February, two weeks after Hironaka was hired, the Tokyo judge granted Carole thirty minutes a day with Ghosn, and told Ghosn's legal team that she could travel to Japan without fear of being arrested. On February 25, she went to Kosuge to visit Ghosn in jail for the first time. In the lobby, she saw other families visiting. Some of the men were heavily tattooed, something most closely associated in Japan with members of Yakuza gangs. Her eyes lingered on the children's grave expressions. She was led to the tenth floor, then down a long gray corridor to a tiny room. She sat down, flanked by two guards.

A few seconds later, Ghosn was brought in by another two guards through a steel door on the other side of the glass. His skin was yellow, and his face was gaunt. His hair was longer than usual and had become whiter. His eyes were tired and sunken.

Carole bit her lip and tried hard not to cry. She wanted Ghosn to see her smile. They talked about how much they missed each other and yearned for a regular life. Ghosn told her that he wished he had realized how happy he had been before his arrest and that he had put up a copy of an interview she had given to *Paris Match* by his bed. Throughout the visit, the guard wrote down everything they said. When the time was up, the two were told it was time to go. They put their palms together on opposite sides of the glass. Ghosn told her that he was very lucky to have love in his life and he was scared of losing her.

"Why do you say that?" Carole asked.

"Because I've lost everything else," Ghosn responded.

After that first visit, Carole went to see Ghosn every day for ten days. She bought Ghosn tangerines from the prison shop to add fruit to his diet, as well as cans of tuna and little chocolates with almonds that he liked. Carole, who had been at her wit's end at the start of the year, began to feel hopeful again. She could visit her husband, and Takano was racing to prepare a new bail request.

Bail works differently in Japan from the way it does in the United States. Offenders' movements aren't tracked by ankle monitors, and there is no probation officer assigned to check on them. The challenge is to satisfy the court that a suspect will not flee or manipulate witnesses if released. Takano knew how to create a set of conditions for Ghosn that would not only satisfy the court but also allow him to live with some degree of freedom. Takano proposed that Ghosn's home have a camera installed outside the door to monitor who went in and out. Ghosn would also have to go to his lawyer's office every weekday from 9:00 a.m. to 5:00 p.m., which he would do anyway to prepare for trial, but it also meant that there was an officer of the court to monitor him. He would also have to surrender his smartphone, using only a simple cell phone and court-approved electronic devices. He would have internet access only at his lawyer's office and all calls to and from that cell phone would be logged. Ghosn would also pledge not to contact anyone connected with his case. The application was filed on the last day of February. Less than a week later, bail was granted.

Ghosn posted bail of around $9 million in cash. After 108 days behind bars, he walked out of the Tokyo Detention Center on March 6, 2019, at 4:30 p.m. Journalists from every news outlet in the country and the foreign media corps were waiting to capture the moment the auto titan finally got out of jail. First a trolley was wheeled out carrying a stack of blankets, which was loaded into a waiting van. That was the cue for the shooters to begin snapping. Then came half a dozen jail officers flanking Ghosn's lawyer, Takano. The cameras began snapping more furiously.

But where was Ghosn?

Surrounded by wardens, all in dark uniforms and wearing medical face masks, was a group of what appeared to be workmen. One of them wore a light blue cap, dark blue overalls, an orange reflective vest, thick-rimmed glasses, and a face mask.

Was that Ghosn? It was hard to tell through the mask.

By the time the group had walked over to a small Suzuki van with a ladder on top, the press had figured it out. Through Tokyo streets and via helicopters above, reporters chased Ghosn's van for more than an hour until it stopped at Takano's office, where more press cameras captured Ghosn's exit from the vehicle. This time he had a suit jacket over his overalls.

Ghosn's attempt at disguise was the talk of the town. The next morning, news programs instructed people how to re-create Ghosn's outfit with products bought on Amazon.

The plan to keep Ghosn's departure a secret had obviously failed. Takano, who had suggested the deception as a way to give Ghosn some breathing space, apologized to Ghosn and his family. He was worried that he had humiliated Ghosn in a fashion unbefitting his past career. Ghosn couldn't have cared less. He was simply grateful to be out.

That evening, Ghosn and Carole went to their new home, a five-hundred-square-foot one-bedroom apartment near central Shibuya. Finding a landlord willing to rent to a criminal defendant, especially one as famous as Ghosn, had been a challenge. A horde of media was permanently stationed outside wherever he stayed. In the end, a woman who worked at the French embassy had agreed to rent them a small apartment. Carole had tried to decorate the place and make it as cozy as possible before Ghosn's release. Ghosn and Carole stood in the hallway, hugging silently for several minutes.

One of the first things Ghosn did was take a shower for a very long time. In jail, he could shower only twice a week. The towels there were so thin—a measure to prevent people from hanging themselves with them—that he could never get himself dry. He picked the thickest towel he could find.

*   *   *

On the outside, Ghosn traveled to his lawyer's office, where he could use the internet and communicate with his family on weekdays. He would reserve Monday and Wednesday for personal things, and on Tuesday, Thursday, and Friday he would pore through documents, preparing his defense with the help of a translator. In the evenings, he watched films with his wife. Snuggling up on the sofa, Carole sometimes felt as though they were playing the role of a young married couple.

On March 9, Ghosn celebrated his sixty-fifth birthday with his three daughters and Carole in the private room of a nearby hotel. He had been through a traumatic experience, but he was out of jail and hoping to open a new chapter in his life.

Scenes from Ghosn's life outside Kosuge were frequently splashed on the front pages of Japanese tabloids. He had been seen going out to dinner in restaurants and taking long strolls in a park. He and Carole had bought bikes that they rode around town.

As the weeks passed, the theme faded, but not the Ghosn story. More and more articles focused on what reporters called "the Oman route." Tokyo prosecutors had broadened their investigation and were now looking into why Nissan had paid tens of millions of dollars to its Oman-based distributor, SBA. Prosecutors suspected that the money Nissan had sent to SBA had transited through SBA's general manager, Divyendu Kumar, and landed in Ghosn's pocket. They had information suggesting that some of the money had been used to acquire shares in startups through a fund called Shogun Investments and also to buy a yacht, which was now in Carole's name.

Ghosn said that all the payments by Nissan to SBA had been legitimate dealer incentives and that neither he nor his family had benefited from them in any way. None of the CEO Reserve payments to SBA were discretionary, he added, and all of them had followed stringent internal procedures involving several high-ranking executives. Furthermore, the amounts were part of an appropriate and reasonable strategy to expand Nissan's business in the Middle East.

Anthony, who managed Shogun Investments and had always assumed that the cash he invested had come from his father, had only recently learned that in fact it had come from Divyendu Kumar. Earlier in the year, Anthony had flown to Beirut to meet with Kumar and Ghosn's Lebanese lawyer, Carlos Abou Jaoude. As the chairman of Good Faith Investments, Kumar was the source of the $27 million that had been sent to the United States for Anthony to invest. Anthony had been unnerved, but he trusted his father enough that he had figured there must be a good explanation.

As for the 120-foot *Shachou*, Carole remembered Ghosn asking her to sign some papers related to the boat the previous summer, but she hadn't asked any questions. She was unaware of the source of the funds and had no idea that she owned a yacht, at least on paper.

The Tokyo prosecutors' headway on the Oman route stemmed from a key source: the hard drive that Nissan had found in the offices of its main distributor in Beirut on the day of Ghosn's arrest and handed over to Japanese authorities. With its thousands of files and emails, the hard drive had enabled prosecutors to piece together the alleged flow of money from individuals in Oman to Ghosn. To prosecutors, it was clear what had happened: Ghosn had paid Bahwan through bonuses from Nissan's coffers and received a kickback in return.

The Ghosn side fought to prevent the use of the hard drive by the prosecutors, arguing that it had been stolen and that the communications it contained were protected by attorney-client privilege. Nissan countered that its legal team had taken it with the explicit consent of both Amal Abou Jaoude and the local car distributor who owned the premises.

In Japan, the authorities had no qualms about using the material.

On April 3, Japan's *Yomiuri* newspaper and several other Japanese outlets reported that the Tokyo prosecutors were preparing to indict Ghosn again, this time for allegedly defrauding Nissan. Shortly after the reports were published, Ghosn took to Twitter to announce a press conference in a week's time. "I'm getting ready to tell the truth about what's happening," he wrote.

He then recorded a video message to be aired in case he was re-arrested. Wearing a white shirt and a dark suit, he sat at a desk with his hands clasped. He accused Nissan executives of "playing a very dirty game."

"This is about a plot. This is about a conspiracy. This is about backstabbing," he said, adding that he was innocent of the charges.

The next day, April 4, he was in bed when the doorbell rang. Carole looked over at the clock. It was 5:50 in the morning.

Ghosn went to the door in his pajamas. Standing outside were around twenty prosecutors. "Get dressed," they told Ghosn.

Carole panicked. She watched as Ghosn asked if he could take a book he was reading and a piece of chocolate. The prosecutors said no. Ghosn sought to put on a brave face. As he walked out, the press cameras were waiting to capture his latest arrest.

After Ghosn was carted away, some of the prosecutors stayed to search the apartment. Carole was still in her pajamas—a pair of pants and a camisole. She asked to change, but the prosecutors wouldn't allow her to be in a room alone. One of the women on the team of prosecutors shadowed her everywhere, even when she used the toilet.

The Japanese officials rifled through and took many of the papers in the house, including a book of letters that Ghosn had written to Carole while he was in prison. They took her phones, her computer, her tablet, and her Lebanese passport. They photographed the contents of her wallet, including her credit cards and a membership card for Barneys, a department store in New York.

Outraged, she confronted one of the prosecutors.

"Are you allowed to do this?" she asked.

"This is Japan," she was told simply.

That night, she slept on the sofa of her neighbor's apartment. The first stay in jail had been so hard for Ghosn, and he had been out for less than a month. Now he was caught in the jaws of Japan's judicial system again. How long would he be in this time?

The day after Ghosn's rearrest, Carole came to the conclusion that it would be safer to leave the country. Perhaps she could travel with her US passport, which the Japanese prosecutors hadn't taken. In the evening, the French ambassador, Laurent Pic, met her at the airport. They went through passport control without a hitch, and Carole boarded a plane to Paris. As the aircraft taxied toward the runway, she felt as though she were reenacting the escape scene from the movie *Argo*, in which a group of Americans escape Iran following the revolution there.

Days after she reached France, however, Japanese media reported that Tokyo prosecutors wanted to question her. They were casting a wider net and wanted to question her and Anthony about their knowledge of the so-called Oman route. For now, she and Anthony were regarded as witnesses. If she didn't return to Japan, prosecutors might consider her a suspect, which would complicate her efforts to secure another bail for Ghosn.

The week after Ghosn's rearrest, Carole flew back to Japan to meet with the Tokyo prosecutors. Asked about the source of the funds used to buy the yacht, she said she didn't know. They asked about meeting SBA's managing director, Kumar, in Lebanon and accused her of trying to manipulate testimonies in Ghosn's favor; she denied that any of that had happened.

Meanwhile, Ghosn was back at the Tokyo Detention Center; back to square one, sleeping, reading, and doing sudoku puzzles. Visits were stricter. Searching Carole's phone, prosecutors had found video messages that Ghosn had recorded during his first stint in jail and passed to his wife through the Lebanese ambassador. Now diplomats had to leave their phones at the detention center's entrance.

The interrogations resumed. This time, Ghosn followed orders from his new legal team not to say a word, not even hello. Ghosn had been told that the prosecutors were professionals at making people talk and that if he started with something, he might not be able to stop talking. There was a new prosecutor asking the questions this time, but Ghosn kept silent.

After more than a week of trying and failing to extract a word from Ghosn, the prosecutors turned back to Yoshitaka Seki, who had conducted the first round of interrogations. Seki again sought to cozy up to Ghosn. He tried to come at him from a more casual angle, asking what Ghosn thought about music. What kind of music did he like? Ghosn kept mum. "Or let's talk about sports?" When Ghosn sat in silence, Seki conveyed disappointment: "We can't even talk about that?"

Seki told Ghosn that he just wanted to get to the truth. "If you don't make a statement, you will be prosecuted with one-sided evidence," he said. "We don't want to prosecute without truth."

In the background, Ghosn's legal team was working feverishly to get Ghosn out before the annual Golden Week, which encompasses four national holidays. That year, Golden Week would be extended to mark the enthronement of a new emperor. During the ten-day break,

Ghosn would be locked in his cell without being able to walk on the roof of the prison each morning, and there would be no visits from lawyers and ambassadors. Again his food would be served through a hatch in the door. Ghosn's family was anguished over the mental torment and enduring trauma that would inflict on him. Pulling no punches, Takano accused prosecutors of torturing Ghosn by pressuring him for hours each day to answer their questions when he had clearly chosen to exercise his right to remain silent. On the opposite side, prosecutors were adamant that Ghosn should not be let out on bail, arguing that he might tamper with evidence. To back up their claims, they produced text messages from Carole's phone showing she had been in touch with people tied to the case. They also produced a letter Ghosn had written from jail a few months earlier, intended for his Lebanese lawyer, in which he suggested strong-arming a witness to obtain a favorable statement.

Takano countered with a statement from Carole denying the accusations and pledges from witnesses in Lebanon, Oman, and France promising that they would not contact Ghosn if he were released. But the bail application he filed on April 22 was denied.

The Japanese lawyer didn't give up. Days later, he submitted additional documents explaining that Ghosn's letter to his Lebanese lawyer was tantamount to an SOS by a desperate inmate who had lost faith in his previous legal team.

Takano was successful. Despite fierce opposition from the prosecutors, Ghosn was granted bail on April 25, two days before the start of the holiday break. Long after dark that night, he walked out of the Tokyo Detention Center for a second time and got into a black van. As the vehicle sped away, Takano told Ghosn about the bail conditions he had agreed to. As was the case the first time, Ghosn's communications and movements would be closely monitored to prevent his fleeing the country or tampering with evidence. He would have to keep a record of everyone he met as well as his internet use and telephone calls.

This time, however, there was an extra condition, which Takano had been told about only hours earlier: Ghosn would not be allowed to meet or communicate with Carole, who was considered a potential witness in the latest criminal charges. Ghosn issued a statement that night: "Restricting communications and contact between my wife and me is cruel and unnecessary."

21

War Gaming

Michael Taylor knew almost nothing about Carlos Ghosn when his cell phone rang in mid-2019 with a call from Beirut. The voice on the other end was an old client from his days working private security in Iraq after the 2003 US invasion. Taylor had once organized a convoy of SUVs and brawny guys armed to the teeth to take his client, a Lebanese insurance magnate, from Baghdad Airport to the Green Zone. Now, a decade and a half later, the executive needed his services again. For a friend.

Without mentioning Ghosn's name, the voice on the other end of the line explained that the person was being wrongfully detained in Japan. "He's a great guy," he told Taylor. Something had to be done to save him. Would Taylor be interested in providing assistance?

Square-jawed and still muscular at almost sixty, Taylor had been a military contractor and security operative since the 1980s. He was now a settled family man and beloved mentor in his community, one who had always maintained a weak spot for those who needed to be saved.

While he had been working in private security, his specialties had included rescuing hostages. As savvy as he was tough, he didn't need his contact to elaborate on what kind of assistance he had in mind.

From a quick Google search, Taylor surmised that the target had to be Carlos Ghosn. He had his own Lebanese connections. Taylor's wife also belonged to the tight-knit Maronite Christian community in

Lebanon. Her sister's husband was even a distant relative of Ghosn's mother; Taylor's wife had been to dinner at Ghosn's apartment in Paris some ten years earlier.

When the insurance magnate called again, he confirmed what Taylor already knew. He and a number of his friends in Lebanon were outraged by how the Japanese were treating Ghosn. They had all responded with fierce loyalty in the months that had followed the arrest, a movement of sorts led by Ghosn's wife, Carole, who was now banned from seeing her husband. Convinced of her husband's innocence, she had lobbied world leaders from US president Donald Trump to French president Emmanuel Macron, filed a complaint with Human Rights Watch about the way the Japanese authorities were treating her husband, and appeared on numerous TV broadcasts to plead his case.

The legal fight was also being quarterbacked from Beirut. Days after the arrest, the Lebanese lawyer Carlos Abou Jaoude resigned from his contract with Nissan to fight Ghosn's case, pulling all-nighters to coordinate the lawyers in Japan, France, and the United States. Others in Lebanon had pitched in to help sway public opinion and alter the narrative being pumped out by the media in Japan. The slogan "We Are All CARLOS GHOSN" was plastered across eighteen billboards across Beirut, ordered up by a local advertiser, Dany Kamal, whose hedge fund tycoon sister had hosted the Ghosns at her Lebanese chalet.

Reporters covering the case got briefings from Ghosn's friends on the defendant's down-to-earth honesty. They painted the portrait of a gracious man who loved home cooking and going for walks, had long stayed at a "humble beach house" when visiting Beirut, and was "simply the opposite of what the Japanese press is trying to portray him." The insurance executive was himself a member of a Facebook group called "Comité de Soutien à Monsieur Carlos GHOSN."

Carole had become increasingly distressed. A judge had refused to try all the charges against Ghosn concurrently, so just reaching an initial verdict could take up to five years. An appeal might take another five. Ghosn, who was sixty-five, might be a very old man before he could be back in Lebanon with her. Lobbying efforts were getting his Lebanese supporters nowhere. It was time for more direct action.

Would it be possible to escape? If it was, who could accomplish such a feat?

Ghosn's friends needed someone with the ingenuity to plan the job and the bold tenacity to believe he'd get away with it. They made some discreet calls to contacts in the global security sector, but no one would touch such a hot mission. Japan had security cameras everywhere, and Ghosn was one of the most newsworthy and recognizable criminal defendants on the planet. The solution, as it often did for problems in Ghosn's Beirut circle, emerged at a dinner party.

The insurance executive was having dinner with a real estate tycoon and his wife, when conversation turned to their trapped friend. The real estate tycoon's wife suddenly remembered that one of her childhood friends was married to a guy who had been involved in some hair-raising rescues. "Wait," she said. "Why didn't I think of Mike?"

The insurance executive volunteered to call Michael Taylor.

*   *   *

For an American, Michael Taylor had an unusually tight bond with Lebanon. He had been one of the first US soldiers deployed to the country after the assassination of the Lebanese president-elect in 1982, the ensuing Israeli invasion, and some of the fiercest fighting to follow. When the US embassy in Beirut was bombed on April 18, 1983, killing sixty-three people, he had survived only because he was across the street buying orange juice.

During that time, Taylor had met his wife, Lamia. They were both out one evening at the yacht club in Jounieh, a small town to the north of Beirut. Lamia had accompanied a friend who knew several US Army personnel. The two quickly started dating, and Taylor began work as a private contractor training the Lebanese Christian forces.

Taylor took that experience back to the United States. In 1985, when the couple moved to Massachusetts, he worked for several security companies. In 1988, he and a partner established North America Security Consultants before he struck out on his own.

Starting in 1988, he worked as an undercover agent in a US investigation into international money laundering and hashish trafficking. The operation culminated with the seizure of more than six thousand pounds of hash with a street value of more than $100 million. In 1992, Taylor helped the United States with an investigation into a scheme to forge and distribute counterfeit $100 bills that involved people in Lebanon and Iran.

Over the next two decades, Taylor built a reputation as the go-to person for resolving seemingly unsolvable security situations, serving an impressive roster of corporate clients including ABC, Delta Air Lines, and 20th Century Fox. He also worked for the US government, both as an informant for US security agencies and as a subcontractor on various projects. Among the most notable subcontracting work he did was during the war in Iraq, where he trained local forces and provided weapons maintenance and bookkeeping services. He had also worked on the rescue of *New York Times* reporter David Rohde from the Taliban in Afghanistan and other daring operations.

Still, Taylor had a seeming propensity for taking on shady projects, with numerous bizarre episodes checkering his past. In the late 1990s, he had planted marijuana in the car of a client's estranged wife in an apparent bid to discredit the woman during a custody dispute. He eventually pleaded guilty to misdemeanor charges of breaking and entering and making a false police report.

In 1999, Taylor's name was linked to a scandal in Boston Harbor that involved a woman lifting her top and exposing her breasts during a boat cruise. Captured by a photographer, the scene landed on the front page of the *Boston Herald* the next day and led to the resignation of the head of the Massachusetts Port Authority. The chief suspected that the incident had been orchestrated by Taylor, whose security firm had been turned down for a lucrative consulting contract for the port. Taylor denied any involvement.

Years later, in 2008, Taylor became the head coach of the football team of Lawrence Academy, a preppy Boston-area public school that quickly developed a reputation for one-sided victories. He would pay tuition for talented inner-city kids, helping him to assemble a feared team, with several players weighing over three hundred pounds. In one year alone, more than half a dozen Lawrence Academy players were awarded scholarships to play football at Division 1 college programs on scholarships—something completely abnormal for the teams in that league.

In 2010, Taylor made national headlines when an opposing team forfeited a game rather than risk the safety of its players against his team. The following year, he left the position. Shortly after his departure, the school was stripped of two league titles won during his tenure for violating scholarship protocols and banned from postseason play for three years. Taylor maintained that he had done nothing wrong.

Time and again, Taylor was accused of rule breaking, but he always appeared to have a good excuse. What had happened was never his fault, or at the very least he was never held to account for it.

For all the trouble Taylor had been involved in, everyone at home knew his name. He helped neighbors with snow shoveling and home repairs. When one ex-employee fell on hard times after her husband was injured at work, Taylor appeared with a check to cover her mortgage payments, no questions asked. He gave away money so liberally that his personal assistant took to lying to him about his bank balance, saying it was smaller than it really was.

Taylor's Teflon coating, however, had started to wear in recent years, as he had been drawn once more into intrigue in the Middle East. In 2012, he was charged with bribing a Pentagon official to pass on secret bidding information that was instrumental in winning military contracts in Afghanistan worth $54 million. In addition, he was charged with trying to bribe an FBI agent to make the case go away.

He sat in a county jail for fourteen months, awaiting trial. Then he received an offer from the prosecution: if he would plead guilty to just two charges, they would drop sixty others and release him immediately, in time to join his family for Thanksgiving.

While inside, he "could not exercise, go outdoors or even see day-light," he wrote years later, adding that he "could only meet his family through plexiglass or on a video screen, while shackled at the waist, feet and hands." He had taken the plea "only to avoid a longer stay in the brutal jail."

By the time he got home, he was jaded and overweight. He had put on thirty-seven pounds. He was in such bad shape that he couldn't walk down his driveway to pick up the mail without becoming short of breath. His business, built over seventeen years, was gone. And so was his faith in the US justice system—that from a man whose work-places were always papered over with the Stars and Stripes and whose wife said that the national anthem is his favorite song. He slowly re-built himself. With help from his sons, the wounded patriot started a vitamin water business and set himself to move forward with his life. Vitamin water wasn't going to keep Taylor's blood pumping, though.

*   *   *

On July 1, 2019, weeks after receiving the call from the insurance exec-utive, Taylor flew to Beirut, where he met with Carole Ghosn.

Everything about Ghosn's situation sounded familiar. Carole told him about her husband's stay in jail, how he had been held in a cell alone and could go outside for only thirty minutes a day. The pros-ecutors were now going after his family, she said, meaning that her husband couldn't have any contact with her or his son, Anthony. She called it "hostage justice."

If Taylor was going to extract Ghosn from Japan, he would need a team he could trust with his life. On July 8, Taylor's youngest son, Pe-ter, flew to Tokyo to meet Ghosn. The twenty-seven-year-old brought a present from one of Ghosn's friends, a DVD of the complete series of *Game of Thrones*.

Peter recognized how concerned Ghosn was about the way the prosecution was harming his reputation. Having set up a marketing firm in Beirut only that year, Peter offered to help with search engine optimization, so that sympathetic articles would rank higher in internet searches.

In addition to Peter, Taylor recruited an old friend from the battlefields of the Middle East. George-Antoine Zayek, a former Christian militiaman, had fought alongside Taylor in Lebanon in the 1980s. After Zayek had been shot multiple times in the leg, a doctor had told him he would need to have it amputated. Taylor had helped him get an operation in the United States. Zayek had then started to work for Taylor's security company and in the 2000s had been his operations director in Iraq. Jack Holly, a retired Marine Corps colonel who ran the US civilian logistics operation, called Zayek "the most pure gunslinger I've been around."

But although Taylor trusted his son and Zayek, his sharply trained eye saw a potentially fatal weakness in the operation: the Beirut rumor mill. Chatter traveled faster there than anywhere he'd worked before or since. Out of nowhere, Ghosn's friends started offering Taylor unsolicited advice or worse, telling him that the mission was impossible. Though he was back in the United States at that point, he fretted that too many people knew. He also wondered why people needed to be in touch via WhatsApp, creating a digital trail. As much as possible, he wanted communication to be conducted in person and only through reliable people such as Ghosn's family members who visited him in Japan.

Even Carole needed managing. He was troubled by her habit of taking notes during their meetings. "Oh, I'll destroy it afterwards," she would tell him. "It's because I'll forget a lot of the stuff you tell me." He knew she would remember just enough to land him in trouble. Yet he felt an obligation to keep her updated, as he could see she was struggling, and he regarded her as the underdog and a wife who deserved his compassion.

"It's worse when the doctor doesn't tell you what's wrong," he thought.

*   *   *

During the summer, Taylor started war-gaming. There are only two ways out of Japan: by air and by sea. Security at the airports is much tighter than at the seaports, so Taylor toyed with hiding Ghosn in some sort of container and smuggling him by ship to South Korea or Thailand. But that wouldn't get him all the way home. At some point, he would still need to clear security and board a plane. Just in case, he spent thousands of dollars to secure a fake Swedish passport for Ghosn in Lebanon; he would find out only later just how shoddy it was.

Flying out of Japan had its advantages. Taylor had done some security work for Logan International Airport in Boston and knew exactly where to look for holes: at the private jet terminals. He knew that security checks are much looser at the private terminals because of the lower terrorism risks. So he started exploring them on Google Earth, looking for an out-of-the-way airport that might not have heavy traffic. He was concerned that surveillance and security at the Tokyo airports were way too tight.

He started searching for more provincial airports, even though they would require multiple means of travel, and found Kansai International Airport in Osaka, 250 miles from Tokyo. The private jet terminal was new, and it was apparently very quiet. Nobody seemed to be manning the private side of the airport unless a flight was coming in or going out. Taylor described it as "vacant."

Ghosn gave the green light for the next phase of moving ahead. On October 9, $540,000 was wired from his bank account at HSBC on the Champs-Elysées to a Delaware-based company called Promote Fox LLC, managed by Peter Taylor and one of his brothers. Four days later, Zayek landed in Japan on an Emirates flight from Dubai for the first of two reconnaissance trips. On October 25, a second transfer was made from Ghosn's account in Paris to the Bank of America account of Promote Fox, this time for $322,500. Though he expected he'd be well compensated, Taylor told associates that he hadn't agreed to a success fee, out of principle. He didn't like to negotiate with people in desperate situations. In the 1990s, he had helped two American women extract their children from the Middle East. For each, he had received $20,000, even though one of the cases had taken two and a half years. "He never asked for a penny more. I couldn't believe he would do all of this for two and a half years," said the amazed mother in California who had hired Taylor to get her daughter back.

Now flush with cash, Peter Taylor used a chunk of the money to subcontract some reputation management work for Ghosn. He hired a Beirut-based digital marketing agency called Coddict, which pledged to give higher priority on Google searches to articles painting Ghosn in a favorable light by sending fake traffic to those stories. In two wire transfers in October, Peter paid Coddict more than $30,000 for its work, using the money sent from Ghosn's account. Some of the money also funded counterintelligence services for Ghosn, who had told Peter that he was being watched by Nissan and the prosecutors.

In Beirut, meanwhile, the elder Taylor spent another chunk of Ghosn's money on a pair of black metal-reinforced Penn Elcom roadie cases, designed to transport audio equipment. Taylor knew from Carole that Ghosn was about five feet six, and he figured he would be able to fit.

He drilled around seventy small holes in the bottom of the larger box so that Ghosn would be able to breathe, being careful not to weaken the box so much that it wouldn't support his weight. Taylor thought about what he might say if the box should crack and an arm or a leg suddenly dropped out. He joked that one possible response could be, "Don't worry about it, guys, it's one of the mannequins for a production we're doing. Why don't you get me some duct tape?"

Once he was done, Taylor wheeled the box around the house he owned north of Beirut, which had become a makeshift base for the Ghosn operation, to make sure it was solid. The plan was coming together, but Ghosn was pressuring him to speed things up. Taylor promised Ghosn that he would be free by Christmas. They communicated with each other via brief, simple messages over WhatsApp passed back and forth by Ghosn's visitors.

*   *   *

Now the team had to find a charter company, and a broker in Beirut booked two jets from the Turkish charter firm MNG Jet. The company was perfect for the job, because it had a reputation for not asking too many questions; one of its planes had recently been used to transport gold out of Venezuela. The two planes set them back $350,000. MNG provided a long-range Bombardier Global Express to fly from Dubai to Osaka and then back to Istanbul, from which one of its smaller planes would handle the Istanbul-to-Beirut leg.

Jetex, the Dubai firm handling the flights, applied for slots arriving at Kansai International at 10:00 a.m. local time on December 29 and departing at 11:00 that evening. The team would have thirteen hours to pull the operation off. If all went according to plan, Taylor and Zayek would land in Osaka in the morning on a private jet and stash two large boxes at a nearby hotel. They would then make their way to Tokyo, pick up Ghosn, bring him back to Osaka, and put him into one of the boxes in the hotel.

Then they would wheel him past airport security and onto the waiting private jet.

Taylor was a meticulous planner, and this was the kind of operation for which he'd usually want to do a dry run. He'd done some daring things in his time but never anything like this. Also, unlike Peter and Zayek, he'd never been to Japan. He wasn't sure whether they'd get Ghosn out on December 29, or whether they'd have to go back a second time after picking up more information. He repeatedly told his associates that if they were discovered, he would simply hand himself over rather than resort to violence.

Now Taylor needed a cover story. He read online that a renowned Japanese violinist, Taro Hakase, was performing in Osaka on December 29 and told the ground handlers at Kansai's private jet terminal that the purpose of his visit was to attend the concert. But little problems kept cropping up. One handler asked whether the flight was personal or for business, pointing out that he needed ten days' notice for approval from the transport ministry if the flight was personal. Taylor told him that the two passengers would be traveling on business.

The handlers' next issue was that the signature on the flight contract was of one Ross Allen, but the passengers were Michael Taylor and George Zayek. So MNG hustled together a new contract, this time bearing the signature of George Zayek.

When the Kansai International Airport employees did their due diligence on Taylor, even discovering that the man ran a security company in the United States, the suggestive intel failed to raise any alarms.

*   *   *

At 12:56 p.m. on December 27, Taylor and Zayek cleared immigration in Dubai after arriving from Beirut on Middle East Airlines flight 426. Their checked baggage included the two roadie cases. One of them contained a dented old speaker that had been kept in Taylor's relative's garage for several years.

While in Dubai, Taylor dropped by a music shop. For the sake of appearances, he also wanted to carry a guitar case. Rolling through a private terminal with roadie cases was one thing, but he felt that people needed to see instruments to really buy the whole show. "If you don't have the guitar case, people see boxes," he thought. With the case, "It sends an optic: okay, these guys are musicians."

Taylor picked out a heavy, top-of-the-range case and paired it with the cheapest guitar he could find. No one was going to see the instrument, but the case couldn't be empty. The music store employees seemed confused, but Taylor knew that there was a method to his madness. At the very least, he figured, even if the ground staff didn't believe they were musicians, they might think they were producers of some sort.

"The music I produce," he thought, "you don't wanna hear it."

The following evening, Taylor and Zayek checked in the boxes at the airport, cleared immigration in Dubai on their own papers, and boarded the Bombardier Global Express. The Turkish pilots spotted the boxes and didn't think anything of them—the two passengers had said that they were going to a concert. They had flown Hollywood celebrities as well as Saudi princes and rich businessmen. The pilots knew that VIP clients paid a lot of money and didn't expect to be bothered with questions.

Dressed casually, Taylor and Zayek came on board. They introduced themselves as musicians headed to a concert in Japan, adding that they would use the night flight to sleep.

At 8:35 p.m., they were wheels up for Osaka. Taylor felt his usual twinge of nerves—not because of the mission but because he'd gotten used to flying with a parachute in the Special Forces. He felt naked on a plane without one. His usual remedy was a little drop of Champagne, just something to take the edge off.

22

The Escape

The Bombardier Global Express jet touched down at 10:10 a.m. at Osaka's Kansai International Airport. Michael Taylor and George Zayek disembarked and were greeted on the tarmac by Tomoyuki Matsui, the manager of the private jet terminal's ground service team. He had already been informed that the purpose for their trip was to attend a concert by Taro Hakase.

The ground staff unloaded suitcases, a guitar case, and two large black boxes. Matsui ushered the men to the terminal bus, which took them to the posh Premium Gate Tamayura, where Kayoko Tokunaga, a thirty-year-old employee, was waiting to greet them. Tokunaga was fluent in English and comfortably struck up conversation with Taylor and Zayek as they waited for their passports to be stamped. "Your stay is so short," she remarked.

Ever the thorough operative, Taylor didn't hesitate to lay the groundwork of their cover story. They were violinists who would be performing nearby, he told her. Unfortunately, their stay would be brief, as they had an important meeting outside Japan the following day. But he planned to come back for the Olympics in Tokyo the following summer. From the little that Zayek contributed, he struck Tokunaga as blunt and disagreeable.

As the luggage was wheeled into the terminal, Matsui and Tokunaga started discussing the odd couple they were dealing with. As Matsui spoke, Tokunaga eyed the massive cases that she figured must contain amplifiers, even though they looked too large for the purpose. She also saw the guitar case. Why were violinists carrying a guitar? That the two men were musicians at all came as a surprise. Tokunaga had thought that the passengers were meant to be attending Hakase's concert as guests rather than as performers.

Furthermore, they were about the least likely pair of violinists imaginable. Taylor looked like, well, a former Special Forces operative. If you were to ask anyone to spot the soldier in a lineup of people, he would be the guy. Fitter than men half his age, with closely clipped salt-and-pepper hair and a square jaw, he was straight out of central casting.

George Zayek painted an even more striking image. He openly bore the scars of his former life as a Lebanese militiaman. He was partially deaf in his left ear and partially blind in one eye and walked with a pronounced limp, the result of the leg injury decades ago.

From the airport, Taylor and Zayek took two vans to the Star Gate Hotel, where they checked in at 11:12 a.m. Taylor was given room 4009, where hotel staff dropped off their suitcases and the guitar. Zayek checked into a room six floors above, to which hotel staff brought the two large black boxes.

Zayek returned to the lobby and waited for Taylor. While he sat there, an anxious employee from the terminal showed up with a suitcase they had forgotten on the plane. The worker bowed and apologized for the mistake. The employee noticed that Zayek turned his head as the employee was speaking. Zayek the "concert violinist" explained that he had difficulty hearing out of his right ear, then told him not to worry about the delayed suitcase.

Taylor and Zayek hadn't determined whether they would get Ghosn out that day or the whole exercise would turn into a dress rehearsal. As seasoned operatives, they tried to make sure that there would be no surprises or unpredictable scenarios on such a high-stakes, high-risk mission. Just in case, Zayek took the opportunity of chatting with the employee to seed their cover story more fully, asking whether airport staff had screened their luggage. "The boxes contain amplifiers," he explained, adding that the cargo was fragile and would be compromised if put through an X-ray machine.

Taylor came down a few minutes later, and just before noon, they flagged a taxi and headed for Shin Osaka Station, a hub of the *shin-kansen* bullet train. Zayek had traveled to Japan twice before the escape and had learned his way around the Japanese train system. He walked to the counter and purchased two tickets for Tokyo, a three-and-a-half-hour ride.

*　　*　　*

Meanwhile, Ghosn was having a leisurely morning with his young-est daughter, Maya. He packed some bags. Maya's return flight to the United States provided a convenient cover to send out some of Ghosn's personal belongings ahead of his escape.

They went to lunch, probably for the last time in Tokyo. If anything went wrong, it would be the last meal Ghosn would eat outside a jail cell for a long time—maybe forever. The pair chose a restaurant called We Are the Farm, a trendy farm-to-table eatery in a former dry cleaner located in the chic Azabu Juban neighborhood. The Ghosns loved this side of Japan. The food was excellent and the atmosphere lively. After lunch, they stopped by the house again to drop off Ghosn and pick up Maya's luggage. Ghosn pushed five suitcases to the garage, where his driver was waiting. Maya looked at the unusually large amount of bag-gage. She told the driver that she had too much and would need to drop some off for a friend to carry back to the United States.

Before they drove off, Ghosn told the driver that he could take the rest of the day off. He would call him again in two days, he said. At 2:05 p.m., the car carrying Maya pulled up in front of the Grand Hyatt, where Peter Taylor was waiting. They shook hands, and he took two of Maya's suitcases up to his room. She got back into the car and headed for nearby Haneda Airport.

*　　*　　*

At 2:30 p.m. precisely, Ghosn pushed open the front door of his two-story home and stepped outside. The moment before he crossed the threshold, he was Carlos Ghosn, revered auto executive fighting to clear his name. As soon as he stepped across it to execute his plan, at best he would become Carlos Ghosn the international fugitive. If he was caught, it would be back to jail, perhaps for the rest of his life.

Dressed in a dark jacket and scarf with a woolen cap and sunglasses, he walked west on the main road. He paused and looked over his shoulder before continuing. He had recently complained to a court that Nissan's security contractors spied on his every move.

Nissan wasn't the only monitor. Cameras had been installed outside and inside the foyer of the home by the court, checked once a week by the prosecutors. In addition, a constellation of security cameras on homes and buildings captured every step of Ghosn's twenty-five-minute stroll from his spacious rented house to the Grand Hyatt.

It was a brisk, sunny winter Sunday ahead of the New Year's holiday, one of the few times when Japan shuts down. It was the perfect time to escape. Within a half hour, Ghosn had reached the Grand Hyatt in Tokyo. Keeping his head down, he made his way through the lobby to the guest room elevators. He got out on the ninth floor, walked down the hall, and entered room 933, where Peter Taylor was waiting.

*   *   *

The Nozomi express pulled into Shinagawa Station in Tokyo at 3:22 p.m., and Taylor and Zayek, both wearing baseball caps, got off and headed for the north ticket gate. They exited the station on the western side and boarded a taxi for the Grand Hyatt.

For more than thirty minutes Ghosn had been in Peter's room, where he'd changed clothes and was making small talk. Peter was a sociable young man and had always been good at schmoozing with older, powerful people. He had a precociousness and entrepreneurial streak that caught the eye of accomplished men. He'd turned one hedge fund tycoon into a mentor after meeting him in a bar in the Bahamas.

Spending time alone in a room with one of the world's top business executives right before he would attempt to escape Japan in a box didn't
particularly faze him.

By the time Taylor and Zayek reached the lobby of the Grand Hyatt, Peter was there waiting, having come down shortly before their
arrival. When the two older men appeared, Peter immediately made
for the elevator. The trio wanted to appear to be strangers in case the
surveillance camera footage was reviewed. More than anything, Taylor wanted to ensure that his son wasn't seen as an accomplice.

Taylor, Zayek, and Peter entered the ninth-floor room. It was the
first time Ghosn had met his would-be rescuers face-to-face.

"It's time to go home," Taylor told Ghosn, greeting him with a large
smile.

Seven minutes later, the four men left the room with Ghosn's luggage. Peter headed to the hotel parking lot and took a taxi to the airport, where he was booked on a flight to China. Taylor wanted his son
to get out of the country before anything potentially illegal happened.

Ghosn, Taylor, and Zayek left through the main entrance of the hotel and hailed a cab to Shinagawa Station. Ghosn now wore a pair of
black thick-rimmed glasses and a surgical mask, a common sight in
Tokyo during flu season, as a convenient means of preventing people
from recognizing the face of Japan's most notorious criminal suspect.
The station was packed with holiday travelers. The three men headed
for the train platform.

Ghosn entered carriage 1 with Zayek. Taylor entered carriage 2. The
train left the station for Osaka at 4:55 p.m. The men tried to regularly
keep on the move during the journey. Ghosn's face had been a fixture
on TV and plastered on magazine covers for two decades. Seeing him
there would be like spotting Steve Jobs on a New York subway. Taylor
had given him advice about how to behave, urging him not to speak in
case people recognized his voice. Do not catch anybody's eye, he counseled. Keep walking, but look straight down to the ground.

The bullet train arrived at Shin Osaka Station at 7:20 p.m. The
men filed out and headed to the south ticket gate. They walked with

military precision in single file, a few paces apart: Taylor, then Ghosn, then Zayek.

They piled into another taxi bound for the Star Gate Hotel, with Ghosn and Taylor in the back seat and Zayek up front, next to the driver. Once in the taxi, Ghosn, who had remained bundled up for nearly three hours on the train, removed his mask to take a few deep breaths of fresh air. He also took off the hat but put them both back on a few minutes later.

At 8:15 p.m., the trio walked through the entrance of the Star Gate Hotel. Ghosn and Zayek went directly to the forty-sixth floor, where the boxes were kept, while Taylor went to the front desk before going to his room on the fortieth floor, grabbing a piece of luggage and the guitar case before heading up to meet the other two.

Ghosn took his time, inspecting the box carefully. He turned to Taylor and Zayek, resolute. He wanted to get out of Japan that night. There would be no dry run.

*   *   *

While Ghosn and Zayek rested and made preparations in the hotel room, Taylor returned to the private jet terminal to ensure that the plane would leave as planned and to double-check that the personnel there had received the message that their bags shouldn't be scanned. Most charter airlines don't require bags to be checked, so passengers can choose their level of security. Obviously, if the airport were going to insist on opening the case containing Ghosn, the trio might never leave Japan. Taylor walked into the terminal at 9:00 p.m., catching the staff by surprise.

Tokunaga, the English-speaking terminal worker, asked what he was doing there. Passengers who fly on private jets don't often show up ninety minutes before departure.

"Are we going through a security check when we leave?" Taylor asked.

Tokunaga told Taylor that there would be no security check. She then called Matsui, her manager, who was with the pilot. The pilot and Taylor talked briefly on the phone. Taylor hung up and said he would head back to the hotel, but not before handing Tokunaga an envelope.

"Here's a tip for you," he said. Inside, Tokunaga saw a stack of 10,000-yen notes, each worth roughly $100, held together by an elastic hair band. She had never seen that much money at once. She figured there must have been at least $10,000 in there.

Tokunaga told him she couldn't take it. Tips were forbidden. Taylor declined to take back the envelope and told her to share it with everyone. He reminded her that he was returning for the Olympics. Tokunaga didn't want to offend Taylor, so she held on to the envelope.

Shortly after Taylor left, Matsui, the terminal manager, dialed Tokunaga. He had been surprised by Taylor's sudden appearance and wanted to know what was going on.

"I think he just wanted to check the status of the aircraft," Tokunaga said. Matsui asked to talk to Taylor, but he had already left for the hotel. Matsui made his way to the terminal and again asked why Taylor had come so far ahead of the departure time. Tokunaga told Matsui about the envelope of cash. It presented Matsui with a conundrum. He had handled ground services at the terminal for the past three years. He was used to foreigners who flew in and started handing out cash, not understanding that that was not done in Japan. But no one had ever handed him an envelope stuffed with such a huge amount.

Matsui dialed a manager at another agency to discuss whether they could accept the money. They decided it should be returned politely and in a way that wouldn't offend Taylor and potentially jeopardize future business. Matsui decided to wait until the last moment to return it to minimize any conversation.

*   *   *

When Taylor got back to the hotel, he asked for a luggage trolley to be sent to his room. A few minutes later, porters removed two suitcases from Taylor's room and took them to the lobby.

Taylor headed to the forty-sixth floor and entered the room around 9:30 p.m. The private jet was due to leave the Osaka terminal, bound for Istanbul, in one hour.

Ghosn stood contemplating the four-foot-long box that was supposed to smuggle him aboard the jet. It was the last hurdle—and by far the biggest. Up until now, he had not technically done anything wrong. He was allowed to travel around the country. But he couldn't explain this away. Nonetheless, it was the box he had chosen. It was that or a jail cell.

Taking a final deep breath, Ghosn lay down on the base of the box, and Taylor pulled a sheet off the bed and laid it over him. Taylor then put his guitar on top of Ghosn and tried closing the box. It fit, but the guitar pressed down on Ghosn. He would have to spend at least an hour in there, and he needed to be comfortable. The sheet stayed. It would be the only camouflage if airport staff decided they needed to look inside. The guitar case would be placed on top of the box.

Taylor could sense that Ghosn was nervous. "His butthole is tight," he thought.

"Have you ever gone scuba diving?" he asked Ghosn.

"Yes," said Ghosn.

Taylor told him to imagine that he was scuba diving and mimed taking slow, controlled breaths. He looked him in the eyes, communicating calm and confidence.

"Breathe slowly," he reminded Ghosn.

Taylor lowered the top of the box, and everything went black.

*   *   *

Shortly before 10:00 p.m., Taylor wheeled the big black box out of the room. Zayek followed closely behind, pushing the smaller box, which contained an old, dented speaker that had been kept in Taylor's relatives' garage for years.

They pushed the cases out the entrance and to the driveway, where two vans were waiting. The drive to the airport took only a few minutes, but they were anxious minutes for Ghosn. He could see nothing; he could only hear the voices around him and feel every bump and jolt of the ride. In his heightened state of awareness, the sound of the van door opening after it pulled into the terminal was thunderous. This was it.

Narikuni Kawada, a worker at the terminal, had loaded the cases into the van when Taylor and Zayek had arrived that morning. Kawada and another worker had been able to lift them easily. Now one of them weighed a great deal more. It took five men to lift the awkward case. As they grunted and struggled, they mused about what might explain the difference. "Maybe there is a beautiful young lady in the box," one staff member joked.

Taylor and Zayek walked into the wood-paneled terminal at 10:20 p.m., just ten minutes before their scheduled departure time.

"We're late," Taylor told the employees in a manner meant to induce a flurry of activity. Workers scrambling to get the VIPs onto their private jet would be even less inclined to look closely at their luggage. Two security guards showed up for the departure, even though they had been briefed that Taylor and Zayek didn't need a security screening. They stood by as Taylor walked through the metal detector carrying his backpack, which set off the warning light. Zayek simply walked around it. Then they boarded a shuttle bus to the airplane.

As the bus pulled up to the plane, Matsui's moment came to return the tip. "In Japan, we have no custom of receiving tips," he told Taylor. "We are sorry, but we cannot accept this." Matsui could see that Taylor was disappointed, but the former Green Beret took back the envelope. Matsui pitched in to help load the cases. Along with the captain, he took charge of the smaller case, the one without Ghosn in it. The two men lifted it two steps at a time up the gangway. Matsui pulled the box from the upper steps, while the captain pushed it from below. When they made it to the main cabin, the captain told Matsui to move the case to the back of the plane. It wouldn't roll through easily, so the captain suggested that they flip it end over end until it reached the back of the plane. Matsui listened carefully as he repeatedly flipped it over. Everything seemed fine. Still, he thought it was a callous way to handle delicate audio equipment.

Around the back, the box with Ghosn had gone up the luggage conveyor belt to the rear hatch, but there was a gap between the belt and the entrance to the plane. Taylor walked to the rear of the plane and started barking orders to the crew. He lifted it from one end, while three or four luggage handlers standing on the luggage belt lifted the other.

Inside the box, Ghosn was freezing, trying to fight his rising panic. He was inches from freedom, thwarted by a luggage belt. He heard the urgency in everyone's voices as they jostled the box, trying to maneuver it into the plane. Ghosn pushed all thoughts out of his head, refusing to allow himself to feel any hope until he arrived in Beirut. So many things could still go wrong: the plane might not work, or someone could sell him out before he arrived.

With one final heave, the crew and Taylor pushed the box into the aircraft. It fit through the rear hatch of the plane with barely any wiggle room and was left wedged between the seats.

"No need to strap it in," Taylor assured the workers, motioning them away with his hand.

As the plane made its final preparations to leave, the pilots received a message from Okan Kosemen, the airline manager back in Turkey. "The important cargo should stay at the back. Upon landing, I will welcome the plane," he wrote.

"The separation door will be closed after takeoff; they don't want to be disturbed," one of the pilots responded. After the doors closed, the ground crew headed back to the terminal.

Then nothing happened.

Taylor and Zayek had asked the ground staff to move their departure time forward to 10:30 p.m., and there had been a rush to get everything loaded so they could leave on time. Matsui had expected the engines to fire up the second the doors closed. Instead there was silence.

The plane sat there for around half an hour.

Matsui was about to pick up the phone to call the control tower to see if there was a problem when he heard the engines turn on, just after 11:00 p.m. The plane moved toward the runway. In the box, Ghosn breathed a sigh of relief. Shortly afterward, he felt a lift as the plane's wheels left the ground. He was no longer on Japanese soil.

*   *   *

With the plane in the air, Taylor went to the box and unfastened it. Ghosn clambered out. He was cold. As he warmed up, he sank into the plush leather seats in the rear of the aircraft. The wood paneling was polished to a mirrorlike finish; a diffuser spread a relaxing scent throughout the cabin. He was back in familiar territory.

He accepted the glass of Champagne Taylor offered. He knew he wouldn't be able to relax fully until he reached the safety of Beirut. As they drank, Taylor told Ghosn that the two of them had been through similar experiences. He, too, had been a hostage in an unfair system and had been forced into a confession a few years earlier. After the conversation, Ghosn fell asleep.

Taylor watched him, basking in the glow of a job that was going well. Those were the moments he loved about the job. From everything he had heard from Carole about life in a Japanese jail, Taylor didn't see this job as any different from springing someone out of North Korea.

Having pulled off the caper thus far, Taylor turned his thoughts to covering his tracks. He had spent months planning the minutiae of getting Ghosn out of Japan but barely any time thinking about what would come next. The truth was that although Taylor had worked on daring rescues in the past—whether of a *New York Times* reporter held by the Taliban or of American children held in the Middle East against their mothers' wishes—he hadn't had to worry about hiding his involvement once they were returned. This time was different. The Japanese authorities would attempt to figure out who was behind the escape, and Taylor hoped—perhaps rather naively—that he would be able to throw them off the scent.

He went to the front of the plane to use the bathroom and struck up a conversation with the pilots, asking them where the plane was heading after Istanbul. When the pilots told him they were going back to Dubai for their next job, Taylor asked whether they could deliver the flight boxes there. That wouldn't be possible, it turned out, because the plane was booked by a different client. Taylor didn't have many options. He asked whether he could leave the boxes in the plane, together with the guitar. They said that was fine.

Nothing about the exchange struck the pilots as particularly odd. They were used to dealing with the world's superwealthy, who tossed expensive items aside with little thought. One of them had once picked up clients in Colorado returning from a ski holiday who had simply ditched their gear on the plane when they had landed in the Caribbean for a beach vacation.

*   *   *

It was raining heavily as the plane approached Atatürk Airport just outside Istanbul in the early hours of the morning. Okan Kosemen, the airline's operations manager, climbed into the plane and walked up to the cockpit to tell the pilots that he would handle the passengers.

He directed Ghosn into a car, and the two of them traveled about a hundred meters to another waiting jet. It was before 6:00 a.m.; the place was deserted. Since the opening of Istanbul's new airport some months earlier, even during peak hours, Atatürk's only traffic had been cargo planes and private jets.

Taylor and Zayek had booked a separate flight out of Istanbul, hoping to avoid association with their smuggled human cargo. They watched Ghosn board the plane while the ground staff processed their passports. After the immigration procedures were completed, the men grabbed their bags and headed to Istanbul Airport, a half-hour drive away. They had a commercial flight to catch for Beirut.

Ghosn and Kosemen, meanwhile, climbed into the Bombardier Challenger that would fly him to Beirut and freedom. When they came aboard, the flight attendant sprang to attention. She had been at the back of the plane texting with a friend and rushed to greet the men. "Merhaba," she said to Ghosn, thinking he was Turkish. "Uh, hi, welcome on board," she tried again after she realized that she was dealing with a foreigner.

Ghosn took a seat at the back of the plane with a cup of coffee. The flight took off at 6:03 a.m. Once in the air, he said he was starving. The flight attendant served him a traditional Turkish breakfast that included a cheese plate, a bagellike bread called *simit*, brioche, olives, and eggs.

Ghosn struck up a conversation with Kosemen about the jet he was in, asking the price of the aircraft and how much it cost to rent. As for why he was on the plane, Ghosn offered only a brief explanation. "The Japanese are bad people," he told Kosemen.

Less than half an hour later, he was finally able to relax as he felt the wheels of the jet touch down in his hometown.

Shortly after, Carole got a call from a friend: "Get up and go to your parents' house. I have a surprise for you."

23

Collateral Damage

The line of half-empty wine and Champagne glasses glittered in the light of the candles on the dinner table. The new year was hours away.

Carole and the host, May Daouk, had decided against organizing New Year's Eve festivities in the customary Lebanese way, with hundreds of guests, piles of food, and ear-piercing Arabic music. The two women had instead opted to gather a small party of six at Daouk's home to celebrate their guest of honor, Carlos Ghosn, who had just shocked the world with his daring escape from Japan.

Daouk had cooked, preparing her signature dish—an "upside-down" of eggplant and chicken with cracked wheat. She had grabbed bottles of Champagne from the stock she kept in the house as well as red wine from Ghosn's wine estate, Ixsir, which she had on hand because Carole regularly sent her cases.

The room had blue walls that bore architectural etchings of ancient Lebanese ruins on one side and a large painting with a burst of colors on the other. It was a far cry from the Tokyo Detention Center. For a moment, the clock stopped. The small group was ecstatically happy; they would be fine if time stopped for longer, allowing them to savor and relish a reality they had never thought possible.

In another corner of Beirut, Michael Taylor was in his apartment with a few friends and relatives. Sitting on a sofa, he was watching news programs rehashing the twenty-four-hour-old breaking news of Ghosn's escape. Reporters had only sketchy details of how the former

Nissan chief had managed to jump bail and reach Lebanon. Reports said he had flown on board one business jet from Osaka to Istanbul and on another from the Turkish megalopolis to Beirut. One Lebanese broadcaster said that Ghosn had hired a music band to perform a live concert at his Tokyo residence and had sneaked out, hiding in a music instrument case. It was wrong but not *that* far off, Taylor thought.

As some of his relatives and their friends drank whiskey, they speculated about who could have pulled off such an operation. One thought that perhaps the Lebanese Special Forces had done it. Another speculated that it had to be the Mossad, Israel's spy service. Taylor kept mum. He didn't want any publicity for the job; that was why he'd taken a separate plane from Ghosn's back to Beirut. The former Green Beret retired to his downstairs bedroom before midnight.

The immunity would not last.

*   *   *

In Turkey, Ghosn's escape was sparking particular interest because the tycoon had transited through Istanbul, flying on jets operated by a Turkish company. One of the pilots was in bed on the morning of January 1 when his phone rang. It was Kosemen, the operations manager of MNG Jet. "Our names are in the newspapers, bro," he said. "We have a problem."

At first the pilot wasn't too worried. His duty was to fly the plane, not to inspect the cargo or police the people sitting in the cabin. If Ghosn had boarded his plane, someone above his pay grade bore the responsibility.

But later that day, the pilot and other MNG Jet personnel involved in the two flights were summoned to a police station. After questioning, the manager and the four pilots were charged with migrant smuggling and were sent to jail pending trial. The flight attendants, who were accused of failing to report a crime, were allowed to return home.

A continent away, in Japan, Greg Kelly was in a Tokyo apartment, where he was living while out on bail. He had entered the New Year alone. His wife, Dee, had flown to the United States for the birth of a grandson. Kelly's initial reaction to Ghosn's escape was shock—not just because the American wondered how his former boss had pulled it off but also because he would now have to prepare for his trial without his star witness. He had been left holding the bag, forced to face the accusations alone.

Kelly knew as well as anyone else what an uphill battle they faced to achieve a not-guilty verdict. Neither he nor Ghosn was a young man. They faced the prospect of a lengthy trial and a possible prison sentence. It burned Kelly that he hadn't been able to be at home for his grandson's birth. But he could understand why Ghosn would want to run away.

*   *   *

A celebrity on the lam, Ghosn settled in at the pink house and began organizing his new life in Lebanon. Family members flew in, including Anthony, who arrived from San Francisco. The young man had avoided traveling to Japan for the past fourteen months because he was tied to one of the criminal charges. Anthony and Ghosn met with Michael Taylor at a shooting range. The young man hugged the former soldier and thanked him for bringing his dad home.

It had happened in a way Ghosn never could have imagined, but basing himself in Lebanon for his retirement had always been the plan. He had envisioned keeping a role in the Alliance, perhaps as honorary chairman, while being able to spend more time with his loved ones, giving lectures to students, and traveling the world. The work with his former companies was clearly off the table. But he was looking forward to dialing back, surrounded by friends. He also had the support of swaths of the Lebanese establishment, who venerated him as one of the country's most successful ambassadors.

A few days into the new year, Japanese officials made a statement about the Ghosn escape. "Ghosn broke his own promise that he would definitely appear before the court and fled the country. What this shows is simple: He didn't want to submit to the judgment of our nation's courts and sought to avoid the punishment for his own crimes," said the Tokyo deputy chief prosecutor, Takahiro Saito. "There is no room to justify such an action."

Japanese authorities turned to Interpol, asking the international police organization to issue a red notice under which Ghosn could be detained and sent to Japan if he ever left Lebanon. A few days later, they issued one for Carole as well, alleging that she had lied during her sworn testimony the previous April. Lebanese officials assured them both that they would be safe as long as they remained in the country. Both were Lebanese citizens, and the country doesn't extradite its own nationals.

Of course it stung that they would no longer be able to travel. Ghosn was very close to his mom, Rose, who was in Brazil. Now ninety years old, she continued to live in her own home in Rio, in Barra da Tijuca. She had Alzheimer's and three nurses rotated so that she had 24/7 care. It was a great tragedy for Ghosn to no longer be able to visit her.

Carole, meanwhile, was a US dual national and loved her frequent trips to New York to see her children. That would no longer be a luxury afforded to her. Still, the couple were delighted to have been reunited and were confident that they could challenge the Interpol red notice in the courts.

Ghosn had felt muzzled while on bail in Japan, concerned that he would be sent back to jail if he defended himself too forcefully. Now, however, he would use the court of public opinion.

On January 8, he made his opening arguments.

Flanked by bodyguards, he arrived at the head office of the Lebanese Press Syndicate, where the media had gathered to hear him speak. The story of his sensational escape was gripping the world. In the space of fourteen months, he had gone from the top of the business world to jail in Japan to celebrity fugitive in his ancestral homeland. Reporters had flown in from far and wide, with broadcasters in countries from China to the United States prepared to air the event live. Japan had dispatched the biggest contingent, but only a few of that contingent were allowed inside the building. Dozens of Japanese reporters stood outside in the January rain.

The head of the press syndicate sought to make a lengthy introduction to the packed event, but as the top of the hour approached, he was hounded off the podium. At precisely 3:00 p.m., the perennially punctual Ghosn went on air, wearing a dark suit and bold red tie. "As you can imagine, today is a very important day for me," he said, "one that I have looked forward to every single day for more than four hundred days, since I was brutally taken from my world as I knew it, ripped from my family, my friends, my communities."

Facing the cameras, he was back in his element. "For the first time since this nightmare began I can defend myself, speak freely," he said. "I'm here to clear my name." He launched into an hour-long presentation recounting his arrest and decrying what he claimed was the brutal Japanese justice system. He called the Nissan executives responsible for the plot against him "unscrupulous, vindictive individuals." Prior to the press conference, the Lebanese Ministry of Justice had reminded him that harming Lebanon's relations with a foreign country was a criminal offense, so he was careful to steer clear of direct attacks on Japanese politicians.

Ghosn then moved to a point-by-point rebuttal of the Tokyo prosecutors' charges against him:

His alleged plan to collect tens of millions of dollars after retirement? Nothing had been decided and nothing had been paid.

The payments to billionaire friends in the Middle East? They had been for valid business reasons.

The funds he had received and used to buy a yacht? They had not been company money.

"These allegations are untrue, and I should have never been arrested in the first place," he said.

He pointed to several documents from the Japanese court case projected onto a wall behind him, which he said supported his innocence. Most of the reporters in the room had no clue what the documents referred to, and those who did couldn't read the small font from afar.

For two and a half hours, Ghosn put on quite a show, a sort of looking-glass version of his performances as the head of the Alliance. He gesticulated energetically, his eyebrows moving up and down as he conveyed emotions ranging from anger to surprise to earnest conviction. He answered questions in French, English, Portuguese, and Arabic, depending on which language a reporter had used. He opined about the state of the car industry, criticizing Renault and Nissan for their dismal performance and for missing out on a deal with Fiat Chrysler. "They missed the unmissable," he said.

He declined to address the issue that had drawn the large press corps: his escape. "I'm not here to talk about *how* I got out of Japan, I'm here to talk about *why* I got out of Japan," he said to audible groans from his audience.

*   *   *

Once the whirlwind of media attention subsided, Ghosn returned to his new routine. Every day, he woke up before 6:00 a.m. to do a few hours of work on his defense, the books that he was writing, and his investments. He then had a long breakfast with Carole, a sacred luxury after the months of being apart and the meager prison rations of pickled vegetables and rice. Personal trainers came to the house to help them exercise. He visited his vineyard and enjoyed going for walks in the mountains and riding his bike around Beirut. Two days a week, he visited his lawyer's office, where he was given a small room in which to work on his defense. He was already in advanced discussions to contribute to a documentary and a TV series about his life. To reporters who flew in to interview him, he said that he was more motivated than ever: he was fighting for his reputation, his legacy, and his rights. He would turn the tables on Japan and set the record straight.

But he faced a daunting task: the Japanese criminal case had metastasized, and he was now facing more than two dozen global legal cases and investigations. In France, an investigative magistrate was probing whether Ghosn had misused Renault funds. In the British Virgin Islands, Nissan was alleging that Ghosn had purchased his yacht with stolen company funds and registered it in the Caribbean territory. In the Netherlands, the Japanese carmaker was arguing that he had unlawfully received a secret salary from a joint venture with Mitsubishi and it wanted the money back. He was also being sued by Nissan itself in Japan. In early February, the carmaker filed a civil suit claiming more than $90 million in damages from its former chief. In addition, his Japanese insurance company said it would no longer cover his legal fees following his escape. Worse, it was now trying to recover the tens of millions of dollars it had already paid his lawyers since his arrest.

Despite loudly proclaiming his innocence, Ghosn was becoming a pariah. Banks such as ABN Amro, HSBC, and JPMorgan all asked him to move his money out, saying that he was an unwanted business partner. In the wake of his escape, Ghosn had been excited about a proposal from the student-run Harvard Association for Law and Business to speak about his experiences in the Japanese justice system. But his hopes were dashed: after internal deliberation, the association informed Ghosn that on second thought, his contribution wasn't desired.

Further clouding Ghosn's horizon, Beirut was no longer the sun-kissed haven that he had known during his childhood. The Lebanese capital was buffeted by antigovernment protests over runaway inflation, poverty, and corruption. On some days, it was dangerous even to move around.

*   *   *

Like Ghosn, Michael Taylor was stuck in Beirut. He had lived in the same Massachusetts house for three decades and was desperate to go home.

But Taylor's name was now all over the press as the ex-soldier who had helped Ghosn escape. He had been captured by CCTV cameras at passport control in Turkey. Taylor feared that the Japanese authorities would issue an arrest warrant for him at any time. If he was going to face legal issues, he wanted to face them in the United States. He had done a lot of work for the US government over the years and didn't think it would hand over one of its citizens—particularly a military veteran—to a foreign country.

Ghosn counseled the former soldier to hunker down in Lebanon, but Taylor was losing his mind after so many weeks away. "I'm not a runner," he told a relative. Instead, he asked Ghosn for help to cover his legal fees. Ghosn agreed to send the Taylors some money in crypto-currency to keep the transfer secret. The sixty-five-year-old Ghosn had never handled Bitcoin before, so he asked Anthony to process the transfer.

On February 16, Taylor had finally had enough. Having booked and not boarded three flights since landing in Lebanon, he decided to take a chance and hopped on a flight home to Massachusetts via Dubai. He made it home without issues. Back in the United States, he picked up his old activities, including playing basketball on Wednesday and working on expanding his vitamin water business. Within a few weeks, the COVID-19 outbreak was forcing countries around the world to shut down one after the other. Taylor's son Peter decided to ride out the pandemic at his father's place near Boston rather than in Beirut, where he had lived for the past year and a half.

The family was back together again, and there was still no sign of a red notice. Taylor felt secure enough to tell the story of Ghosn's escape to a *Vanity Fair* reporter, which only added to the evidence that Tokyo prosecutors had been quietly gathering. Almost every minute of the operation had been captured on security cameras: at hotels, in the street, in taxis, in the train, and at airports. Japanese authorities had documents pointing to a trail of money linking Ghosn to the Taylors. By May, as the COVID-19 restrictions eased, Peter Taylor decided to fly back to Beirut to get back to work. He booked a flight for May 20.

That very morning, he was awakened by a loud knock at the door. He went down in his underwear and saw more than a dozen members of the US Marshals Service in fatigues toting assault rifles. Half a dozen SUVs and an armored vehicle were parked farther down the street.

He opened the door and immediately asked whether the officers had come because of a Japanese arrest warrant. "Yes," the reply came. The officers climbed the stairs to find Michael Taylor asleep in his bedroom. They drove the father and son to the local county jail, where the pair was ordered to observe strict quarantine.

When their fourteen-day period in isolation ended, the Taylors joined the other incarcerated men, mostly alleged drug dealers and violent criminals. They woke up at 6:00 a.m. when their cell door loudly buzzed open. They rolled off a thin mattress and headed down to the canteen for a breakfast of three boiled eggs or a bowl of cereal and a doughnut, depending on the day. They killed time by playing cards, reading books, or playing pickup basketball in the yard, which sometimes got rough. "There's no fouls in jail," Peter told one family member.

Michael Taylor struggled to understand how it had come to this. He had expected that people would celebrate him for reuniting a man he saw as a hostage with his wife and kids. Instead, he was rotting in a jail cell at the hand of a US government he had served at the risk of his life. The feeling of injustice was made far worse because his son was being held in the same jail.

Still Taylor held onto his optimism that US judges would see things his way. He assembled a sharp team of lawyers whose first job was to get him and his son bail. Because of the outbreak, the bail hearing took place via video link. The Taylors appeared side by side in orange jumpsuits, wearing jail-issued face masks. The government described Ghosn's escape as "one of the most brazen and well-orchestrated escape acts in recent history," arguing that the Taylors shouldn't be accorded bail because they were a flight risk. At the risk of stating the obvious, Assistant US Attorney Stephen Hassink said that if the Taylors were to attempt to flee, they were "some of the best defendants that I'm sure this court has seen positioned to actually succeed in that flight."

The defense countered that the Taylors would never have come back to the United States if their plan had been to evade justice and that they should be released like other nonviolent inmates who had been let out amid the pandemic. Michael Taylor, the lawyers said, was at particular risk of complications if he contracted covid. He was nearly sixty and had only one lung left after an operation decades earlier. Peter was a college grad with no prior convictions or expertise in special ops. Fleeing would be absurd because he would then face more serious charges than the ones he was facing in Japan.

On July 10, the judge denied them bail, rejecting the arguments that they weren't a flight risk. The Taylors appealed to a second judge, who also ruled against them, duly noting the irony of arguments about why the Taylors would respect their bail when they had been arrested precisely for helping somebody else jump theirs.

Michael Taylor's wife, Lamia, heard the ruling and her heart sank. She wasn't allowed to visit her husband and youngest child at the jailhouse because of the COVID-19 outbreak. The Taylors put all their efforts into avoiding extradition. They argued that they had no chance of a fair trial in Japan and that jumping bail wasn't a crime in that country. (The prosecution countered that although jumping bail isn't a crime in Japan, assisting someone to jump bail is.)

As the weeks passed, the evidence linking the Taylors to the escape kept piling up. In the extradition file prepared by Japanese prosecutors and passed on to US authorities, a document showed that Anthony Ghosn had made six transfers to Peter Taylor using the Coinbase cryptocurrency exchange platform for a total of more than $500,000.

When those details became public and reporters sought comment from Anthony, he was angry. He was back in the news, this time for financing an international caper. He had sent the Bitcoin to help out his dad, with no idea that the beneficiary was Peter Taylor.

He didn't want that kind of attention.

*   *   *

Greg Kelly, at sixty-four years old, was finally going to have his first day in court. He had been fighting to get his trial started for nearly two years and was eagerly waiting for a chance to defend himself against what he regarded as trumped-up charges. He was accused of plotting to pay Ghosn secret, deferred compensation after the Nissan chief had taken a 50 percent pay cut in 2010. Kelly had tried to tell the prosecutors that they had it all wrong and that the payment to Ghosn after retirement were going to be for real consultancy work for the company. Anyhow, no money was ever paid. It irked Kelly that he had not managed to persuade the prosecutors, but at least now he would have the opportunity to make his case before a judge. He had counted on having Ghosn there by his side, backing up his story, but Ghosn would not be returning.

On the morning of September 15, Kelly got out of bed early but didn't bother with breakfast. He could never eat at times like this. When the car carrying him pulled up to the gray stone monolith housing the Tokyo District Court, he strode in quickly behind his lawyers, barely acknowledging the bank of cameramen.

The Japanese prosecutors, with the help of Nissan executives such as Hari Nada, had mobilized huge resources in going after Ghosn; now all that force was bearing down on Kelly alone. In Japan, his trial had become a proxy for Ghosn and his legacy.

Courtroom 104 was an imposing chamber with a thirty-foot-high ceiling. Kelly sat at a long table with his attorneys. The Nissan team was behind him. The panel of three judges who would decide his fate sat on a dais at the rear of the room. The scene would play on repeat once or twice a week for the next nine months—an unusually long trial by the standards of Japanese justice. One reason was the mountain of documents that the prosecution had pushed to enter into evidence. Another was the language barrier.

Instead of a concurrent translation, which Kelly had requested, two English-speaking Japanese translators took notes as a person spoke, then communicated what they had said to the court. Occasionally, discussions broke out over how to translate basic English phrases such as "count toward," "focused on," or "consistent." As the trial stretched on, the translators lost steam, frequently imploring speakers to slow down. By the end of the trial, they were so exhausted that the court sessions ended an hour early.

Kelly vehemently denied the allegations. At Nissan, his concern, shared by many others at the company, had been losing Ghosn to a competitor or to early retirement. To avoid that, he had looked at ways to keep Ghosn around as an executive or consultant. That was all, he said.

The tension in the courtroom spiked when Nada and other former colleagues went to the bar to provide witness testimony. Although they had worked with him on some of the plans, they had turned into his accusers. Kelly refused to look them in the eye. They didn't deserve it.

*   *   *

On March 2, 2021, the Taylors were on a flight from Boston to Japan after exhausting all legal avenues to stop their extradition. After arriving, they were driven to the Tokyo Detention Center in Kosuge, the same one where Ghosn had been detained. They had, in effect, spirited Ghosn out of the country only to trade places with him. When Michael Taylor later appeared in a Japanese court, the former Green Beret bowed in apology as he wiped away tears. "I deeply regret my actions and sincerely apologize for causing difficulties for the judicial process and for the Japanese people. I'm sorry," he said.

Both father and son pled guilty to the charge of aiding the escape of a criminal. In July 2021, Michael Taylor received a two-year sentence, while Peter received one year and eight months. The judge didn't give them the maximum three-year sentence because, he said, the Taylors had shown remorse for their actions.

*   *   *

In Lebanon, Ghosn's day-to-day life was becoming more difficult. Like the rest of the population, he was subjected to lockdown measures. That meant he had to forgo one of his favorite pastimes, bridge games with pro-level players at a tony club in Beirut. Instead, he logged on to an online gaming platform.

Around Ghosn, Beirut was in meltdown. In the summer of 2020, horror struck the Lebanese capital. A fire in a warehouse had detonated an abandoned stockpile of ammonium nitrate, causing a massive blast in the port area. Some of the liveliest neighborhoods of Beirut were flattened and thousands of people were made homeless. Ghosn's pink house was damaged, but the Ghosns were unhurt.

The international community rushed to help, but matters continued to deteriorate. Waves of covid-19 infections knocked down the country, and the ongoing financial crisis raged harder still, pushing large swaths of the population below the poverty line. Covid-19 struck Carole's parents. Her mother recovered, but her stepfather passed away.

Among the patients in Beirut's covid-19 wards that spring was George Zayek, the former militiaman who had helped Ghosn escape. He recovered, although he suffered the effects of the virus for months. He desperately wanted to go back to a war zone, perhaps in Libya. But the red notice issued against him by Japan meant that he was stuck in Lebanon, unable to work.

Ghosn finished two books and a TV documentary. The first book, coauthored with a former journalist, recounted his successes at the head of the Alliance and claimed that he had been ruthlessly brought down by a clique of nationalists at Nissan. The second book, which he worked on with Carole, was titled *Together Forever* and featured a collection of letters between them that focused on their experiences at the hands of the harsh Japanese justice system.

Meantime, the wheels of justice kept turning—mostly to Ghosn's detriment. In May 2021, a Dutch court ordered Ghosn to repay nearly €5 million in salary to an Amsterdam-based company co-owned by Nissan and Mitsubishi, NMBV, saying that his work contract hadn't been valid because it didn't have the required consent from the boards of Nissan and Mitsubishi. Ghosn said he planned to appeal, and that he was in fact owed €15 million for unfair dismissal.

Another battle was taking place in the Caribbean to determine whether the yacht that Ghosn had used to cruise the Mediterranean and that had recently been renamed *Twig* had been purchased with funds stolen from Nissan.

Ghosn denied the charge, claiming that the yacht had originally been bought by his Lebanese lawyer, Fady Gebran, for his own use. The ownership of the yacht had been transferred to Ghosn in summer 2017, days before Gebran's death. No money had changed hands, he said, and none of the money had come from Nissan or Renault.

In France, the probe by the French investigative magistrate, Serge Tournaire, was shifting into a higher gear. Ghosn hadn't yet been charged, and Tournaire wanted to hear his version of events. Since Ghosn couldn't leave Beirut, his lawyers proposed that Tournaire go to Lebanon to conduct his interrogation, saying that their client was willing to cooperate with his probe. Tournaire agreed.

Ghosn's French legal team, led by the Paris-based Jean-Yves Le Borgne and Jean Tamalet of the US firm King & Spalding, worked their client through a number of hourslong sessions ahead of the visit. As the interrogation got closer, however, they changed tack: rather than answer all Tournaire's questions, their client would refuse to engage on information gleaned from Gebran's hard drive.

The lawyers argued to Tournaire that the hard drive had been obtained illegally. Since it hadn't been collected and sealed by a sworn judicial officer, it was impossible to guarantee the authenticity of the emails and other documents it contained, they said. For those reasons, the lawyers argued that the French investigative magistrate should remove from the case file all material related to the hard drive. Tournaire said that Ghosn was free to pursue this fight in court. As far as he was concerned, the documents were admissible, and he could ask questions about their content.

As the hearing date neared, Tournaire ordered a raid on Suhail Bahwan's apartments in France. Five French officers raided his homes, taking paintings off the wall, examining his safes—even calling in an expert to crack those that only he had the key to open—and going through all his vehicles and belongings. Though they had confirmed his extreme wealth and material assets, they had found nothing that they deemed relevant to the Ghosn probe.

The investigators hadn't gotten more than that from Bahwan himself. Whenever people asked him about the Japanese and French investigations, he would become angry—always quick to point out that it was his money and he was free to do whatever he wanted with it.

On June 2, 2021, Tournaire arrived at Beirut's main courthouse to question Ghosn in a hearing supervised by Lebanese judicial officials. Once Ghosn had read his opening remarks, Tournaire charged in on the one topic Ghosn had always sought to avoid: the so-called Oman route. Over the course of seven hours the first day, Tournaire asked Ghosn about his relations with Suhail Bahwan. Ghosn said it was based on mutual admiration. He loved that Bahwan was a "self-made man." Tournaire pressed Ghosn with questions about the loan that the fallen tycoon had taken from Bahwan in 2009. Had Ghosn paid it back? He hadn't. Bahwan had extended the loan indefinitely. He and Bahwan had discussed the terms of the arrangement only orally, in Arabic. There were no documents.

As Ghosn's hearing extended into a second day, he increasingly reached for his trump card: he wouldn't answer any questions about information stemming from Gebran's hard drive. Tournaire plowed on with his questions, but Ghosn kept stonewalling: "Same answer."

Following the final day of questioning, Ghosn's lawyers told the press that their client had answered "hundreds of questions" and that the questions had been "fair."

In April 2022, after more than three years of investigation, French prosecutors formally said they suspected Ghosn of having funneled millions of euros from Renault, and issued an international arrest warrant for him. Ghosn again denied the accusation. He added that he was eager to be tried in France, but that he couldn't leave Lebanon because authorities there were holding his passport.

In addition to Ghosn, French prosecutors issued warrants for the arrest of Suhail Bahwan, two of the billionaire's sons, as well as Divyendu Kumar, the former general manager of the Omani car distributor.

Epilogue

BEIRUT, LEBANON

Tucked away behind wrought-iron gates on a quiet side street is a 1930s mansion called the Hotel Albergo. It is an oasis of calm and luxury away from the hustle and bustle of Beirut. It's become Carlos Ghosn's headquarters in the Lebanese capital.

On a spring morning long after the escape, Beirut was a ghost town. Muslims were celebrating the end of Ramadan with a holiday known as Eid al-Fitr. Everyone else was taking the day off. Roads were empty. Shops were closed.

Carlos Ghosn was open for business. One of us, Nick, was there to interview him for the sixth time since his arrest more than two years earlier. The circumstances and Ghosn's general state were far different from those when we had conducted our first chat via video link from his lawyer's office in Tokyo. Back then, he wasn't supposed to talk to journalists. Now he was free to meet with anyone he liked, so long as it was in Lebanon.

Given Ghosn's ferocious punctuality and expectation that the courtesy be reciprocated, Nick arrived thirty minutes early for the hour-long interview. A year and a half after Ghosn's escape—time he had pledged to spend clearing his name—we were eager to learn how the former captain of industry was coping with his new life as an international fugitive.

Nick approached the concierge and asked if he could do him a favor and open the top-floor bar for the visit. He got a strange look. "The bar, sir, is closed." Nick told him whom he was there to meet, and the concierge's expression shifted instantly. For Mr. Ghosn, the rules were different.

"If it's for Mr. Ho-ssen, we can open it," the man said (using the Arabic pronunciation). "We cannot say no to Mr. Ho-ssen."

At 10:30 a.m. on the dot, Ghosn strode through the wrought-iron gates, having made the short walk from his pink house, shadowed by his personal security detail. "Hi, Nick," he said.

Nick remarked that he still had the same bodyguard as when they'd met in the wake of his escape. He shrugged. "Same threats."

They squeezed into the elevator and took it to the bar on the sixth floor. In Arabic, Ghosn greeted the waiter and ordered a couple of espressos. After bringing the coffees, the waiter left them alone.

They began with small talk, covering how Ghosn spent his time now, the state of Lebanon, and the toll the pandemic had taken on his friends and family. He spoke about how he was trying to help his country by getting involved in a number of charities. He still woke up at the crack of dawn to work.

When the conversation turned to his legal situation, his eyes narrowed, and he shifted forward in his seat. He attacked the "thugs" at Nissan for investigating him. He attacked the French for abandoning him by launching investigations of their own and for freezing his assets. He attacked Japan for refusing to send his legal file to Lebanon so he could be tried there. He attacked the banks for asking him to remove his money in the wake of his escape.

It was Carlos Ghosn against the world.

Nick moved on, broaching the one subject we anticipated he would resent having to address: Oman.

He had never been very expansive on that topic. Six months earlier, Nick had asked him numerous questions about the funds he'd used to buy a yacht and invest in startups, and the conversation had gone nowhere. Instead, he had sought to move that interview off the record, insisting that he would reserve his answers for the French magistrates investigating him, which was his right.

It was time to try again. "Has your defense on Oman evolved at all since we talked in December?" Nick asked.

"We're not playing games," he said. "We're telling the reality as it is. And it's going to be very steady. We're going to give more explanations, we're going to give more details, and we're going to answer all the questions about it."

Nick asked him if he continued to claim that his late lawyer had originally bought the yacht for himself. Ghosn deflected the question by commenting that the question was fundamentally whether there had been any company money involved—and there wasn't. "That's it. That's it. The rest, it's not a legal problem," he said.

Did his position on the various companies at the heart of the legal case—Good Faith Investments, Brasiliensis, Beauty Yachts—remain that he hadn't been the beneficiary?

"No change."

"Those were not your companies?"

"No change."

At that stage, there seemed little prospect of Ghosn ever facing trial. Judicial authorities from France to Japan were bogged down. He didn't want to be tried in Japan, saying he had zero faith in that country's justice system. He didn't want to be tried in France, either, saying his case there had been tainted by the Japanese evidence. His strategy was to try to have the damning evidence from his late lawyer's computer thrown out of the case file, rather than trying to explain it away. France could try him in absentia, but there was little appetite in the country to stage a big trial without the man at the center of the allegations showing up for his day in court. Ghosn, for his part, could simply stay in his ancestral homeland of Lebanon.

That placed Ghosn and the prosecutors into a kind of holding pattern—potentially forever. Failing to address the Oman allegations in detail was unlikely to get Ghosn out of his gilded cage anytime soon.

Once the Oman topic was out of the way, Ghosn was back on the attack. He took aim at the Japanese judicial system, comparing the predicament of the Taylors to that of ISIS hostages. He then moved on to berating the "so-called management" at Renault and Nissan for their dire performances.

"Frankly, when you look at the numbers, the whole Alliance collapsed," he said.

His only regret was not taking the General Motors job when it was offered to him in 2009.

One of Ghosn's associates had once told Nick that they'd pleaded with Ghosn to apologize for something—*anything*—after his escape. But Ghosn wasn't about to apologize for anything. That was not how his narrative worked: the odyssey, the slights, the obstacles, the villains. For Ghosn, the tale relied on the hero's purity.

Did he still think the escape was worth it? Nick asked.

"Oh, yeah. . . . I would have died in Japan. I was finished," Ghosn said emphatically.

How had he gone from Carlos Ghosn the keen observer, eating andouillette and drinking red wine with common workers on the factory floor at Michelin; to the Carlos Ghosn depicted in manga comics and tailored suits, towering over the global auto industry; to Carlos Ghosn trying to breathe slowly, escaping Japan in a potential coffin of his own making; to Carlos Ghosn the local storyteller and emperor of Beirut's Hotel Albergo? When had he gone from the revered turnaround manager with legendary attention to detail to the thirty-thousand-foot executive with a sixteen-foot-tall statue dedicated to his visionary legacy but no idea his lieutenants were plotting against him? Where had he lost himself?

There is something tragic about learning deeply about this man and his craft, then recounting his epic life.

At the start, everything he touched turned to gold. And there's almost a point where you wish he hadn't been as celebrated as he was in Japan. The Nissan turnaround led the public to deify a man who in many ways was not equipped to be treated with such reverence.

He leveraged his fame to overreach for power and shirk account-ability. In the end, the toxic combination of ego and drive precipitated Ghosn's downfall and left a trail of destruction.

Among the wreckage is Michael Taylor, whose two-year sentence began in the summer of 2021. While Ghosn enjoys freedom, his res-cuer spent months sitting on the floor of a tiny cell tearing bits of paper into the size of a matchstick head. Like most foreigners and danger-ous criminals in Fuchu Prison, located on the western edge of Tokyo, Taylor spends much of his day in solitary confinement. His son Peter received a slightly lighter sentence and was held in the less rigid Yo-kohama prison.

For Greg Kelly, a three-day visit to Japan for a board meeting turned into a three-year stay in what felt very much like a prison. He was found guilty of one charge related to his actions in 2017 and 2018, and was cleared of others. He received a six-month sentence that was suspended for three years. His disappointment with being found even partially guilty was softened by eagerness to flee Japan.

Ghosn's wake also swallowed the boardrooms and factories that belong to Renault and Nissan. Battered by the scandal left behind by the former boss, the two carmakers today are a fraction of the size that they were when Ghosn was at the helm. Ghosn ran his compa-nies like a pressure cooker and the high-stress environment pushed these companies to grow, sometimes beyond their means. The minute he walked out the door, they deflated, seemingly at a loss for a future direction.

And what of the Alliance that was supposed to be Ghosn's legacy? Today it is a hollow shell of its former self, seldom mentioned even by the companies that are supposed to be a part of it.

Tragically for Ghosn, the repercussions extended to his family. At-tempts to lift Carole's red notice have proved futile, and she remains trapped in Lebanon with him, unable to travel to see her children. Ghosn's sister Claudine, his son Anthony and his daughter Maya have all been caught up in the criminal investigations, their names plastered across newspapers around the world. Ghosn's mom hasn't seen her only son in more than five years.

It wasn't supposed to end this way. Ghosn had intended to retire in Lebanon in a blaze of glory, going down in history books as one of the greatest automotive executives and a business innovator. Instead, Ghosn will forever be known for his most audacious act: escaping Japan in a box.

As Nick and Ghosn were parting ways at Hotel Albergo, the former celebrity CEO was recognized by a young Lebanese couple on their honeymoon who were staying in the hotel. "Carlos, do you mind if we take a picture with you?"

His face softened. Of course, he was happy to oblige, he just requested that they not post the photo on social media. He stood smiling between the two of them.

"Mabrouk," Ghosn told the couple after posing. He walked back toward Nick, seeming glad to have had a witness to the moment.

As he was about to get in the elevator, Ghosn offered one last thing: "I had yesterday an interview with the *Harvard Business Review*. You know the editor in chief? Smart guy. He's writing a big article about the case."

Then he was gone.

ACKNOWLEDGMENTS

We're indebted to a small army of people without whom you wouldn't be reading this book. Colleagues, friends, and mentors went above and beyond to help us, sacrificing evenings and weekends to get this project over the finish line. We got so much support that we've budgeted for rounds of red wine and sake to be on us for the next several years.

The foundation of this project was the *Wall Street Journal,* our professional home, and our amazing colleagues around the world.

Covering a story like Ghosn's for the *Journal* required a truly global team. Thank you to Mark Maremont in Boston and David Gauthier-Villars in Istanbul, who are two of the very best reporters in the business today. Their scoops allowed us to get ahead of the competition. Sam Schechner in Paris, the entire Tokyo bureau (Phred, River, Chieko, Miho, Kosaku, Alastair, Surya, and Megumi), Nazih Osseiran in Beirut, Rory Jones in Dubai, Bradley Hope in London, and Patricia Kowsmann were invaluable teammates as we worked to discover new facts about what was happening and why it was happening.

Peter Landers, the *Journal's* bureau chief in Tokyo, Stacy Meichtry, the Paris chief, and Chip Cummins, the business editor in Europe, spent months working on this story and deserve huge credit. Together, they were always on call to encourage us, guide our coverage, and make our copy fly higher.

The *Journal's* "Page 1" editors (or "enterprise editors," as they're now called), Matthew Rose and Tammy Audi, as well as Jamie Heller, the business editor, were passionate about the story and expanded the reach of our work. Erwin Shrader deftly juggled time zones while editing dozens of our stories. Thank you to the senior editors who run the empire: Matt Murray, Jason Anders, Grainne McCarthy, Thorold Barker, and Drew Dowell. They recognized a great story and gave us the time and latitude to see it through.

The initial idea for writing a book came from Joshua Robinson, a sportswriter at the *Journal*. He had recently published an excellent book on soccer, full of his fast-flowing, smooth prose that made the process seem like a walk in the park. How hard could it be . . . ? Ridiculously hard, as it turned out. Thankfully, Josh was incredibly generous with his time, and always made himself available to boost our morale and polish our drafts.

As we labored with the scope and complexity of the Ghosn story, we were able to count on two people in particular who had our backs:

Now our former colleague, David Gauthier-Villars stepped in to help us bring structure and clarity to the book, one chapter at a time. Under COVID-19 lockdown in Istanbul, David pulled off Ghosn's greatest trick: forging an alliance between Paris and Tokyo that got results.

From Los Angeles, Domenica Alioto also stepped in, moving into her signature "hyperdrive mode" to help us tie the whole book together in a short amount of time. Her care and sensitivity for human characters and attention to detail were priceless.

John Stoll, the *Journal*'s former autos editor in Detroit, reviewed key chapters. Jason Chow, who spent a number of years covering Ghosn for the *Journal*, provided thoughtful feedback and encouragement. Walter Hemmens, a wry Irish journalist, was invaluable in helping us beat the fear of a blank page and getting this project moving. Clément Lacombes, a hugely talented and dogged reporter, shared his knowledge and his archive collected over many years of covering Ghosn.

It's one thing writing the book, it's quite another putting it out into the world. We're grateful to our brilliant agent, Eric Lupfer, at Fletcher & Co., who was with us from inception to publication. Thank you also to Hollis Heimbouch, Kirby Sandmeyer, William Adams, and the rest of the team at HarperCollins for taking a chance on two first-time writers. You've enabled us to realize one of our major professional ambitions.

Finally, Nick would like to say a huge thank-you to his fiancée, his three sisters, his parents, grandparents, and friends. They all patiently, heroically put up with missed weekends and changing deadlines for way longer than they should have.

Sean would like to thank his wife and fellow *Journal* reporter, Suryatapa Bhattacharya, for her constant support and advice. He would also like to thank his son, Amartya, who doesn't really understand what his father does for a living but can spot a Nissan on the road, because "Daddy is always talking about Nissan." He would like to apologize to his family for all the late nights and canceled vacations while he chased this story.

NOTES

1: Self-Made

7 John Dunlop and the Michelin family: Wade Davis, *One River: Explorations and Discoveries in the Amazon Rain Forest* (New York: Simon & Schuster, 1996).

8 Rubber barons had started: Ibid.

8 finest materials in the world: Joe Jackson, *The Thief at the End of the World: Rubber, Power, and the Seeds of Empire* (New York: Penguin, 2008).

9 One in ten would die: Carlos Pousa, ed., *Porto Velho: A Journey Through Its Economic Cycles and History* (Rio de Janeiro: Canal Comunicação & Cultura, 2012).

9 arrived a decade earlier: Roberto Khatlab, "Un mariage au Liban réunit trois générations d'émigrés," *L'Orient–Le Jour*, February 17, 2014, https://www.lorientlejour.com/article/854882/un-mariage-au-liban-reunit-trois-gen erations-demigres.html.

9 Thousands of workers had died: Gary Neeleman and Rose Neeleman, *Tracks in the Amazon: The Day-to-Day Life of the Workers on the Madeira-Mamoré Railroad* (Salt Lake City: University of Utah Press, 2013).

10 within a matter of decades: Ibid. The first viable *Hevea* seeds arrived in London in 1876, and portions of seedlings were sent to Singapore. Production rose in the 1890s along with the increased demand for rubber. In 1905, Malaysia sold only 230 tons of rubber but fifty thousand acres were planted. The amount of rubber sold doubled by 1906. Rubber trees can be tapped after seven years.

10 at a premium: John Tofik Karam, "Lebanese in the Brazilian National Market," North Carolina State University, January 23, 2015, https://lebanese studies.news.chass.ncsu.edu/2015/01/28/lebanese-in-the-brazilian-national -market/.

11 On October 10, 1939: John Tofik Karam, photograph of Abidao Bichara's grave, University of Illinois at Urbana-Champaign, https://0.academia-photos .com/49025337/12912867/14295094/s200_john.karam.jpg.

11 his parting words of advice: John Tofik Karam, *Another Arabesque Syrian-Lebanese Ethnicity in Neoliberal Brazil* (Philadelphia: Temple University Press, 2008).

2: The Father

16 a priest named Boulos Masaad: "Reconstitution du Crime de Majdel Baana," *L'Orient–Le Jour*, April 27, 1960.

17 leading him to believe: "G. Ghosn et S. Abdel-Khalek condamnés à mort," *L'Orient–Le Jour*, January 10, 1961.

17 He forced the priest out of the car: "Peine de mort requise contre G. Ghosn et S. Abdel-Khalek pour le meurtre du Père Masaad," *L'Orient–Le Jour*, July 14, 1960.

17 fired a second bullet: Ibid.

17 Georges always maintained: "Ghosn rejette sur Abdel-Khalek toute la responsabilité du meurtre du Père Masaad," *L'Orient–Le Jour*, October 7, 1960.

18 given them the license plate number: "G. Ghosn et S. Abdel-Khalek condamnés à mort."

18 seeking the death penalty: "Peine de mort requise contre G. Ghosn et S. Abdel-Khalek pour le meurtre du Père Masaad."

18 She was put: "Mme Georges Ghosn—Impliqué dans l'évasion des détenues de la prison de Baabda—est arrêtée," *L'Orient–Le Jour*, August 11, 1960.

18 never faced charges: "Mme Georges Ghosn est remise en liberté," *L'Orient–Le Jour*, August 12, 1960.

19 the supply of which had been cut off: "G. Ghosn—qui a financé l'opération—a été transféré à la Prison de la Citadelle pour avoir incité les détenus de Baabda a une grève de la faim," *L'Orient–Le Jour*, August 9, 1960.

19 Three buses and fifteen taxis: "Ghosn rejette sur Abdel-Khalek toute la responsabilité du meurtre du Père Masaad."

19 The killing was ruled an accident: "La cour de cassation annule la peine de mort rendue contre Georges Ghosn," *L'Orient–Le Jour*, December 21, 1962.

19 He was found guilty: "Sélim Abdel-Khalek condamné aux travaux forcés à vie," *L'Orient–Le Jour*, June 28, 1968.

21 Following his release: "Georges Ghosn trouvé porteur de 34,000 faux dollars," *L'Orient–Le Jour*, March 7, 1971.

21 Georges pleaded not guilty: "Georges Ghosn plaide non coupable," *L'Orient–Le Jour*, March 1, 1972.

21 sentenced to another three years: "Jugement confirmé," *L'Orient–Le Jour*, November 28, 1972.

4: Wartime General

34 Ghosn was put into command: Carlos Ghosn and Philippe Riès, *Shift: Inside Nissan's Historic Revival* (New York: Currency, 2006).

35 Kléber-Colombes was losing: "L'activité de l'usine des Hauts-de-Seine de Kléber-Colombes sera maintenue," *Le Monde*, January 22, 1982, https://www.lemonde.fr/archives/article/1982/01/22/l-activite-de-l-usine-des-hauts-de-seine-de-kleber-colombes-sera-maintenue_2898717_1819218.html.

38 "The old married couple": Carlos Ghosn, "Carlos Ghosn (6) Turbulence and Triumph in Brazil," *Nikkei Asia*, January 7, 2017, https://asia.nikkei.com/Spotlight/My-Personal-History/My-Personal-History-Carlos-Ghosn/Carlos-Ghosn-6-Turbulence-and-triumph-in-Brazil2.

43 "somewhat of a mystery man": "'We Did Not Acquire Any Brand to Elim-

inate It.' (Carlos Ghosn of Michelin North America Inc.)," *Modern Tire Dealer*, September 1, 1991.

43 the steely criticism that Lutz cast: Ghosn, and Riès, *Shift*.

5: The Birth of the Alliance

48 largest car industry deal in history: Steven Lipin, "New World Order? Chrysler Might Merge with Daimler-Benz—or Be Taken Over," *Wall Street Journal*, May 6, 1998.

49 produce around 4 million vehicles: Steven Lipin, "Chrysler, Daimler-Benz Announce World's Largest Industrial Merger," *Wall Street Journal*, May 7, 1998, https://www.wsj.com/articles/SB894421909383679000.

49 The company had amassed: Robert L. Simison and Lisa Shuchman, "Daimler-Chrysler Seems to See a Good Deal in Mess That Is Nissan," *Wall Street Journal*, January 12, 1999.

50 a one-in-ten shot: Stéphane Lauer, *Renault: Une révolution française* (Paris: Lattès, 2005).

54 stood up and bowed: Ibid.

56 "We're not in the mood": Chris Knap, "Ford CEO Seeks Closer Customer Ties," *Orange County Register*, February 19, 1999.

56 lose only $5 billion: "They Said It," *Globe and Mail*, March 1, 1999.

57 "Well you know": David Woodruff, "Renault Bets Ghosn Can Drive Nissan," *Wall Street Journal*, March 31, 1999.

6: Turnaround

60 "He looks like Mr. Bean": Frédéric Garlan, "Nissan's French Number Two Gets TV Grilling in Japan," Agence France-Presse, April 23, 1999; Brice Pedroletti, "Le patron qui a conquis le Japon," *L'Express*, May 10, 2001.

64 Nissan Revival Plan: "Nissan Revival Plan," October 18, 1999, https://www.nissan-global.com/EN/DOCUMENT/PDF/FINANCIAL/REVIVAL/DETAIL/1999/fs_re_detail1999h.pdf.

7: Two Briefcases

73 more than fifteen hundred shareholders: "For Investors: 107th Shareholders Meeting," Nissan Motor Corporation, https://www.nissan-global.com/EN/IR/SHAREHOLDER/107_index.html.

73 sales had tripled: "FY05 Financial Results," Nissan Motor Corporation, April 25, 2006, https://www.nissan-global.com/EN/DOCUMENT/PDF/FINANCIAL/2006/0425/060425fy20060425presentationcolor_E.pdf.

73 world's largest Nissan showroom: "Oman Becomes Home to World's Largest Nissan Showroom," Nissan Motor Corporation, June 5, 2005, https://global.nissannews.com/en/releases/release-265936b8190abc85d84741b6049740ab-050606-01-e.

74 "We have enough talent": "Nissan's Ghosn Warns Firm May Miss Sales Target in Yr to March 2007—UPDATE," FinanzNachrichten.de, June 27, 2006, https://www.finanznachrichten.de/nachrichten-2006-06/6622487-nissan-s-ghosn-warns-firm-may-miss-sales-target-in-yr-to-march-2007-update-020.htm.

74 attracted plenty of media attention: David Ibison and James Mackintosh, "The Boss Among Bosses," *Financial Times*, July 7, 2006, https://www.ft.com /content/530603e4-0de3-11db-a385-0000779e2340.

75 "Please be confident": "Nissan's Ghosn Warns Firm May Miss Sales Target in Yr to March 2007—UPDATE."

75 at 8:30 a.m. in Paris: Joann Muller, "The Impatient Mr. Ghosn," *Forbes*, May 12, 2006, https://www.forbes.com/global/2006/0522/020.html?sh=3ae8 15151328.

75 swapped back on return trips: Monica Langley, "For Carlos Ghosn, Fast Lane Gets Bumpy," *Wall Street Journal*, October 28, 2006, https://www.wsj .com/articles/SB116200109759906779.

81 "I'm glad to see": James B. Treece, "Ghosn to GM: Be Serious or Begone," *Automotive News*, October 15, 2006, https://www.autonews.com/article/200 60925/SUB/60922064/ghosn-to-gm-be-serious-or-begone.

8: Swap Deals

90 an extended standing ovation: Sylviane Zehil, "Carlos Ghosn à «L'OLJ»: «Il n'y a jamais de crise sans fin,»" *L'Orient–Le Jour*, November 28, 2008, http://jamhourus.com/wp-content/uploads/2017/06/press_article_2008 .pdf.

90 "Forgive me, Carole": Carole Ghosn and Carlos Ghosn, *Ensemble, toujours* (Paris: Éditions de l'Observatoire, 2021) (author's translation).

9: Spillovers

97 Carole laughed and accepted: Ghosn and Ghosn, *Ensemble, toujours.*

99 private lessons three times a week: Toshiaki Ohnuma court testimony, October 29, 2010.

100 Ghosn sought a number: Toshiaki Ohnuma court testimony, November 11, 2020.

103 "Why is Ghosn's salary": Yoshio Takahashi, "Nissan CEO Made $9.8 Million," *Wall Street Journal*, June 23, 2010, https://www.wsj.com/articles/SB100 01424052748704853404575323780460252438.

10: Figure Out a Way

105 "Listen, we have certainties": Reuters, "Renault a de multiples certitudes sur l'espionnage, dit Ghosn," BFM Business, January 23, 2011, https://www.bfmtv .com/economie/entreprises/transports/renault-a-de-multiples-certitudes-sur -l-espionnage-dit-ghosn_AN-201101230013.html (author's translation).

106 none of the accounts referenced: "Renault: La DCRI n'a trouvé 'aucune trace d'espionnage,'" *L'Express*, March 3, 2011, https://lexpansion.lexpress.fr /entreprises/renault-la-dcri-n-a-trouve-aucune-trace-d-espionnage_1426610 .html.

106 "I got this wrong": Matthieu Lauraux, "Carlos Ghosn sur TF1: Le PDG de Renault s'excuse," TF1, March 15, 2011, https://www.tf1.fr/tf1/auto-moto/news /carlos-ghosn-tf1-pdg-de-renault-s-excuse-9962589.html (author's translation).

107 and gave the men a dressing-down: Mathieu Suc, *Renault, nid d'espions: Le livre qui révèle la face cachée de Carlos Ghosn* (Paris: Editions du Moment, 2013).

108 Ghosn became unusually heated: Toshiyuki Shiga court testimony, January 12, 2021.

112 all the Beirut jet set: "Garden party aux caves d'Ixsir," *Noun*, November 1, 2012, 318–20.

11: Hall of Mirrors

113 "You can be happy with the flirt": Video highlights from Ghosn-Zetsche press conference, Paris, 2012, https://www.alliance-2022.com/blog/video-high lights-ghosn-zetsche-paris-press-conference/.

12: Money Canals

125 praising Lebanon's decision: Élie Masboungi, "Colloque sur l'environne- ment juridique et fiscal du commerce franco-libanais," *L'Orient–Le Jour*, May 13, 2011, https://www.lorientlejour.com/article/703756/Colloque_sur_l%2527en vironnement_juridique__et_fiscal_du_commerce_franco-libanais .html.

13: Double Vote

136 to a Renault plant in France: "Nissan to Build Micra at Renault Plant in France," Nissan Motor Corporation, April 26, 2013, https://reports.nissan -global.com/EN/?p=11216.

136 wanted to close two blast furnaces: Reuters Staff, "French Parliament Passes Law Punishing Plant Closures," Reuters, October 1, 2013, https://www .reuters.com/article/france-industry/french-parliament-passes-law-punish ing-plant-closures-idUSL6N0HR3KJ20131001.

144 "As the good Lebanese sheik": Dita Von Bliss, "Quelqu'un m'a dit . . . ," *L'Orient–Le Jour*, October 11, 2016, https://www.lorientlejour.com/article /1012007/quelquun-ma-dit.html.

144 "We wanted it to feel": Leena Kim, "Carole and Carlos Ghosn Threw a Wedding Fit for a King and Queen," *Town & Country*, March 3, 2017, https:// www.townandcountrymag.com/the-scene/weddings/a9634/versailles-wed ding/.

144 "That's why we wanted": Raphaëlle Bacqué, "Feu d'artifice, porcelaine et vin d'Ixsir: Le jour où le couple Ghosn a convié sa cour à Versailles," *Le Monde*, February 22, 2019, https://www.lemonde.fr/m-le-mag/article/2019/02/22 /feu-d-artifices-porcelaine-et-vin-d-ixsir-le-jour-ou-le-couple-ghosn-invitait -a-versailles_5426881_4500055.html (author's translation).

15: Global Motors

155 "Good art": Nissan, "Nissan Unveils 'Wheels of Innovation' Sculpture," You Tube, July 2, 2017, https://www.youtube.com/watch?v=mCLqEI8VURo.

155 It had cost: Amy Chozick and Motoko Rich, "The Rise and Fall of Carlos

Ghosn," *New York Times*, December 30, 2018, https://www.nytimes.com/2018/12/30/business/carlos-ghosn-nissan.html.

156 "It's game over": Marie Bordet and Clément Lacombes, "Carlos Ghosn, confidences du n° 1 mondial," *Le Point*, July 19, 2017, https://www.lepoint.fr/economie/carlos-ghosn-confidences-du-n-1-mondial-19-07-2017-2144381_28.php (author's translation).

157 it wanted to sell 14 million: John D. Stoll, "Carlos Ghosn Bets Big on Sales Growth," *Wall Street Journal*, September 15, 2017, https://www.wsj.com/articles/nissan-renault-seeks-to-boost-annual-vehicle-sales-to-14-million-1505456101.

161 "My responsibility is": Groupe Renault, *Annual General Meeting of Shareholders— Palais des Congrès (Paris—France)* | *Groupe Renault*, YouTube, June 17, 2018, https://www.youtube.com/watch?v=GhpolIvAt6Q&t=1308s.

163 "People are ready": Sophie Fay, "Pour Carlos Ghosn, rien n'arrêtera la mondialisation," *L'Obs*, October 28, 2018, https://www.nouvelobs.com/economie/2018 1028.OBS4583/pour-carlos-ghosn-rien-n-arretera-la-mondialisation.html (author's translation).

164 "On my way": Chozick and Rich, "The Rise and Fall of Carlos Ghosn."

18: Boxed In

192 The first full day of interrogations: Takashi Takano, "Thinking about Criminal Trials," Takashi Takon @blog, January 11, 2020, http://blog.livedoor .jp/plltakano/archives/65953931.html.

192 "Fighting Against the Darkness of Injustice": Megumi Fujikawa, "Ghosn's Lawyer, a Former Prosecutor, Knows His Way Around a Courtroom," *Wall Street Journal*, November 27, 2018, https://www.wsj.com/articles/carlos -ghosns-lawyer-is-familiar-with-prosecutors-tactics-1543314606.

194 "I don't have my suits paid for": Carlos Ghosn and Philippe Riès, *Le temps de la vérité* (Paris: Grasset, 2020).

195 through business deals with Nissan: Sean McLain, "Carlos Ghosn Investigators Focus on Ties to Saudi Businessman," *Wall Street Journal*, December 27, 2018, https://www.wsj.com/articles/ghosn-investigators-focus-on-ties-to-saudi -businessman-11545935009.

196 "You are my ray": Ghosn and Ghosn, *Ensemble, toujours*, 259.

197 His daily interrogations were suspended: Nick Kostov and Sam Schechner, "Carlos Ghosn's Lawyer Said He Had a Fever in Jail, Is Feeling Better," *Wall Street Journal*, January 10, 2019, from https://www.wsj.com/articles/wife-of -jailed-ex-nissan-ceo-carlos-ghosn-asks-about-his-health-11547149610.

199 "Your Honor, I am innocent": Reuters Staff, "Statement by ex-Nissan Chairman Carlos Ghosn in Tokyo Court," Reuters, January 7, 2019, https://www .reuters.com/article/us-nissan-ghosn-text-idUSKCN1P205I.

199 promised he would deliver it: Ghosn and Ghosn, *Ensemble, toujours*.

199 At retirement, Ghosn was due more than €30 million: Laurence Frost and Gilles Guillaume, "Renault Scraps Ghosn's 30 Million Euro Parachute with Government Backing," Reuters, February 13, 2019, https://www.reuters.com /article/cbusiness-us-nissan-ghosn-renault-exclus-idCAKCN1Q213D -OCABS.

201 "The key is to move on": "Carlos Ghosn Is Out as CEO of Renault," Bloomberg, January 24, 2019, https://www.bloomberg.com/news/videos/2019-01-24/ghosn-resigned-from-top-job-at-renault-last-night-france-s-le-maire-says-video.

19: Scorched Earth

205 "This is a big step forward for Nissan": "Jean-Dominique Senard, Chairman of Renault, Hiroto Saikawa, CEO of Nissan, Thierry Bollore, CEO of Renault and Osamu Masuko, CEO of Mitsubishi Motors, Announce the Intention to Create a New Alliance Operating Board," *Official Global Newsroom*, March 12, 2019, https://global.nissannews.com/en/releases/release-bf2bf1e053fd301abd3ca437660b544d-190312-02-e.

206 Later in April, Nissan said it would miss its profit target: Sean McLain and Nick Kostov, "Renault Merger Plan for Nissan Triggers New Tension," *Wall Street Journal*, April 26, 2019, https://www.wsj.com/articles/renault-to-propose-merging-with-nissan-11556265370.

213 "The brutality and the totally unexpected character": Anne Feitz, Julien Dupont-Calbo, and David Barroux, "Renault: Thierry Bolloré dénonce « un coup de force stupéfiant ,»" *Les Echos*, October 10, 2019, https://www.lesechos.fr/industrie-services/automobile/renault-thierry-bollore-denonce-un-coup-de-force-stupefiant-1139074.

213 "The alliance needs a bit of fresh air": Nick Kostov and Stacy Meichtry, "Renault Board Votes to Remove CEO Thierry Bolloré," *Wall Street Journal*, October 11, 2021, https://www.wsj.com/articles/renault-chief-executive-thierry-bollore-to-step-down-11570785214.

20: Inside Out

217 Carole bit her lip and tried hard not to cry: Ghosn and Ghosn, *Ensemble, toujours*, chapter 16.

217 "Because I've lost everything else": Ibid.

218 The plan to keep Ghosn's departure a secret: Sean McLain, "'It Failed': Ghosn Lawyer Fesses Up to Dress-Up Drama," *Wall Street Journal*, March 7, 2019, https://www.wsj.com/articles/it-failed-ghosn-lawyer-fesses-up-to-dress-up-drama-11552020876.

219 hugging silently for several minutes: Ghosn and Ghosn, *Ensemble, toujours*, chapter 18.

220 in fact it had come from Divyendu Kumar: Nick Kostov and Sean McLain, "Carlos Ghosn Ran a Tech Fund—Using Millions from an Executive at a Nissan Partner," *Wall Street Journal*, August 26, 2019, https://www.wsj.com/articles/carlos-ghosn-ran-tech-fundusing-millions-from-an-executive-at-a-nissan-partner-11566836112.

221 "This is about a plot": Sean McLain, "Carlos Ghosn Assails Nissan Executives for Playing a 'Dirty Game,'" *Wall Street Journal*, April 9, 2019, https://www.wsj.com/articles/carlos-ghosn-says-nissan-executives-played-a-dirty-game-11554795423.

221 Carole panicked: Sean McLain and Megumi Fujikawa, "'It Was Scary as Hell': The Rearrest of Carlos Ghosn Opens New Front in Inquiry," *Wall Street*

Journal, April 4, 2019, https://www.wsj.com/articles/new-suspicions-against-ghosn-present-most-serious-threat-11554381414.

222 she felt as though she were reenacting the escape scene: Bruna Basini and Hervé Gattegno, "Carole Ghosn: 'Tout le monde a lâché Carlos,'" *Le Journal du Dimanche*, April 6, 2019, https://www.lejdd.fr/Economie/exclu-jdd-carole-ghosn-tout-le-monde-a-lache-carlos-3887537.

223 "We don't want to prosecute without truth": Takashi Takano, *Hostage Justice* (Tokyo: Kadokawa Shinsho, 2021), author's translation, from chapter 2: Carlos Ghosn's detention, bail, and escape.

224 The Japanese lawyer didn't give up: Ibid.

225 "cruel and unnecessary": Sean McLain, "Carlos Ghosn Leaves Jail Again in Release on Bail," *Wall Street Journal*, April 25, 2019, https://www.wsj.com/articles/carlos-ghosn-is-granted-bail-by-tokyo-court-again-11556161288.

21: War Gaming

231 In 2010, Taylor made national headlines: Mike Carraggi, "St. George's Calls an Audible," *Boston Globe*, October 5, 2010, http://archive.boston.com/sports/schools/football/articles/2010/10/05/st_georges_calls_an_audible/?rss_id=Boston+High+School+Sports.

232 "only to avoid a longer stay in the brutal jail": Mark Maremont and Nick Kostov, "Behind Ghosn's Escape, an Ex-Green Beret with a Beef about His Own Time in Jail," *Wall Street Journal*, January 18, 2020, https://www.wsj.com/articles/behind-ghosns-escape-an-ex-green-beret-with-a-beef-about-his-own-time-in-jail-11579323661.

22: The Escape

243 "It's time to go home": May Jeong, "How Carlos Ghosn Escaped Japan, According to the Ex-Green Beret Who Snuck Him Out," *Vanity Fair*, July 23, 2020, https://www.vanityfair.com/news/2020/07/how-carlos-ghosn-escaped-japan.

248 "The important cargo should stay at the back": David Gauthier-Villars, "Ghosn's Escape from Japan Leaves Seven Facing Trial in Turkey," *Wall Street Journal*, July 1, 2020, https://www.wsj.com/articles/ghosns-escape-from-japan-leaves-seven-facing-prison-in-turkey-11593634188.

23: Collateral Damage

255 "Ghosn broke his own promise": Peter Landers, "Japanese Officials Break Their Silence on Ghosn's Escape," *Wall Street Journal*, January 5, 2020, https://www.wsj.com/articles/japanese-officials-break-their-silence-on-ghosns-escape-11578204876.

257 "As you can imagine": euronews, "Carlos Ghosn, Nissan's ex-boss, gives a press conference in Beirut," YouTube, n.d., https://www.youtube.com/watch?v=5WvRDV67mDU.

261 "some of the best defendants": Nate Raymond, "U.S. Fights Bail Bid by Men Accused of Helping Former Nissan Boss Escape," Reuters, June 22, 2020, https://www.reuters.com/article/us-nissan-ghosn-idCAKBN23T351.

264 the Taylors had shown: Sean McLain, "Ghosn Escape Planner Michael Taylor Is Sentenced to Two Years in Prison," *Wall Street Journal*, July 19, 2021, https://www.wsj.com/articles/ghosn-escape-planner-michael-taylor-is-sentenced-to-two-years-in-prison-11626669860.

267 Ghosn's lawyers told the press: Agence France-Presse, "Ghosn Grilling in Lebanon by French Investigators 'Fair,'" RFI, June 4, 2021, https://www.rfi.fr/en/business-and-tech/20210604-ghosn-grilling-in-lebanon-by-french-investigators-fair.

INDEX

About the Authors

NICK KOSTOV has worked for the *Wall Street Journal* for the last seven years, covering business and general news from Paris. A graduate of University College London, Kostov lives in Paris.

SEAN MCLAIN has led the *Wall Street Journal*'s coverage of Japan's biggest car companies, including Toyota, Honda, and Nissan, for the past six years. A graduate of St. John's College in Annapolis, Maryland, McLain lives in Tokyo.

In 2019, Kostov and McLain won an Overseas Press Club award for best international business news reporting in newspapers, news services, magazines, or digital for their series, *The Fall of Carlos Ghosn*.